D0494683

# Edinburgh, Lothians and The Borders

*'Know that this heritage*
*Is also theirs, which is why*
*I confess fear for only half of*
*Their future.'*

*Stuart MacGregor*

# FOREWORD

Twentieth-century Scotland has a heritage of human endeavour stretching back some ten thousand years, and a wide range of man-made monuments survives as proof of that endeavour. The rugged character of much of the Scottish landscape has helped to preserve many antiquities which elsewhere have vanished beneath modern development or intensive deep ploughing, though with some 10,200 km of coastline there has also been an immeasurable loss of archaeological sites as a result of marine erosion. Above all, perhaps, the preservation of such a wide range of monuments should be credited to Scotland's abundant reserves of good building stone, allowing not only the creation of extraordinarily enduring prehistoric houses and tombs but also the development of such remarkable Scottish specialities as the medieval tower-house and the iron-age broch. This volume is one of a series of nine handbooks which have been designed to provide up-to-date and authoritative introductions to the rich archaeological heritage of the various regions of Scotland, highlighting the most interesting and best preserved of the surviving monuments and setting them in their original social context. The time-scale is the widest possible, from relics of World War II or the legacy of 19th-century industrial booms back through history and prehistory to the earliest pioneer days of human settlement, but the emphasis varies from region to region, matching the particular directions in which each has developed. Some monuments are still functioning (lighthouses for instance), others are still occupied as homes, and many have been taken into the care of the State or the National Trust for Scotland, but each has been chosen as specially deserving a visit.

Thanks to the recent growth of popular interest in these topics, there is an increasing demand for knowledge to be presented in a readily digestible form and at a moderate price. In sponsoring this series, therefore, the Royal Commission on the Ancient and Historical Monuments of Scotland broadens the range of its publications with the aim of making authentic information about the man-made heritage available to as wide an audience as possible. This is the second edition of the series, in which more monuments, museums and visitor centres have been added in order to reflect the way in which the management and presentation of Scotland's past have expanded over the last decade. The excursion section proved very popular and has been both expanded and illustrated in colour.

The author, John Baldwin, is particularly well qualified to write this volume, for he was formerly an education adviser to Lothian Region's Department of Education and is especially aware of the cultural wealth and diversity of south-east Scotland. With additional experience in the Scottish Country Life Section of the former National Museum of Antiquities of Scotland, in the Scottish Wildlife Trust and the Whithorn Archaeological Project, he has a wide knowledge of Scottish material culture, past and present, and of the interaction of man and environment.

Monuments have been grouped according to their character and date and, although only the finest, most interesting or best preserved have been described in detail, attention has also been drawn to other sites worth visiting in the vicinity. Each section has its own explanatory introduction, beginning with the most recent monuments and gradually retreating in time back to the earliest traces of prehistoric man.

Each major monument is numbered and identified by its district so that it may easily be located on the end-map, but it is recommended that the visitor should also use the relevant 1:50,000 maps published by the Ordnance Survey as its Landranger Series, particularly for the more remote sites. Lothian and the Borders are covered by sheet nos 65, 66, 67, 72, 73, 74, 79 and 80. The National Grid Reference for each site is provided (e.g. NT 628245) as well as local directions at the head of each entry. The Lothian Regional Transport bus and road *Map of Edinburgh and Surrounding Areas* provides valuable assistance in and around the City.

An asterisk (*) indicates that the site is subject to restricted hours of opening; unless attributed to Historic Scotland or the National Trust for Scotland, the visitor should assume the monument to be in private ownership and **should seek permission locally to view it.** It is of course vital that visitors to any monument should observe the country code and take special care to fasten gates. Where a church is locked, it is often possible to obtain the key from the local manse, post office or general store.

We have made an attempt to estimate how accessible each monument may be for disabled visitors, indicated at the head of each entry by a wheelchair logo and a number: 1=easy access for all visitors, including those in wheelchairs; 2=reasonable access for pedestrians but restricted access for wheelchairs; 3=restricted access for all disabled but a good view from the road or parking area; 4=access for the able-bodied only.

Many of the sites mentioned in this handbook are held in trust for the nation by the Secretary of State for Scotland and cared for on his behalf by Historic Scotland. Further information about these monuments, including details of guidebooks to individual properties, can be obtained from Historic Scotland, Longmore House, Salisbury Place, Edinburgh EH9 1SH. Information about properties in the care of the National Trust for Scotland can be obtained from the National Trust for Scotland, 5 Charlotte Square, Edinburgh EH2 4DU. Key abbreviations used in this volume are: NGS National Galleries of Scotland; NMS National Museums of Scotland; NTS National Trust for Scotland; RCAHMS Royal Commission on the Ancient and Historical Monuments of Scotland.

ANNA RITCHIE
Series Editor

# ACKNOWLEDGEMENTS

Exploring evidence in the field is crucial to any appreciation and evaluation of sites, even if the final selection does not include everyone's favourites! I am particularly grateful to my family, to Vivien, David and Richard, for encouraging me so freely to roam and to write! In so doing I have met with many across Lothian and the Borders, whether farmers, dykers, shepherds, museum curators, archaeologists, planners, countryside rangers and others besides, whose kindly interest and local knowledge, tactful clarification and patience have contributed in no small way to the volume.

Equally valuable are the inventories and archives of the Royal Commission on the Ancient and Historical Monuments of Scotland. Together with the holdings of the National Monuments Record of Scotland, Historic Scotland and the National Museums of Scotland, they contain a remarkable record of Scotland's past. In particular I would like to thank Dr David Breeze, Ms Marilyn Brown, Miss Catherine Cruft, Dr Piers Dixon, Mr JG Dunbar, Mrs Lesley Ferguson, Mr Ian Fisher, Mr Gordon Maxwell, Ms Lesley O'Halloran, Dr Graham Ritchie, Ms Veronica Steele, Mr Geoffrey Stell and Mr Joe White. Elsewhere, staff of the National Trust for Scotland, Edinburgh University's School of Scottish Studies and the City of Edinburgh Central Libraries (Scottish Library) were as willing and courteous as ever, Finally, to Anna Ritchie, series editor, a special word of gratitude for her never-failing encouragement, patience and good humour.

Most illustrations originate in the National Monuments Record of Scotland (Crown Copyright). Author and publisher are also grateful to the following for permission to reproduce: Historic Scotland (Crown Copyright) (pp. 21, 24, 27, 30, 33 bottom, 35, 36 top, 38 bottom, 43 top, 44 right, 45, 46, 48, 56, 79 bottom right, 81, 82, 87 bottom, 88 top, 94, 107, 111, 112, 113, 114, 115, 116, 117 bottom, 118 left, 120 bottom, 121 top left & bottom, 122, 123, 128, 140, 143 middle & right, 145, 146, 147, 148, 149, 150, 151, 152, 155, 156, 157, 158, 159, 160, 161, 162 bottom, 163, 167, 172, 173 bottom, 174, 189 bottom, 196, 197, 198, 207, 211 top right & bottom, 212 bottom, 213, 214 bottom pair, 216, 217); Trustees of the National Museums of Scotland (pp. 143 left, 216 top); National Trust for Scotland (pp. 10, 36 middle & top, 44 left, 51 bottom, 61, 72 left, 73, 87 middle, 92, 93, 100, 101, 210, 211 top left); Cambridge University Committee on Aerial Photography (p. 175 left); Cramond Heritage Trust (pp. 28 bottom, 62); Roslin Chapel Trust (p. 34); Caledonian Brewery (p. 60 top); East Lothian Council (p. 86); JR Baldwin (p. 31 bottom); GD Hay (pp. 55, 67 top, 118 right); JR Hume (p. 85); J Sowrey (p. 28 top), B Walker (p. 80); Mrs B Willsher (p. 129).

# INTRODUCTION

**Preston Mill, East Linton**

## Man and the Natural Environment

It is perhaps 8500 years since people first appeared in the landscape of south-east Scotland—some 6500 years BC. Whilst many of the most interesting prehistoric and later sites to have survived are found in places of particular scenic or environmental interest, today's landscape would be unrecognisable to anyone from such earlier cultures. Prehistoric people would be just as astounded at what they would see today, however, as either they or we would be if relocated to c 1700 AD. For the face of the land has undergone quite startling change—not just over 8 or so millennia, but over just 2 or 3 centuries.

The last Ice Age ended c 8000 BC and gradually a bare tundra landscape was colonised first by mosses, lichens, grasses and shrubs, then by trees. Scots pine, then birch, were followed c 7200 BC by hazel; and by elm, oak and ash between 6500 and 6000 BC. By c 5500-3000 BC, the forests were at their most developed in a mild, moist climate; and only the wettest of swamps, the most exposed coastal sites and the highest hills would not have been afforested. At that time, the treeline was perhaps as high as 800 m. Colder and wetter conditions from c 3000 BC led to a decline in overall tree cover, to a decline in elm and Scots pine (and growth in alder), to greater expanses of heathland and grassland and the rapid growth of blanket peat bog in poorly-drained areas.

All the while, woodlands would generally have been mixed, their actual composition dependent upon such factors as slope, exposure, drainage and soil. At lower levels, it was probably mixed oak woodland that predominated; pines and birch scrub at higher levels, with such smaller trees or bushes as rowan and juniper; all interspersed with heather, luxuriant meadows, meandering streams, thickets and wetlands alive with flowers and insects, birds and animals. These woodlands were home to elk and reindeer, to wolf, lynx and brown bear, to wild horse, wild ox, wild boar and wild cat, to lemming and beaver, pine marten and polecat—none of which (any more than the forests or swamps themselves) eventually survived the impact of people. Only animals such as red and roe deer, otter, fox and badger, stoat and weasel, hares, voles, and birds such as ptarmigan, raven and rock dove still manage to cling on in the area, and perhaps an occasional red squirrel.

The first scattered groups of hunters and gatherers had arrived in the landscape by 6500 BC. Their effect on the woodlands was probably minimal, but analysis of pollen grains trapped in peat and loch sediments confirms the presence of open grassland plants, and tiny fragments of charcoal are evidence of fire, whether natural or induced by man. Cereal grains and associated weed species appear by 4000 BC, coinciding with the arrival of the first farmers; thereafter, the evidence shows that over succeeding millennia—albeit initially on a small-scale and temporary, shifting basis—people increasingly cleared, burned, drained and cultivated the land, and their livestock prevented regeneration of woodland in cleared areas. As iron-age populations increased, their technological development hastened deforestation. Although there were still considerable expanses of woodland and forest surviving into early medieval times, many so-called medieval hunting forests were not necessarily heavily wooded, and erosion triggered leaching of nutrients, increasingly impoverished soils and created yet more peat bog in upland areas. Subsequently, the ever-increasing exploitation of timber for house-building, ship-building and fuel further reduced the extent of ancient woodland—as did forest clearance to flush out freebooters, moss troupers and wild animals, sometimes by burning. Although late 17th- and early 18th-century estate plantings—often linked to landscaping—helped to redress the balance, the huge swathes of latter-day blanket afforestation with non-native species can never be an ecologically-sound substitute.

So it is that today's bleak, wind-driven and frequently sodden grasslands and heather moors are essentially people's creation, aided and abetted periodically by fluctuating climatic change. As with Scotland's Highlands, the Southern Uplands are in no sense a 'natural' wilderness, but one brought about by deliberate woodland clearance and increasingly intensive grazing regimes, mainly by sheep but variously, at different periods, by horses, cattle, goats and pigs. And heather burning, whether for sheep or for grouse, has contributed to the spread of bracken as well as thick, matted grasses. The vast expanse of 'improved' lowlands in the intersecting plains and river valleys also represents an entirely artificial, man-made landscape—forged by people's skill in developing increasingly sophisticated technologies for draining wetlands (particularly lowland bogs and lochs), clearing scrub and heathland, and cultivating and fertilising the reclaimed land.

Such continuing landscape change inevitably caused massive change in associated ecosystems, affecting the nature, range and density of the area's wildlife—a reduction and extinction (not to mention introduction) of plant, insect and animal species, forever hastened by the search for food, sport, profit and whatever else passes in the name of progress.

For the environment has been altered in many other ways too. Even if the impact of 20th-century technologies be set aside—whereby hugely increased areas of countryside have been buried beneath buildings, factories, roads and refuse—there are the dykes and hedges, quarries and cultivation terraces, trackways and drove roads of earlier centuries, as well as the many bridges, viaducts and aqueducts, harbours and lighthouses, castles and country houses, churches, tombs and other monuments.

## Sites in Time and Space

South-east Scotland is bewilderingly rich in surviving sites and monuments—evidence of these 6500 years of man's presence in the landscape. To appreciate them is to remember that each is a product of its time and of the technology of its time, so that mere technological comparisons across time are likely to be both simplistic and misleading. Small medieval bridges are at least as impressive and required just as much skill to construct as massive railway viaducts; early burial cairns, stone alignments and multi-ramparted hill settlements taxed minds and bodies, inventive genius and social organisation, in just the same way as elaborate abbeys, vaulted tower-houses and huge curtain-wall castles.

It is helpful to understand something of the respective technologies involved; but it is equally important to understand why buildings are sited where they are found. For buildings are a part of landscape history, of man and his inter-relationship with his environment. Certain elements, needs, problems are common throughout human time—shelter, defence, food, death, belief. It is attitudes, approaches, solutions that vary, according to the patterns and processes of a particular age.

Whilst location is overwhelmingly determined by geography, therefore, it is also tempered by politics and preference. Certain kinds of building occupy particularly prominent sites—hillforts, castles, follies and obelisks (not to mention latter-day communications transmitters and wind farms!). By contrast, 17th- and 18th-century country houses feature in less exposed, less well-defended but scenically-pleasing places, more attractive in times of peace than war. Border Abbeys and early churches are strategically placed at key locations in what would have been largely undrained medieval lowlands; and the upland location of so many stone circles perhaps suggests early settlement in areas of better natural drainage, where a thinning forest edge allowed easier woodland clearance. River valleys attracted industries dependent upon water-power; and the area's other many-varied industries were established alongside their underlying natural resource—coal, oil shale, limestone, sandstone, clay, salt water. In turn, modern settlement has frequently developed around earlier kirktons, fermtouns, market burghs, estate villages, early industrial villages and fisher touns—albeit ever-influenced by the impact of contemporary communications and transport systems, and the over-riding application of modern technologies and economic philosophies to subduing and subjugating natural landscapes and environments.

Most of what survives in south-east Scotland reflects the heritage of the higher echelons of specialised and stratified, organised societies—burial cairns, stone circles, abbeys and churches, castles and country houses. This is hardly surprising, for they alone had the resources and power to use long-lasting materials and to organise others in their careful construction. Even water mills, canals and railways are hardly typical of the majority population, only of their time. And whilst post-improvement farms, farm cottages and steadings, along with the fairly extensive crumbling ruins of a more recent industrial past, mines, mills, factories and their associated housing and settlements, reflect something of the ways of 'ordinary' people, evidence is scarce indeed for pre-improvement pastoral and agricultural life-styles and buildings. It is restricted in the main to a handful of fragmentary field and settlement systems. Notwithstanding such limitations, the range and density is remarkable.

To move rapidly through a landscape, however, stopping briefly to examine a church, a tower, a house, a bridge, a field system, is to appreciate little more than its simplest shape and function. Insight into the distinctive character of a region, into the way past societies thought and acted, how their material culture evolved—this all requires time and energy! Countryside, village and townscape are best walked and explored; artefacts, maps, histories, illustrations, language and tradition examined. Moreover, what man did, where and when, relates directly to the anatomy of the landscape—not just the present or past flesh on the skeleton, but that very basic, underlying, bony structure that has predetermined the main lines of contact, communication and settlement through time.

## Settlement Names

Placenames, whether purely descriptive or indicative of settlement, have an important and all too often under-rated contribution to make to the dissection of a human landscape, to the context for its buildings. In south-east Scotland, French, Norse, Gaelic, Cumbric or British, Pictish names are all represented, in addition to Anglian/Scots/English.

Many are the 18th- and 19th-century Scots/English names in *-ton/-town, -burn, bridge, -hill, -dyke, -head, -muir, -haven, -mouth*; moreover, farms were commonly divided into *Upper and Nether, Easter and Wester* as expansion and development increased. But a number of earlier terms also occur with some frequency. *Spital* was a general term for a hospice or shelter for travellers, particularly on higher ground—though originally referring to an institution established by the Church or the Knights Hospitallers for the sick and the needy. A *mains*, on the other hand, went with a feudal landed estate to distinguish the principal farm from the big house itself or from more humble farming townships.

That much of the countryside was devoted to grazing, rather than arable, is reflected in the many *Her(d)ma(n)stons*; *shiel* confirms that stock and herds moved seasonally to more distant pastures. Particularly in Lothian, however, it may be that Hermand/Hermiston/Herdmanston originates in OE *heierdeman*, a hired man—freeborn retainers (as distinct from menial servants) who were attached to a lord's household and formed the core of the local gentry or freeholder class. In effect they were the local government officials and factors of their time—overseeing and administering.

It is for such earlier historical periods that placenames can be of particular value and fascination in unravelling the cultural heritage—provided that interpretation is not based simply on recent maps or other late evidence, but on the earliest recorded forms.

Of the languages represented in placenames, French, Norse and Gaelic had but a fleeting impact, and they reflect more a linguistic influence than any great linguistic presence. French is the 'youngest' of these. Names such as Prestongrange, Newtongrange, Drygrange incorporate an Old French *grange*, granary—the farm associated with a powerful abbey settled by monks coming either directly from France or by way of England. But even *grange* does not presuppose, if any, more than a short-lived handful of French speakers. Otherwise, French is restricted mainly to personal names associated with castles and estates—Riddell, Melville, Seton. Most of the barons had settled first in England before being invited north by David I, and none of the names pre-dates the mid 12th century, by which time Scots English was pre-eminent.

A little earlier, however, from the 10th century until the 12th century, following the political unification of Scotland under Kenneth MacAlpin, a Gaelic-speaking overlordship drawn from further north and west existed in south-east Scotland. Geographical features may incorporate eg *dùn, beinn, ceann, tòrr, druim, creag, gleann, ord, allt, glac, tairbeart, camus*, particularly in northern and western Lothian and the north-western valleys of Peebleshire and Selkirkshire; settlements are indicated by names in *baile*, a farm, mainly west of the Pentland Hills (eg Balerno, Balbardie, Balleny). East and south of Edinburgh and in the Borders *baile* names are extremely rare; *achadh*, a field (and not necessarily, therefore, a settlement) is even rarer, restricted to West and Midlothian (eg Auchendinny); as also is *dail*, a meadow (eg Dalry, Deloraine) and *eachlann*, a horse paddock (Echline). Names incorporating a Gaelic personal name and Anglian *tun*, by contrast, equivalent of Gaelic *baile*, are more common—*Maelcarf* in Makerstoun and *Maccus* in Maxton, *Colman* in Comiston and *Gille Moire* in Gilmerton. They no more required Gaelic speakers, however, than places incorporating French or Scandinavian personal names presuppose French or Scandinavian speakers; rather were they given by Anglian speakers to lands owned by those bearing 'Scots' names.

**Cat Stane, near Kirkliston**

Anglo-Scandinavian compounds are plentiful in Lothian and the Borders, though less markedly so in Peeblesshire and West Lothian—*Bóndi*, in many Bonningtons, *Dólgfinnr* in many Dolphin(g)(s)tons, *Ormr* in many Ormisto(u)ns, *Kolbrandr* in Cockburnspath and Colinton, *Gamall* in Gamelshiel, *Gunni* in Gunsgreen, *Ulfkell* in Oxton, *Ingialdr* in Ingliston, *Hrafnkell* in Ravelston, *Sveinn* in Swanston and Swinton ('Swein son of Ulfkill held Swinton in 1100'). Few of these are recorded before c 1130; most from only the 13th-14th century. Moreover, in Corstorphine and Kirkettle, the personal names *Torfinn* and *Ketill* are preceded (rather than followed) by Gaelic *crois*, cross and *carn*, cairn—evidence of once Gaelic-speaking communities and presumably coined after about the mid 10th century.

These Scandinavian personal names were fully anglicised before they reached Scotland, and given that the first Vikings did not reach the Northumbrian coast much before the end of the 8th century, they clearly relate to later periods of Northumbrian consolidation in south-east Scotland, not to earlier periods of colonisation. They may represent simply a fashion in first names, or a more genuinely mixed race and culture reflected equally perhaps in the 10th to 12th-century hogbacked tombstones of Abercorn, Old Cambus, Ancrum and elsewhere.

There are, by contrast, just a few indications of settlement by actual Scandinavian speakers. These settlers, though influenced by England's Danelaw, may have been Norse- rather than Danish-speaking, arriving perhaps from around the Solway and Dumfriess-shire. They were concentrated mainly north of and just below the Lammermuir Hills. A handful of names incorporate *-byr*, a farm, hamlet—Humbie, Begbie, Blegbie, Pogbie, Corsbie, 'Schatteby'; one only incorporates *-thveit*, a clearing or meadow—Moorfoot. There are no records earlier than the mid 12th century, though the names were presumably given somewhat earlier; the alternating 12th- and 13th-century forms of old Midlothian Smeaton, however, *-tun* and *-bi*, reinforce the temporary, short-lived nature of such small pockets of Scandinavian speakers in essentially Anglian territory. Other partly Scandinavian names incorporate *gill*, a ravine; the stream name *grain*, a fork, branch; and *fjall*, a hill—particularly in the high lands towards the Dumfriess-shire border.

The main period of Northumbrian colonisation spanned some 200 or so years, from the mid 7th century. The first phase was a military takeover of lands both sides of the Tweed as far west as Dere Street. This was marked by the battle of Degsaston in 603 AD, when the Anglians defeated the Scots and the Picts, probably at Addingston's 'Aedan's Stane' in Lauderdale. (And Eidyn/Edinburgh was captured between 633 and 641 AD.) Simprim (possibly OE *-ingas*, followers of) and *Coludesburh*, a part-translation of British or Cumbric *Caer Golud* (the Celtic fort of Colud on St. Abb's Head) probably represent the first Anglian centres, followed by names in *-ingaham*, a settlement. When Coludesburh moved inland it became Coldingham—the village of the people of Coludesburh. Along with Whittinghame and Tyninghame in East Lothian, these pioneering *-ingaham* names are restricted to the extreme eastern coastal fringe. Subsequently names in *-ingtun*, an enclosure/farm and *-ham*, a homestead/group of homesteads, help trace the spread of settlement further round the east coast and into the lower reaches of the more important rivers—Edington, Edrington, Mersington, Hassington, Re[g]n[in]ton, Upsettlington, ?Haddington, ?Carrington; Smailholm, Yetholm, Birgham, Ednam, Oxnam, Midlem, Edrom, Kimmerghame, Leitholm, Morham, Oldham (-stocks). That several of these settlement names subsequently became parish names emphasises the quality of their lands, and their economic significance as manorial centres.

Most names in *-wic*, Darnick, Fenwick, Hawick, Borthwick, Hedderwick, Prestwick, Fishwick, are likely to be 9th century or later and with the exception of coastal (North) Berwick, barley farm, suggest secondary dependent farms based on cattle grazing and dairying. Other settlements of around the same period incorporate *-worth*, enclosure—Polwarth, Cessford (earlier Cesseworth), Jedburgh (earlier Gedwearde); also *-bot(h)l*, house, dwelling place—Morebattle, Newbattle, Bolton.

Settlement was intensifying along the main rivers and their tributaries, still on the fertile, though increasingly rising ground, not yet into the hills. For example, OE *ceaster*, a fort, was widely used by Anglians in south-east Scotland for locations close to pre-Anglian native fortified homesteads—

Belchester, Darnchester, Chesterhowe, Kerchester, Bonchester, Blackchester, High Chesters, Rowchester, Whitechesters, Chesters. That such names (and most other Anglian names with the exception of just a handful in *-wic* and *-ham*) are found only east of Dere Street (north of the Teviot), underscores Anglian supremacy to the east—where key Anglian townships and farms seem to have been located one for one, close to, but at 1.5-2 km from the forts or home 'farms' of British estates that the Anglians were sequestrating. And if Sprouston (east of Kelso) were the key royal, religious, ceremonial and market centre that has been suggested (like Yeavering in Northumberland), the Anglian phase of Doon Hill hall, superimposed on a British hall, might best be seen as home base for an individual thane or royal official required perhaps to oversee the 'town' of Dunbar. To be used cautiously, the value of such name evidence increases when set alongside the distributional and dating evidence of Anglian crosses and shrines, the Catrail or the Doon Hill halls.

As for the pre-Anglian names, a modest Pictish presence is confirmed in the northern part of the area by such as *pevr*, beautiful/radiant, in Peffer Mill, Peffer Burn; *pit*, piece of land, in Pitcox, Pittendreich; *aber*, river-mouth, in Abercorn, Aberlady. It is a distribution that suggests a restricted, coastal presence of Picts south of the Forth—whether or not this is also echoed in the Pentland (?Pictland) Hills.

By contrast there are considerable records of places associated with the British tribes who were defeated politically by the Northumbrians, who had co-existed with the Romans, and who had created the surviving systems of 'Celtic' fields as well as the iron-age fortified hilltop settlements. Thus, whilst the Anglian called it *ceastor*, the native used *cair* for his own fortified farm or large house (Carfrae, Caerlanrig) or, indeed, for a Roman fort (Cramond). Another key element is *–tref*, homestead—Soutra, Tranent, Traprain, Trabroun/Trabrown, Traquair, Dreva and Trehenna. This is a primary settlement name; less important places, none of them likely to be very early, incorporate *penn*, end/head—Penicuik, Pencaitland, Penmanshiel, Penshiel, Pennygant Hill; also *pren*, tree—Pirn, Pirnie, Primrose, Barnbougle (earlier Prenbowgall). A particular tree, even in a wooded landscape, may have had a specific importance as a meeting place or place of worship. It seems likely that these British names, often in Anglo-British hybrids, were adopted by Anglian speakers only after considerable peaceful co-existence—with the hilly land around Stow on the Gala Water possibly one of the last strongholds of British or Cumbric speakers.

There are, of course, other Cumbric terms to have survived in important placenames — *-ros*, moor, in Melrose (bare moor); *pebyll*, tent, in Peebles; *-cēd*, wood, in (Dal)keith, Bathgate; *-crwm*, bent, in Ancrum. *Egles*, church, is found in Eccles (near Coldstream), Ecclaw (near Duns), Eccles Cairn (Yetholm parish)—'church' names which, in the main, point to the establishment of Christianity in the area before the late 6th century AD. By contrast, the saint's name makes Ecclesmachan unlikely to be older than the 7th century.

## Landform and Communications

The placename evidence is at its most intriguing perhaps for this Dark Age/Early Christian/Early Medieval period. Whilst much denotes actual settlement, much is geographically descriptive of hills, moors and valleys. For Scotland is an essentially mountainous country. Even the lowlands are punctuated with individual hills and extensive uplands, so that communications have always been difficult, and this led to the development of strong local cultures and loyalties. In south-east Scotland, no less than elsewhere, it is the natural obstacles to easy communications that stand out most strikingly—the sea, the hills and the rivers.

The point is well-made by climbing the northern-most summits of the Pentland Hills above Swanston (alternatively, the more accessible Arthur's Seat, Blackford Hill or the Braid Hills within Edinburgh). On a clear, though almost inevitably windy day, the fortified volcanic plugs of West and East Lothian and Edinburgh rise up from the river-riven plain alongside obsolete coal and shale bings. To the north they are bounded by the narrowing Forth, once crossed by ferries, now by its distinctive rail and road bridges. It is a clearly-defined barrier but it also leads inland, north-west, to the 'cradle of the Scottish nation', set about by the steep-edged Ochils and more distant, dominating peaks of Breadalbane and the Trossachs.

Rivers and firths are both real and psychological barriers, but more easily overcome than the dense forests and swamps, once haunts of predatory wolves, bears, wild boars, that occupied the flatter low-lying ground into medieval times—around Lothian's Almond, Water of Leith and Tyne, just as much as the Border's Tweed and its tributaries. The older land routes, therefore, like earlier settlements, kept to the higher ground flanking the hills, or to the coastal strip. In West Lothian, Linlithgow's palace, church and burgh, like much earlier iron-age forts on the hills just south, guarded the main route to the upper Forth and lower Clyde; the more direct route to the Clyde, followed equally by roads and railways but not by the canal, skirts the northern flanks of the Pentlands, then over bleak but low-lying moorland between Shotts and Slamannan. Communications were reasonably easy, and for much of its past West Lothian was very much a 'debateable land', fought over from all sides. It was a gateway north and west, south and east, that no Pict or Scot could afford to leave in Northumbrian or British hands; no Roman could afford to leave unprotected. Yet in all this, the mysterious folds of the Bathgate Hills south of Linlithgow, virtually isolated by the rivers Avon and Almond and the Forth, long provided sanctuary whether at Cairnpapple or Torphichen; and on occasion these low, lumpy hills likely marked a fragile frontier.

Such routes could take only one course eastwards, however—towards that narrow neck of land between the Pentlands and the sea dominated by a scatter of sharply-defined volcanic crags that nowadays contribute so much to Edinburgh perspectives. The modest but steep, rough summits also commanded the sea routes north—whether from the mouth of the Almond, Esk or Water of Leith. Inevitably the hilltops were fortified; inevitably the Romans brought their roads here to meet their maritime supply route.

Subsequently, and equally inevitably, British, Northumbrians, Scots, Anglo-Normans and English all understood the crucial and capital importance of the place. Without physical control of Edinburgh, the whole of the north and the west was at risk from the south—or vice versa.

Edinburgh, thus, was the focus not just for routes from the north and west, but for all main routes east and south of the Pentlands, whether modern roads and railways, medieval roads, Roman roads or prehistoric trackways. They came principally from three directions—across the East Lothian plain, either coastally or hugging the northern slopes of the Lammermuirs, avoiding the marshy flood plain of the Tyne; from the south across Midlothian to the Esk by way of the northern tributaries of the Tweed, notably Lauderdale; from the south-west around the southern and eastern flanks of the Pentlands from the upper Clyde/upper Tweed/Biggar Gap.

Unlike the open prospect north and north-west from a Pentland summit, however, that to the south and east is closed by the long, low line of the steep northerly incline of the Lammermuir and Moorfoot Hills—a knife edge, Lothian edge, the edge of the world, as it were. To all appearances, control of that edge would effectively secure Edinburgh, the Forth and the north. But what of beyond, to the south?

From the Eildon Hills above Melrose (or maybe from the lower rocky outcrops of Smailholm, Brotherstone or Hume) is to appreciate how fully the Borders focus eastwards on the broad and fertile, once marshy Merse and on its natural capital, Berwick. The low straggling outcrops north of the Tweed soon blend into the gently sloping moorlands of the southern Lammermuirs; and these, in turn, with the Moorfoots, obscure all sight of Lothian just as effectively as the Cheviots obscure all sight of England. In a western arc, moreover, from the Teviot to the Gala Waters, long and sinuous river valleys radiate outwards to disappear amongst hilly uplands linking the Cheviots to the Moorfoots. A secure, self-contained little enclave, therefore, of no great threat to a Scottish nation?

But such an apparently solid, mountainous barrier is a deceit. Unlike the Lammermuirs, which terminate around St. Abb's Head in breathtaking sea-cliffs, heavily populated in season with vast colonies of breeding sea-birds, the Cheviots stop short some way from the sea. In physical terms the Tweed Valley is simply a northwards continuation of the Northumbrian plain extending far inland, right up to the base of the Lammermuirs and the Eildon Hills. As a consequence, for so much of its past, it was also a racial, political and economic extension. The neolithic builders of the earliest, unchambered long cairns seem to have come from north-east England rather than from the Irish Sea province; the bronze-age occupants of the round cairns and beaker burials penetrated from the east coast, with northward movement around the eastern edge of the Cheviots. The territories of the later iron-age Votadini, the Gododdin, stretched even further, from Hadrian's Wall to the Forth—a feat emulated subsequently by the Northumbrian Angles and Anglo-Scandinavians. Indeed, the old kingdom of Northumbria eventually stretched from the Forth to the Humber, whilst ecclesiastically St Cuthbert at Lindisfarne seems to have held all the land under Lammermuir between the Leader and the Whiteadder Waters as well as the whole of East Lothian belonging to the monastery of St Baldred at Tyningehame. What a precedent for an emergent, unitary Scotland!

If control of the Forth, Edinburgh and the approaches north of the Lammermuirs were crucial for such a Scotland in the 11th century AD, control of the Merse and the Tweed was equally so. For in addition to its agricultural, wealth-producing potential, this broad, eastward-flowing 'Northumbrian' lowland valley controlled direct access to the heart of Scotland—northwards to Edinburgh, central and northern Scotland along the eastern coastal fringe or through one or other of the long Lammermuir or Moorfoot valleys; westwards up Tweeddale and through the Biggar Gap into Clydesdale, the west-central lowlands and west Scotland (with further transverse routes back north to Edinburgh and the Forth). These upland massifs, in other words, were far from impenetrable. Moreover, the route through Teviotdale not only led to south-west Scotland and the Solway Firth, but also into north-west England. Its control would mean that the 'back door' also was secured.

It was in 1018, after victory at Carham on the south bank of the Tweed, that Scotland's national border was fixed—more or less—to follow the Cheviots and the Tweed. Both 'doors' were secured; Edinburgh ceased to be a Border fortress; the name 'Lothian' referred to the whole area between the Forth and the Tweed. Warring, land-grabbing and cattle-reiving continued of course, but for a couple of centuries or so it was still more a matter of Angles and Cumbrians, of powerful family feuds, than of English and Scots. Only after the death of Alexander III in 1286 and of his heir, the Maid of Norway, was the Scottish Nation finally forged from under the hammer of a predatory Edward I and the long-drawn-out Wars of 'Independence'. In the process, in 1482, Berwick was finally lost. By 1707 of course, by somewhat more subtle means, the whole country was lost—and though that is a different story, the enemy had, as always, been as much within as without.

The point is, rather, that through all this time, through the cut and thrust of political, religious and military diplomacy, the routes across south-east Scotland provided the key to success—or failure. The location of earlier, prehistoric burial cairns and fortified settlements testifies to the long-established value of the area's through-routes. The actual distribution and density of hillforts for example—around Cockburnspath, Coldingham Moor and Bunkle Edge; flanking Lauderdale, Teviotdale and the Cheviots; around the upper Tweed and the Biggar Gap—give a glimpse of the relative importance of different routes during the 500 or so years before the birth of Christ; superimposition of the network of Roman forts, camps, harbours and roads emphasises the different priorities of native and invader. A thousand years later, the threat to an independent Scotland by sea from the south is echoed by the mighty castles of East Lothian; the threat by land by a similar chain along the Tweed from Berwick and across to Biggar—with those in Liddesdale covering the south-western approach. Thereafter in the 14th century, and again in the 16th century, it is rather the ownership of the larger forts and castles that helps identify areas under English or Scots (latterly with French) control. The evidence reinforces, however, the continuing strategic pre-eminence of the coastal and Lauderdale routes.

**Tantallon Castle and the Bass Rock**

The distribution of tower-houses, peles and bastle-houses, by contrast, reflects more specifically the pressures of daily life. Unsuited to siege warfare or highly-mechanised attack, they provided adequate protection from localised raids from the 14th century to the Union of the Crowns in 1603 and later. They were particularly plentiful in Lothian west and south of Edinburgh; there were equally strong concentrations in the Cheviot foothills close to the Border, in the hummocky landscape north of the Tweed between Earlston and Kelso, and also around Peebles, the upper Tweed and the Manor Water. In these areas indeed, they clustered more thickly than almost anywhere else in Scotland—a comment partly on the fertility of the land but partly on the uncertainty of life in key areas straddling important through-routes close to the national border. For throughout this period the land between the Forth and the Border continued to be very much a frontier zone, an encouragement both to petty lawlessness and to brutal, localised, struggles for power.

The majority of tower-houses are found below the 150 m contour; those built before 1600 are a good indicator of the upper limit of cultivation and habitation for they tend to have been built on or even slightly beyond the moorland margin of the period. Pre-Reformation churches, too, stand on lands farmed in the Middle Ages and can extend almost up to the limits of cultivation. The big abbeys, that power block close to the Border and beholden to the Scottish kings, generally held the most favoured and strategically important locations, given that most of the Merse itself would still have been ill-drained. And they paid the price during successive English invasions. That the peak of medieval church building had passed by around 1300 is a reminder of subsequent troubled times and their impact on economic prosperity, for ecclesiastical wealth was drawn largely from local industry and labour, and from trade. There were other reasons, nonetheless, why agricultural expansion had more or less halted by 1500—not just climatic changes and more frequent crop failures, but loss of shelter due to massive destruction of woodlands and loss of fertility due to lack of manure on the more distant of the cultivated lands. Proverbially, the return was never more than threefold—'Ane to saw and ane to gnaw, and ane to pay the laird witha' '. Meantime, the countryside was served by the scattered little burghs, with their mercat crosses, markets and fairs.

Shelter belts in the present-day landscape, on the other hand, often reflect modest extensions of cultivation in the mid 18th-mid 19th century, when improved drainage, liming and other new methods complemented the regular rectangles of new enclosures and new farm-steadings. A more settled society and increased prosperity was also manifest in the shift from tower-house to country house, first mainly in East Lothian from the early 17th century, and gradually across the whole area. The shift was accompanied by a move to a more open, attractive, relatively low-lying and 'indefensible' location.

In other words, from the Union of the Crowns, and more particularly from the Union of the Parliaments a century later in 1707, it is not so much defence that helped determine the predominant characteristics and pattern of major secular buildings and settlements, but fashions, resources and what was considered 'politically correct'. And as food became more plentiful, grown on the larger, more efficient, well-managed farms, so new industries could be manned full-time—whether cottage industries or fisheries in newly-planned villages, or more heavily centralised industries in a new kind of urban settlement serving mills, mines or factories. This, put simply, was the theory, and in practice this is what occurred. Surviving industrial architecture can give some idea, at least, of the social costs involved.

## The More Recent Past

Communications continued to be a vital factor in this brave new world—mill towns, like medieval abbeys, were mostly sited close to the clustering mouths of the Tweed's main tributaries, close to the radial hub. And similarly around Edinburgh. But from the 18th century, man became increasingly able to remodel his communications network to suit his industrial and economic requirements. Roads, canals and railways all made use of natural routes where appropriate, but cuttings, embankments, bridges, viaducts, aqueducts reflect innovative engineering linked to the new technologies; hitherto insuperable natural obstacles could now be overcome.

In just 200 or so years, therefore, man has been able to 'adjust' his environment more fundamentally than at any time during his 8000 years or more occupation of south-east Scotland. Nowadays, moreover, the speed and scale of technological innovation and change is greater than in any previous age. Our traditional, complex and diverse cultural heritage is disintegrating—whether language, traditions, social structures, or built environment; and for so many communities increasingly distanced from a natural environment, the growing ecological imbalance is apparently of little widespread concern. Yet our forbears well understood, if not always respected, the ever-crucial inter-relationship of man and environment; their collective experience, distilled over time, can provide a stable, identifiable cultural base from which to grapple with an uncertain future.

This book does not set out to highlight the more stimulating monuments of the 20th century, but however good and interesting certain individual modern buildings may be, or a handful of larger projects and rehabilitation schemes, the overall impact of today's built environment on much of the landscape remains progressively intrusive—a cancerous growth of housing ghettos, industrial complexes, business and retail parks, power-lines, transmitters, motorways, high-level farm or estate tracks, to add to a largely derelict industrial legacy. It is an increasingly compartmentalised, structure-littered landscape, where the 'improvement' of such countryside features as Edinburgh's Arthur's Seat tends merely to suburbanise and diminish. Earlier ages undoubtedly had their meaner, more squalid features in addition to the higher status structures that have survived. There were fewer of them however, they were of a lesser scale and they were constructed in natural, unobtrusive, assimilable materials.

Until recent times, man in south-east Scotland remained dependent on what was to hand, and it was local materials—stone, slate, clay, timber, turf, straw—that helped give the area its distinctive character. Different kinds of building stone in particular reflected what was below as well as above the ground. Hard, difficult-to-work, dark volcanic whinstone featured in rubble masonry across much of the area, particularly Lothian; so also different and varied kinds of more easily worked sandstone—red, yellowy-orange, rusty-iron sandstones in East Lothian and Roxburghshire; dark greywacke around the upper half of the Tweed; a sometimes rather drab, off-white sandstone from the Craigleith Quarries in Edinburgh's New Town. Building in clay survived longest on Coldingham Moor, whilst brick-making was largely restricted to mining areas within the Lothian coalfield. Bricks were used above all to build the mining villages themselves and the engine-house chimneys on large, progressive farms. As for roofing, thatch was eventually superseded by slates, mainly from the west of Scotland but also from Tweeddale; red pantiles, on the other hand, were common on 17th- and 18th-century buildings in lowland Lothian. Originally imported perhaps as ballast from the Low Countries, they were subsequently made, like bricks, in association with coal-mining, particularly near Inveresk and Prestonpans—though an occasion, as an offshoot of a local drainage tile works. Such localised distinctions in traditional building materials are still very much in evidence across south-east Scotland; they contribute considerably to variety in the landscape and reflect the diversity of a natural environment. Their impact, moreover, is essentially low-key; by and large they do not dwarf or alienate the landscape.

Here then is a quite startling heritage of buildings and other 'monuments' spanning perhaps 50 centuries; maybe 200 generations. The range and richness is remarkable. It remains to be seen how much of this heritage modern man will continue to value and conserve, and it remains to be seen how much he will be able to contribute of comparable, lasting interest and individuality.

Reconstructed tower-houses, water mills and smaller churches, and the occasional water tower, railway station or lighthouse can make attractive and manageable homes and work-stations; and large-scale textile mills or whisky bonds provide much-needed urban flats and offices. Yet the ubiquitous use of glass and concrete, brightly-coloured brick, multi-coloured girders and steel panels in so many new buildings creates an ever-tightening and garish yoke around distinctively Scottish villages, towns and cities. It represents an environmental intrusion fashioned in considerable part by the gallop towards minimum regulation and maximisation of assets. Yet were Scotland to reverse the 18th-century political, social and architectural trends that embraced a new Britain at the expense of an old Europe, and were she—from amongst the ashes of 19th and 20th century British imperialism—to rediscover her cultural and political self-confidence, whether or not within a new Europe, would the degradation be any the less? Would there then be a more sensitive and civilised relationship with the environment and a more sustainable, responsible use of finite resources?

Buildings, monuments, archaeological and historical sites, set within their human and environmental as well as their technological context, form a particularly tangible and accessible key to appreciating and learning from the attitudes, achievements and follies of past societies.

**Eildon Hills, Melrose**

*Grey recumbent tombs of the dead in desert places,*
*Standing stones on the vacant wine-red moor,*
*Hills of sheep, and the homes of the silent vanquished races,*
*And winds, austere and pure.*
*R L Stevenson*

# EXCURSIONS

The environmental setting for surviving prehistoric and later sites and monuments is early 21st century, not that of 300, 3000 or 4000 years ago! What has survived of earlier ecosystems is extremely limited and fragmentary, all-but fossilized within a hugely-changed landscape.

Many of the key conservation sites now have protected status as Sites of Special Scientific Interest (SSSIs) or National Scenic Areas (NSAs). There is a National Nature Reserve (NNR) at St Abb's Head (NTS/SWT); Scotland's first Voluntary Marine Nature Reserve (SWT) lies offshore around St Abbs and down to Eyemouth; the more important local sites are designated Local Nature Reserves (LNRs). The Scottish Wildlife Trust (SWT) manages some 20 wildlife reserves across Lothian and the Borders; the Woodland Trust (WT) has a clutch of woodlands; and access to many of these reserves (some require permits) can be arranged by contacting: The Scottish Wildlife Trust, Cramond House, Cramond Glebe Road, Edinburgh EH4 6NS (tel 0131 312 7765) or The Woodland Trust, Glenruthven Mill, Abbey Road, Auchterarder, Perthshire PH3 1DP (tel 01764 662554).

In Lothian, visitors may well notice enigmatic roadside markings, particularly in rural areas. These mark lengths of roadside verge, some of ancient origin and harbouring groups of decidedly uncommon plants; others simply preserving locally-rare plants (including important water-plants alongside ditches). To help maintain and extend these colonies, special cutting regimes have been adopted by the Local Authorities, in collaboration with the SWT, for both listed and non-listed verges. In both cases, a full cut only takes place in August, after the plants have flowered and their seeds dispersed.

## In and Around Edinburgh

No detailed excursions are offered for Edinburgh itself, any more than Edinburgh's best-known sites feature in the Gazetteer; and this is deliberate! Visitors can explore many walks and buildings in **Central Edinburgh** which are well-documented in innumerable Edinburgh guide books (see also Chapter 10: *A Glimpse of Edinburgh*). These may be in the **Old Town** – perhaps The Palace of Holyroodhouse, Edinburgh Castle, Ramsay Gardens, The High Kirk of St Giles, the Royal Mile with its many other kirks and closes, tenements and townhouses, the Grassmarket, Greyfriars Kirk and Heriot's Hospital – not to mention modern Saltire Court. Or they may be in the **New Town** – the Galleries on the Mound, the Scott Monument, the rune stone in Princes Street Gardens, the superb townhouses of Moray Place, Heriot Row or Charlotte Square, such buildings as (New/Old) Register House and the Headquarters of the Royal Bank/Bank of Scotland, Dean Village, St Bernard's Well beside the Water of Leith, and the monuments on the Calton Hill. Inverleith House and the remarkable Victorian and modern palm houses in the Royal Botanic Garden are but a kilometre or two to the north.

For visitors prepared to venture a little further afield, however, whether by car or by bicycle, bus and foot, there are many architectural treasures and landscapes to discover, many focused on one-time villages outwith the former boundaries of the Burgh. By way of example:

**Edinburgh (N by W to S)**: Caroline Park (late 17th-century Mackenzie mansion); Granton Gas Holders (1902, 1933, 1966); Cramond (no. 5: Roman fort, tower house, 17th to 19th-century Cramond House, remains of 18th-century iron mills, 18th-century village); Lauriston Castle and nearby converted farm steading/octagonal horsegang (c 1840); Corstorphine (15th to 19th-century church, churchyard and 16th-century dovecote); mid/late 19th-century Caledonian Brewery and nearby cooperative housing schemes, Slateford aqueducts/viaducts and early 20th-century slaughterhouses (no. 3); Colinton (mainly 18th to 19th-century church, session house, offertory house, village, early 20th-century Redford Barracks); Currie (18th-century kirk, school, schoolhouse); Balerno (17th-century Malleny House/Gardens, Threipmuir Reservoir, Bavelaw Castle).

**Edinburgh (S by E to N)**: 18th to 19th-century Swanston Farm and Village (no. 20) with prehistoric Hillend hillfort and Caerketton burial cairn; the Caiystane (no. 113); Blackford/Braid Hills (late 19th-century Royal Observatory, cultivation rigs, Hermitage); Liberton (1753 'agricultural' tombstone, 16th-century Tower); Burdiehouse (19th-century limekilns); 15th to 18th-century Craigmillar Castle (no. 48); Duddingston (mainly 17th to 18th-century kirk, village, wildlife sanctuary); Arthur's Seat (Dunsapie hillfort, medieval cultivation terraces, 15th-century St Anthony's chapel, St. Margaret's Well); 15th-century St Triduana's Chapel at Restalrig (no. 66); Leith Docks (no. 12: 17th-century Martello Tower, 16th to 19th-century mercantile/industrial buildings, Victorian steam crane/swing bridge, 19th-century Newhaven harbour, late 20th-century Scottish Office).

## Across the Lothians and Borders

Edinburgh apart, south-east Scotland lends itself to many theme-based explorations, which can be identified quite easily from the gazetteer. For those who prefer a more varied diet, the routes selected serve as an introduction to some of the most attractive and interesting sites and landscapes.

Each excursion forms a roughly circular tour and can start at any point. Several monuments in each tour can be visited very quickly, or easily viewed from the road; others require some walking—occasionally, stiff climbs. As outlined, each is best seen as a two or three day excursion. Season, weather, terrain, composition of the party and individual interests will all help determine how many or how few of the sites can be managed comfortably in a day, but each 'route' is so designed that it can readily be broken down into shorter outings.

Cyclists, ramblers and walkers of the Southern Upland and Pennine Ways can also select, match and mix according to their plans, and visits to specific monuments can often be linked to the many cycleways, town trails and countryside walks that have now been devised for many parts of the area. Local Authorities, Country Parks, Tourist Organisations and Voluntary Groups all publish leaflets detailing walks, cycle tours and wildlife sites, as well as access guides for the disabled. Be sure to enquire locally.

Groups might like to remember that, by prior arrangement, visits can sometimes be made out-of-season to many Historic Scotland/NTS properties and to country houses otherwise closed to visitors at that time. And specifically 'educational' group visits, booked in advance, may be granted preferential rates. In any case, it is always advisable to check in advance that monuments are open and accessible.

**Ceiling boss with mason's mark, St Triduana's Chapel**

**Edinburgh Castle in the snow**

**Cramond Auld Brig**

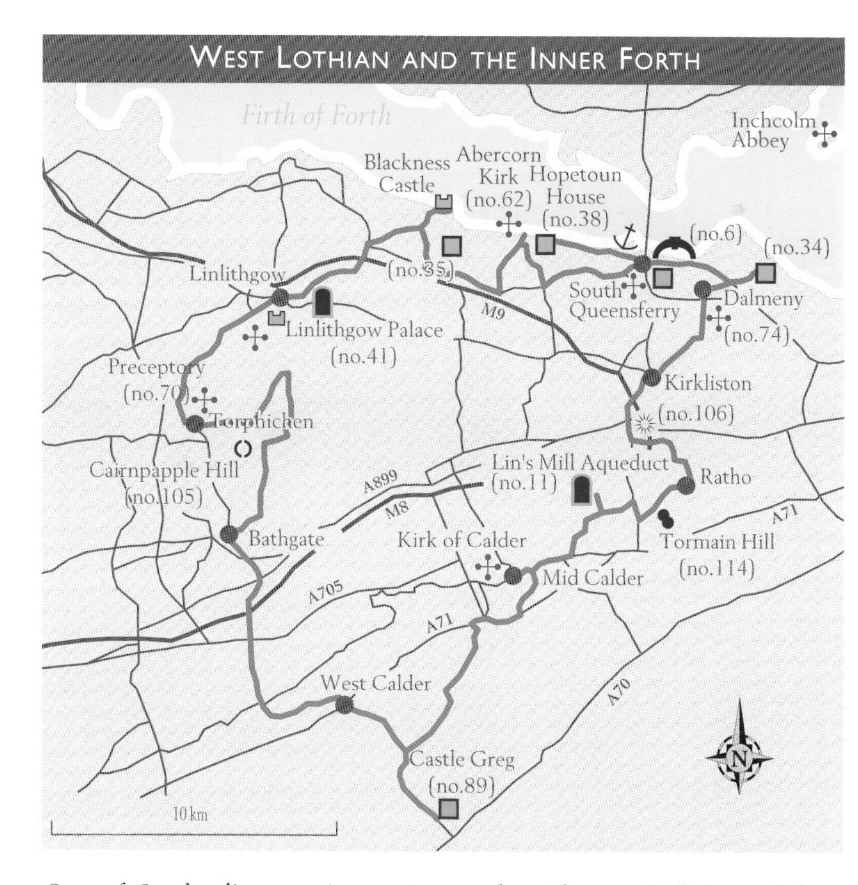


## Key

| | |
|---|---|
| Bridge | |
| Broch, fort | |
| Carved Stone | |
| Castle | |
| Church | |
| Cultivation Terraces | |
| Harbour | |
| Henge monument | |
| House, rural building | |
| Hut circle | |
| Industrial monument | |
| Lighthouse | |
| Long Cairn | |
| Mercat Cross | |
| Miscellaneous prehistoric | |
| Roman fort | |
| Round Cairn | |
| Standing Stone | |
| Stone Circle | |
| Town, village | |

One of Scotland's most impressive royal residences, Linlithgow Palace (no. 41), stands beside Linlithgow Loch close—to St Michael's Parish Church, a remarkable 17th-century Town House and the ornately-carved Cross Well. Look also for the peaceful semi-rural Union Canal Basin, with original stable buildings, just S of the railway in Manse Road. SW of the town, A 706 crosses the Canal at Woodcockdale (canal cottages, stables) a little E of the Avon Aqueduct (c 1820)—Scotland's tallest and longest canal aqueduct (see nos 3, 11).

Continue S on B 792 to the Knights Hospitallers' unique Torphichen Preceptory (no. 70). Take narrow side road E past Gormyre Farm (refuge/sanctuary stone nearby), and work through lumpy hills N (Cockleroy hillfort and good views over Linlithgow), then E and S to Cairnpapple's remarkable and complex henge and cairns (no. 105). This often-bleak, low, rounded hilltop encapsulates thousands of years of prehistory, and the panoramic views help explain why our ancestors selected this particular site for their ceremonial structures.

From Bathgate, B 792 leads through bleak former mining communities to Addiewell (1866 and site of one of James 'Paraffin' Young's largest shale-oil works), and on to West Calder. Look for the long rows of single-storey brick-built cottages and the atypically conical Five Sisters shale bings (shale tips were usually flat-topped). B 7008 leads S to Castle Greg Roman Fortlet (no. 89); minor roads lead back E and N from Harburn (SWT woodland) to A 71 and the conservation village of Mid Calder. The Kirk of Calder represents a final pre-Reformation flourish in what was originally intended as a collegiate church.

East on A 71, then minor roads N to Lin's Mill Aqueduct (no. 11). Walk along towpath to admire engineering prowess, and look N for M 8 and Birdsmill railway bridges at this key, difficult river crossing. Cut SE to B 7030 (Bonnington), then about 1 km NE to shelter-belt and a gently-rising walk to Tormain Hill (no. 114)—intriguing cup-and-ring marks on earthfast boulders around its low, loosely-wooded rounded summit.

Follow B 7030 through Ratho (Union Canal bridge, 1822 inn, cottages), to massive Newbridge roundabout (M8/M9), where minor road gives access to remains of Huly Hill round cairn (no. 106). Then W on A 89 (superb 32 span railway viaduct, 1842, crosses Almond valley), and back N on B 800 to Kirkliston (partly 12th-century church and pleasing square).

At B 9080/B 900 crossroads, turn E and follow minor roads NE to Dalmeny Kirk (no. 74)—Scotland's most exquisite, ornately-carved small Norman church, set back from late 18th- to early 19th-century estate cottages. Continue E to Dalmeny House (1817: no. 34), then W on B 924 to South Queensferry and the stunning Forth Railway Bridge (no. 6). Boat trips from old ferry pier to the very fine Augustinian Inchcolm Abbey on its island in the Forth (see no. 63: *Fife, Perthshire and Angus* volume).

West along the twisting,'two tier' High Street (many 17th to 18th-century townhouses, attractive Tolbooth), past the remains of the Carmelite Priory, take shore road W under Road Bridge to that most palatial Adam mansion, Hopetoun House (no. 38). A little further W, either by estate roads after visiting Hopetoun, or direct from Woodend on A 904, a tiny estate village

**Torphichen Preceptory, Bathgate Hills, West Lothian**

with imposing mid 18th-century factor's house guards access to mainly post-Reformation Abercorn Kirk (no. 62)—early Christian associations, Norman architecture, excellent 18th and 19th-century gravestones and a most aristocratic laird's loft.

Return SW to A 904, then W to B 9109 and N to The House of the Binns (see no. 35: look out for small packhorse bridge in fields near main road), and on to Blackness Castle (see no. 32: *Glasgow, Clydeside and Stirling* volume). The Castle is a 15th to 19th-century fortress, prison and ammunition store, protecting royal Linlithgow's one-time harbour. Return to Linlithgow by B 903/A 803.

**South Queensferry and the Forth Bridge**

**Hopetoun House stables and clock tower**

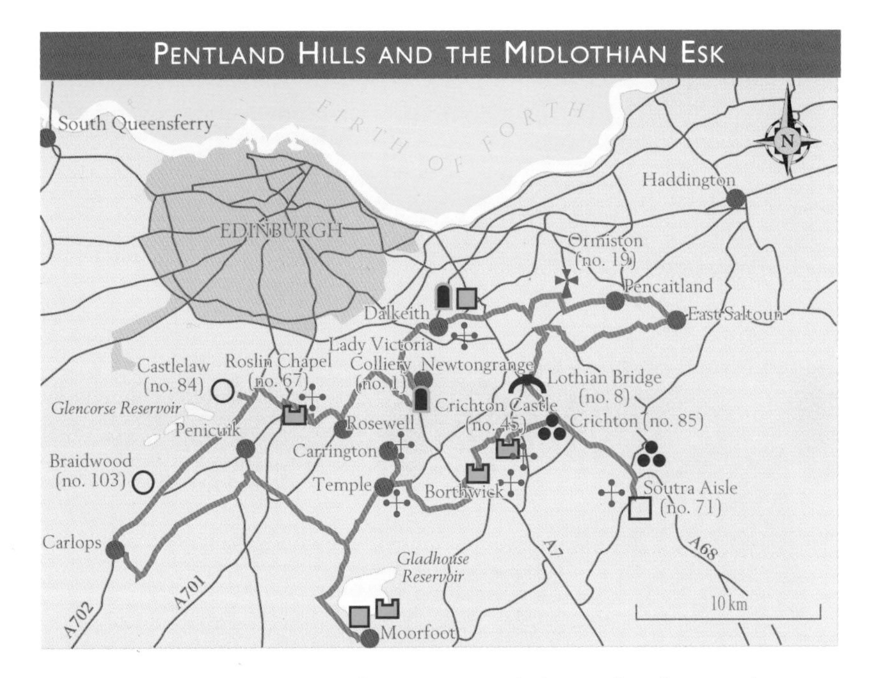


In Dalkeith, look for the Tolbooth, St Nicholas's Church, Watch Tower (1827) and idiosyncratic old Water Tower, now a private house. A 7 leads S under Lothianbridge railway viaduct to Newtongrange—Scotland's largest 19th-century mining village and Lady Victoria Colliery (no. 1). Follow B 704 NW, then A 6094 SW to Rosewell, another classic mining village with a remarkable yellow-brick, 1925 St Matthew's RC Church, priest's house and cloister.

West on B 7003, then down the narrow twisting road into Roslin Glen old gunpowder works), and up through Roslin village to Roslin Chapel (no. 67)—where the sheer eloquence of the 15th-century stone carving is unrivalled in Scotland. Pleasing woodland walk to picturesque, partly-ruinous/partly-occupied 15th to 17th-century Rosslyn Castle, set precipitously on sandstone cliffs high above N Esk. Rights-of-way allow a fine walk NE from the Castle/Chapel through thickly-wooded gorge (LNR/SWT), past 'Wallace's' Cave and 15th to 19th-century Hawthornden Castle to Hewan.

Continue W on B 7003 and minor roads to A 702. S just a little, then W up steep farm road for Castlelaw Fort and Souterrain (no. 84) and fine Pentlands hillwalks. Look S to the Covenanting battlefield of Rullion Green (1738) across Glencorse Reservoir (1819-24). Take A 702 S to Braidwood Settlement (no. 103) and the linear cottage-textile village of Carlops (1784). Stretches of Roman road from Biggar to the Forth can be traced near to Eight/Ninemileburn and across Linton Muir, whilst a major drove road crossed the Pentlands at Cauldstaneslap and down Baddinsgill to West Linton.

Minor roads E from Carlops (Whitfield lime kilns) and NE across Auchencorth Moss, lead to A 701, then E on B 6372, past Roseberry Steading (curious 19th-century building in 18th-century style), to Temple.

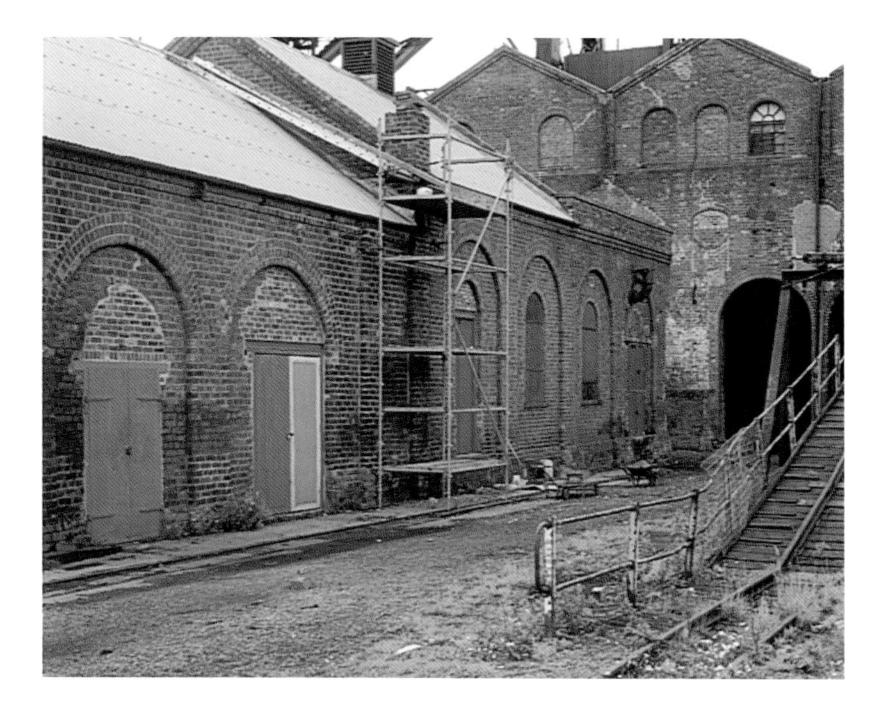

**Pit head, Lady Victoria Colliery, Newtongrange**

**Inner courtyard wall, Crichton Castle**

Consider a detour to Upper Side Limekilns, Gladhouse Reservoir (LNR), Moorfoot Farm and a gentle walk to heavily-ruinous 16th-century Hirendean peel tower. The Reservoir (1879) boasts a weir and embankment, pumping house, metal bridge and reservoir supervisor's quirkily baronial Gladhouse Villa.

Temple is an attractive conservation village with 13th to 14th-century ruined Templar church, subsequently passed to the Knights of St John; also good 17th and 18th-century gravestones. Nearby Carrington (minor road N) is a tiny village with pantiled cottages, T-plan church, the Whitehill Aisle and Carrington Mains Farm. Continue W on B 6372 to Robert Dundas's stately Adam mansion, Arniston House (occasionally open), and SE by minor roads to North Middleton (modern limeworks) and across A 7 to 15th-century Borthwick Castle (vast 'double' towerhouse, now a hotel), and church with 15th-century tomb.

Minor roads meander N/NE, across abandoned Waverley railway line (Edinburgh/Carlisle: closed 1969), to peaceful Crichton village, prehistoric fort and 15th-century Collegiate Church (look for the cast-iron gravestones, one recalling an Edinburgh foundry owner). Gentle track to Crichton Castle (no. 45)—splendidly Italianate inner courtyard wall. Crichton Souterrain is about 1 km E of the village, S on B 6367, then E towards Crichton Dean. Incorporating Roman masonry and in the middle of a field, it generally merits gumboots and a torch, and respect for the farmer's crops.

**The Apprentice Pillar, Roslin Chapel**

Continue E to A 68. Diversion S on the A 68/B 6368, leads to the remains of medieval monastic hospice at Soutra Aisle (no. 71), and a fragment of the Roman road/medieval Dere Street at King's Inch. Return N to 18th-century Pathhead, where the side road NW to Ford reveals Telford's most graceful 5-arch Lothian Bridge (no. 8). Return to Dalkeith along this minor road—the line of the old Roman road, and with stunning views on a clear evening across to the Pentlands, Edinburgh and the Paps of Fife. Alternatively return via the Saltouns, Pencaitland and Cockburn's tree-lined planned village of Ormiston (15th-century mercat cross: no. 19); thence by Cousland (preserved 18th-century smiddy, with tools and fittings).

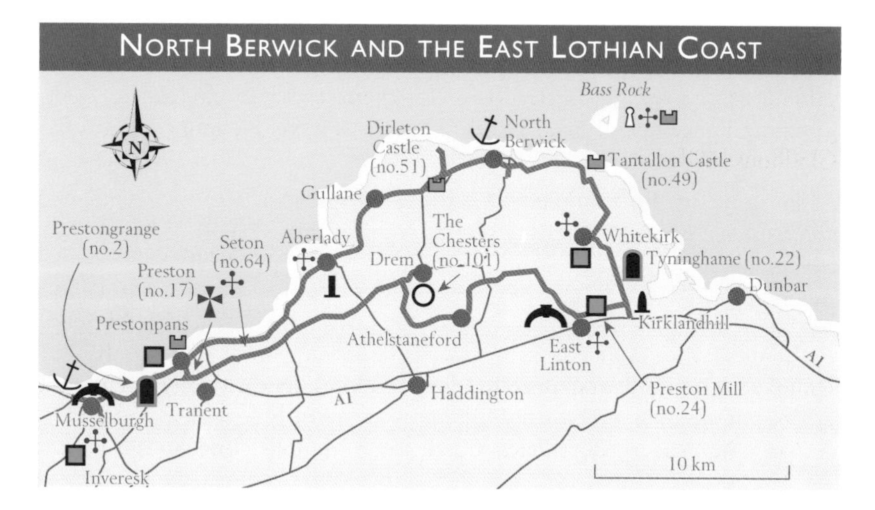


North Berwick Law, a volcanic plug surmounted by a whale's jawbones, makes a superb vantage point both landwards and seawards. W on A 198, Dirleton Castle (no. 51) rises majestically beside a very 'English' village green and typical lowland Scottish 'mains' ('home') farm. Minor road N to Yellowcraig (LNR) gives access to rocky/sandy shore with good outlook to Fidra (lighthouse) and coastal walk W to Gullane and Aberlady Bay (LNR).

Continue W on A 198 to Gullane (Norman chancel arch in ruinous old church) and Aberlady (loupin'-on-stane and replica of 8th-century cross shaft fragment at church; also distinctive Wemyss Estate alms-houses). Road W passes entrance to Robert Adam's Gosford House where shoreline trees, bent and stunted by prevailing W/SW gales, incline gradually higher in the lee of the encircling estate wall. B 1348 runs past Port Seton harbour, coal-fired Cockenzie Power Station and Prestonpans, to Prestongrange Colliery Beam Engine and adjacent disused brickworks (no. 2).

B 1348 leads eventually to Musselburgh (tiny mid 19th-century harbour of Fisherrow; 3-arch early 16th-century bridge across Esk with cutwaters, refuges and a stair each end; 5-arch early 19th-century Rennie bridge). B 6124 S from centre of Musselburgh soon reaches Inveresk (fine 17th-

**Tantallon Castle**

century Inveresk House and Gardens (NTS); other 17th and 18th-century houses/mansions; early 19th-century church with fishermen's loft—all largely overlying site of earlier Roman fort).

At Prestonpans, little survives of the old salt pans and fisheries, but B 1349 leads S uphill to a splendid cluster of 17th to 19th-century buildings—the superb Mercat Cross (no. 17), its rotunda all-but unique in Scotland; also Preston Tower, Northfield House, dovecotes and one of Scotland's very first post-Reformation churches (1596).

**Preston Mercat Cross** (Right)

Rejoining A 198, return E past simple roadside monument commemorating Jacobite victory over the English at the Battle of Prestonpans, 1745, to tree-shrouded Seton Collegiate Church (no. 64) and Longniddry; thence B 1377 to Drem (tiny estate village with pleasing warm-coloured single-storey cottages). The multi-ramparted, atypically low-lying Chesters Hillfort (no. 101) and the Hopetoun Monument on the Garleton Hills lie a little to the S; or if you prefer, make E/SE to the early 19th-century planned village of Athelstaneford, built for craftsmen and smallholders, and traditionally the place where Angus MacFergus saw a saltire (now Scotland's national flag) in the sky following a Pictish victory over the Northumbrian Athelstane.

**The kiln at Preston Mill** (Right)

East Fortune retains part of its wartime airfield, where some of the old RAF hangars now house Scotland's national Museum of Flight (NMS). Thereafter B 1377 continues to East Linton (good bridges and village centre, and a Prestonkirk Parish Church with largely 13th-century chancel). B 1407 leads E to pretty, albeit atypical (for Scotland) Preston Mill and nearby Phantassie Doocot (no. 24), and on to the airy planned estate village of Tyninghame (no. 22) and the ruins of St Baldred's Norman church. At junction with A 198 (diversion S to Kirklandhill Standing Stone), turn N to Whitekirk's reconstructed church and prominent Teind Barn (see no. 25).

**Phantassie doocot** (Right)

Continue N to Tantallon Castle (no. 49)—a mighty cliff-top promontory stronghold facing the precipitous, gannet-covered Bass Rock, complete with ruinous castle, chapel and 1902 lighthouse (boat trips from North Berwick). On a good day consider coastal cliff walks S towards Auldhame and Seacliffe. Back to North Berwick by A 198.

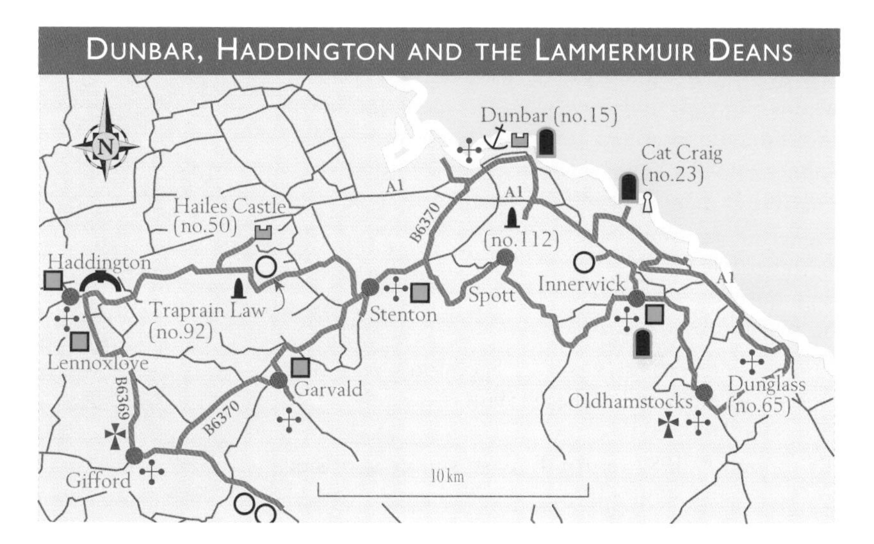


Dunbar (no. 15) has an attractive harbour with ruinous castle and 19th-century fort. See also the 1991 post-inflagration interior of 19th-century parish church (with 1611 alabaster monument to the Earl of Dunbar), and the simply-furnished John Muir's House (High Street)—birthplace of the father of modern conservation. Then take minor road S off A 1087, across A 1, to Easter Broomhouse Standing Stone (no. 112), before following A 1 (S) and left at East Barns for Cat Craig Lime Kilns (no. 23), Barns Ness Lighthouse and a geologically-interesting shoreline (fossils). Coastal walk (or drive via A 1) to late 18th-century Skateraw harbour, where today's landscape is dwarfed by massive, four-square bulk of Torness Nuclear Power Station.

Continue SW to Dunglass Collegiate Church (no. 65) and the many narrow gorges or 'deans' twisting down from the Lammermuirs to the sea; thence by minor roads W/N of Cockburnspath to Oldhamstocks—pretty village green with 18th-century pump, mercat cross and church. Meander around hummocky hills via Thornton to pink-stoned Innerwick. Look for 18th-

**Dunbar harbour and castle**

19th-century church, early 19th century farm buildings at Temple Mains (W end) and Innerwick Farm (W end), and inscribed 1887 cast-iron Jubilee horse trough just W of village. Possible diversion via Meikle Pinkerton to Doon Hill outline of 7th-century timber Northumbrian hall. Follow narrow country lanes W by early 19th-century Thurston Mains, Elmscleugh and The Brunt (fords) to Spott (early 19th-century Kirk and Manse).

**St Mary's Church and the Nungate Bridge, Haddington** (Right)

Left (W) at Spott to Pitcox and B 6370 to Stenton (rood well and reconstructed tron; fine pantiled/slated vernacular buildings/steadings; village greens; 1829 neo-Gothic church). There are forest trails at W end of Pressmennan Loch and Wood (WT). Continue W through rich, rolling farmland to Nunraw (16th-19th-century baronial mansion; severe mid 20th-century Cistercian Abbey of Sancta Maria), and on to Gifford—attractive, early 18th-century planned village erected by Giffords away from early 18th-century Yester House (and earlier Collegiate chapel of St Cuthbert). Look for white-harled T-plan church, Mercat Cross (1730) and public well.

**Hailes Castle, beside the River Tyne** (Right)

B 6355 leads SE to clearly-defined prehistoric forts of Black Castle and Green Castle, and on into Lammermuirs. Otherwise B 6369 leads N past Lennoxlove (16th to 19th-century country house, open seasonally), to the busy market town of Haddington. Here the vast Collegiate/Burgh church of St Mary's (no. 68), with its remarkable Lauderdale Aisle, lies close to medieval Nungate Bridge and ruins of St Martin's Kirk. Nearby, a 19th-century iron water-wheel is preserved at renovated/converted Poldrate Mill. Take minor roads E from Haddington on S side of Tyne to Hailes Castle (no. 50); then S to the fortified 'town' on Traprain Law (no. 92)—a tribal capital at the time of the Roman invasions and a fine viewpoint after a short steep climb. Look for the Loth Stone SSW.

Return to Dunbar by Luggate, Bielmill, Pitcox and Belhaven—a coastal village with attractive, stone-built, 19th-century and still-operational 'real ale' brewery and kilns. Bracing coastal walks and picnics in John Muir Country Park, accessed from West Barns!

## COASTAL BERWICKSHIRE AND THE MERSE

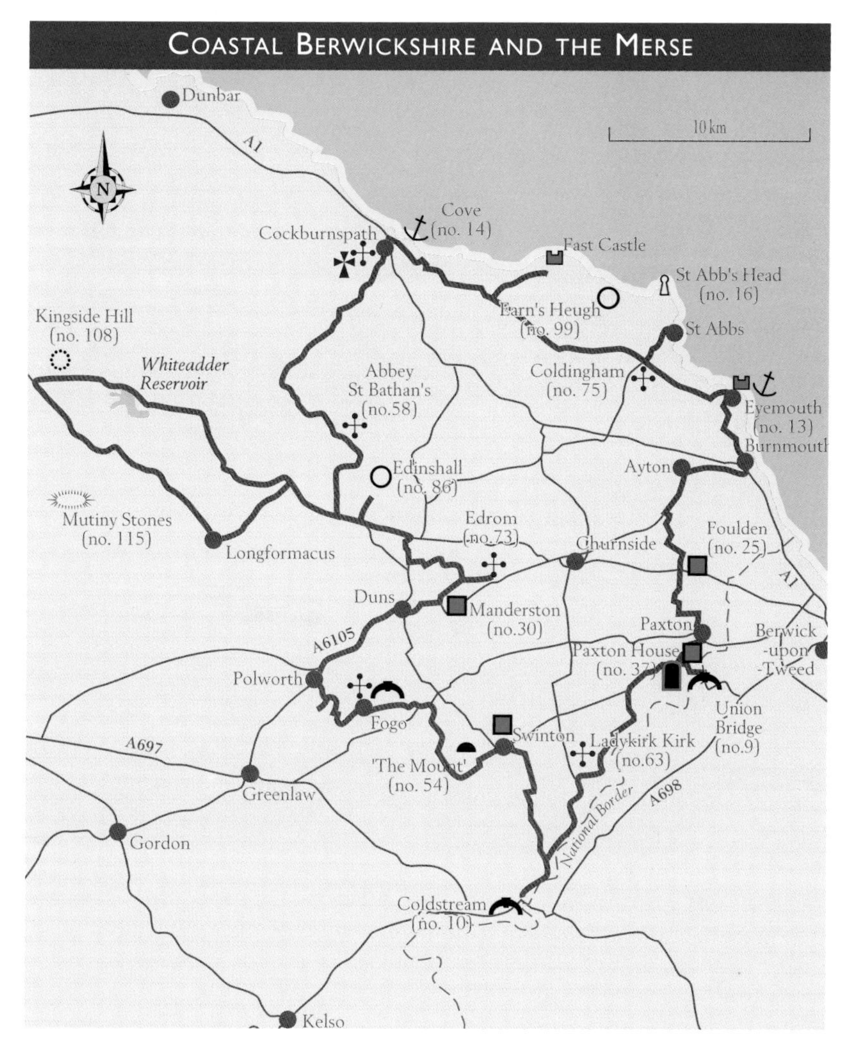


Eyemouth (no. 13) is a bustling North Sea fishing community set around a river mouth with multi-period piers and fortifications. At Coldingham, NW on A 1107, the Benedictine Priory (no. 75) and pleasing, one-time handloom weaving village lie a little inland. Nearby coastal cliffs offer spectacular and bracing excursions to Coldingham Sands or St Abb's Harbour; to the lighthouse, vestigial ecclesiastical remains and National Nature Reserve on St Abb's Head (no. 16); or cliff-top Earn's Heugh Forts (no. 99).

Continue NW on A 1107, across Coldingham and Penmanshiel Moors, then E at Old Cambus Wood for fragmentary Fast Castle, set romantically on a precipitous promontory reached on foot by a track and narrow walkway. Minor road N to Pease Dean (SWT) passes farm/quarry track to ruins of 12th-century St Helen's/Old Cambus Kirk. Close by N end of Cockburnspath by-pass (A 1), take minor road E to tiny cliff-top settlement of Cove. Walk past landslips to tiny atmospheric harbour, now all-but abandoned (no. 14).

**St Abb's Head lighthouse**

**Cove Harbour**

Return S on old A 1 to Cockburnspath (medieval mercat cross, distinctive parish church with round tower, good pantiled cottages and outhouses), then take minor road SW just beyond village to Ecclaw and over Dunglass Common—a fine hill road—to the attractive estate village and church of Abbey St Bathan's (no. 58). Continue S to B 6355, then E; and take Cockburn Farm track N from junction with B 6365 (motorable with care almost to Cockburn East). Walk across gentle pastures to Edinshall Broch (no. 86), a remarkably fine and rare southern Scottish example set steeply above the twisting Whiteadder Water, with Cockburn Law hillfort behind.

On a good clear day, a lengthy but exceedingly fine drive may be taken into the heart of the Lammermuirs. Follow B 6355 NW through Ellemford and Cranshaws to the Whiteadder Reservoir; then W past Mayshiel and back along minor roads to Longformacus. Treated as a day excursion in its own right, this would allow hill walks to eg Gamalshiels, Whitestone Cairn, the Mutiny Stones Long Cairn (no. 115) or the Twinlaw Cairns. Considerable care is needed on these somewhat featureless hills in poor weather with mist or fog.

Continue E on B 6355 to Preston, S on A 6112 over the Whiteadder Water Bridge with 'cuddy jail' below (for imprisoning witches!); then E at Cumledge along minor roads to ornate late Norman arch at Edrom (no. 73), and on to the neo-classical, Edwardian magnificence of Manderston (no. 30).

**Coldstream Bridge across the River Tweed**

**Cockburnspath Church, near Coldingham**

For Marchmont House (yet another fine mid 18th-century house, now a Sue Ryder Home for the disabled, but with partial access), drive W on A 6105 through Duns, the planned village of Gavinton (1760) and Polwarth, then S along minor roads. Continue S and E to mid 18th-century Fogo Kirk and 17th-century burial aisle, not far from single-arched Fogo Bridge (1641); then meander along minor roads S to 'The Mount' motte (no. 54), and E to Swinton (stump of former windmill once used to power farm threshing mill). At A 6112, go S to Smeaton's elegant Coldstream Bridge (no. 10); or make E along B 6470 direct to heavily-vaulted Ladykirk (no. 63). Flodden Field and Wark Castle on the English side of the Tweed can readily be visited from Coldsteam; Norham Castle from Ladykirk.

On the return to Eyemouth do not miss the pioneering Union Chain Bridge (no. 9); thereafter continue NE along B 6461 to Paxton House (no. 37: partly an NGS outstation). Both places are well-known Tweed salmon-netting stations, retaining evidence of icehouses, boathouses and fishing shiels/bothies. Foulden Teind Barn (no. 25) might be a final stop, at the meeting of the minor road N and A 6105; thereafter N by mainly minor roads to Burnmouth harbour and Eyemouth.

## Below the Cheviots

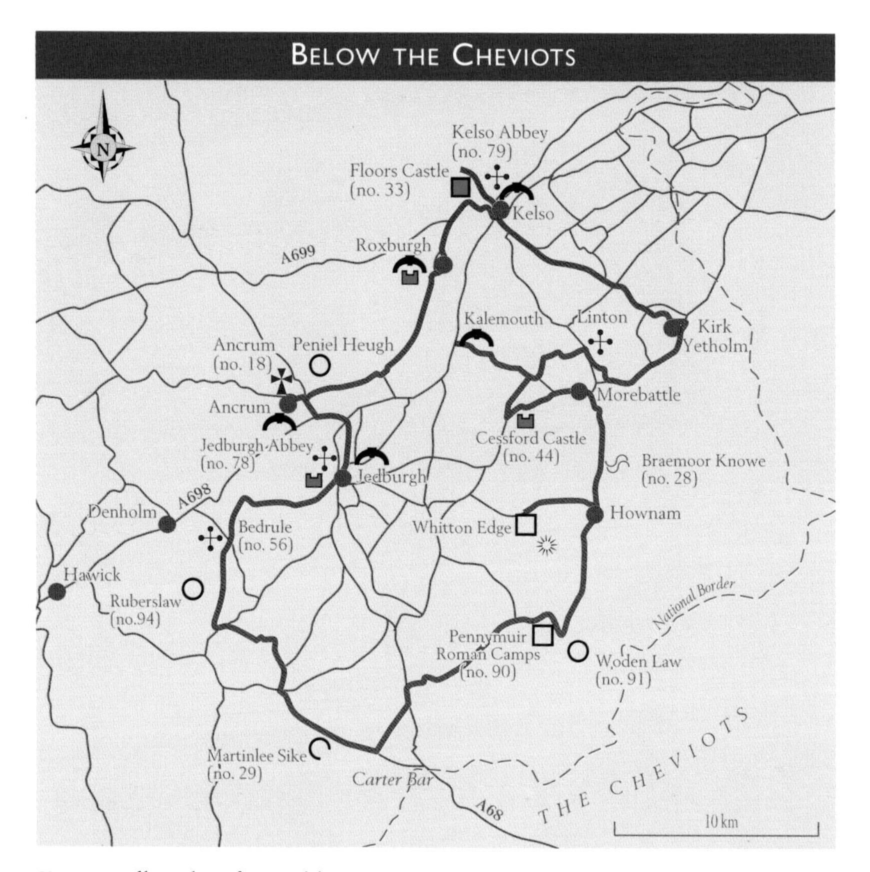


From Jedburgh's fine Abbey (no. 78), 16th-century bridge and T-plan bastle-house (Mary, Queen of Scots' House), it is but a short drive W over B 6358 and S to Bedrule (no. 56), a tiny village whose church contains fragments of Anglo-Scandinavian hog-backed tombstones and powerful stained glass windows commemorating World War I. The climb to Ruberslaw prehistoric hillfort (no. 94: or alternatively to Bonchester Hill fort) is rewarding if time permits; otherwise S along minor road to A 6088, past the ruins of Abbotrule and Southdean churches. This is Border country, close by Carter Bar—a land of long-abandoned medieval hamlets and landscapes, many of them easily explored on foot (Martinlee Sike: no. 29).

Near Hass, N just a little on A 68, side roads lead E across high moorland to Pennymuir Roman Camps (no. 90). For the fit, Woden Law (no. 91) provides a unique blend of native and possible Roman fortifications set close to the Cheviot ridge—alluring in summer, but bleak and raw in a blizzard on a wind-swept winter's day! The delightful drive N down the Kale Water could include an attractive diversion W to Whitton Edge and a gentle high-level amble S along part of the Roman road/medieval Dere Street. Here you will come across Cunzierton hillfort, the Five Stanes Stone Circle and Trestle Cairn.

Back beside the Kale Water, at Braemoor Knowe (no. 28) just N of Hownam, a fine set of likely medieval cultivation terraces is clearly visible from the road. And in the hills behind, there is a fine fortified settlement on Hownam Law.

**Arcading in the nave, Jedburgh Abbey**

**Woden Law hillfort and siege works**

From the pleasing village of Morebattle, Cessford Castle (no. 44) and Kalemouth Suspension Bridge (c 1830) can be visited to the W; to the N, Linton's partly Norman church stands on a mound of pure sand—the flat valley below being a vast freshwater loch in earlier times. E along B 6401, Kirk Yetholm boasts a village green, the one-time home of the gipsies, and the N end of the Pennine Way. And like the Kale Valley, the Bowmont Valley, twisting high into the Cheviots S of the Yetholm, is peppered with hillforts and medieval settlement sites just waiting to be explored!

B 6352 leads back N to the market/abbey town of Kelso (no. 79)—look out for the 17th-century Turret House (NTS); 18th-century Abbey Court, Ednam House (Hotel), Cross Keys and octagonal parish church; and 19th-century Woodmarket. And a little N on A 6089, stately Floors Castle (no. 33) sweeps down to the river.

The route towards Jedburgh, however, lies back across Rennie's elegant early 19th-century bridge (and toll-house), and W on A 699 as it curls round the foot of the hill that once supported a massive Roxburgh Castle, squeezed in between Tweed and Teviot. The side road SW leads through Roxburgh village (interesting skewed railway viaduct/footbridge), on through Nisbet, past Monteviot House/Home Farm (Waterloo Monument and hillfort on Peniel Heugh), to Ancrum (no. 18)—whose late 16th-century mercat cross and bridge give focus and perspective to an attractive village green. Jedburgh lies but a short way S on A 68.

**The 17th-century Turret House, Kelso** (Below)

**The nave and west entrance, Kelso Abbey** (Bottom right)

## Melrose, Lauderdale and the Middle Tweed

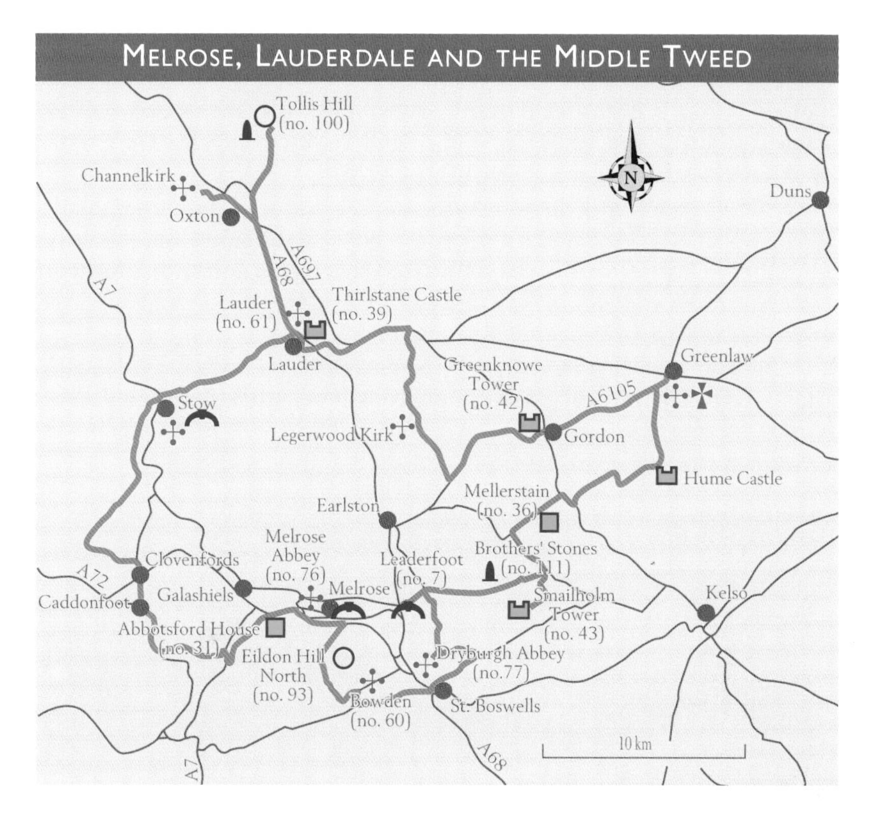


Sheltering below the Eildon Hills, and not far from the chain bridge and well-proportioned toll-house, Cistercian Melrose (no. 76) is a fine introduction to the peace and beauty of the Border Abbeys. Approach Eildon Hill North (no. 93) from B 6359 at golf course. It gives outstanding views around the Tweed Valley to the present-day settlements of Darnick, Gattonside, Newstead and Eildon, sites of late 13th/early 14th-century monastic granges/farms (little evidence above ground, however, of Roman Newstead).

**The Cistercian Abbey at Melrose**

Take B 6359/B 6398 from Melrose Mercat Cross to Bowden, an attractive conservation village with a remarkable wooden laird's loft within the Kirk (no. 60). Cross A 68 at St. Boswells, E along B 6404, then N on B 6356. Those especially interested in abbeys will wish to explore Dryburgh's romantic riverside ruins (no. 77). A little further N along B 6356, close to the roadside stands a splendidly bold and little-known 7 m high statue to William Wallace, 14th-century guardian of Scotland. And not far from Bermersyde, Scott's view looks out across the Tweed to the 6th to 11th-century ecclesiastical promontory site of Old Melrose. Continuing N, the sentinel Brothers' Stones (no. 111) stand on a low hill N of the minor road E to Smailholm, where Smailholm Tower (no. 43) occupies a low rocky knoll a little S of the village. Its prominent tower (housing an interesting display of miniature historical/Border ballad figues) is set in the remains of a medieval landscape, attractive also for short walks and picnics.

**Road bridge and railway viaduct over the Tweed at Leaderfoot**

**Statue of William Wallace** (below)

Return direct to Melrose by way of the Leaderfoot Bridges (no. 7), a superbly graceful 19-arch 1865 railway viaduct, with later 18th/later 20th-century road bridges close to the former Roman crossing of the Tweed. In the longer days of summer, however, continue N from Smailholm by B 6397, and branch E for the Adam mansion of Mellerstain (no. 36), thence E by minor roads to Hume Castle (late 18th-century 'toy fort' on 13th-century site, overlooking tiny linear village and 18th/19th-century agricultural landscape: eye of faith may detect traces of major medieval settlement on S slope below/around castle!). Continue N on B 6364 to Greenlaw (17th-century kirk and Old Mercat Cross), then W on A 6105 to Gordon and Greenknowe Tower (no. 42).

Continue NW from A 6105 along side-roads to Legerwood's peaceful, partly Norman church with 12th-century grinning demon, and on to palatial, turreted Thirlestane Castle (no. 39) just outside the little town of Lauder—a classic medieval burgh layout with later 18th-century tolbooth and 17th-century cruciform kirk (no. 61). The early 19th-century country church at Channelkirk is not far away to the N, on a bluff above the W side of the valley, close by the Roman road/Dere Street over Soutra; nor is Tollis Hill (no. 100) with its prehistoric fort and standing stone, high up under Lammer Law. Look out for and perhaps explore some of the many other hillforts lining both sides of Lauderdale, a key, ancient through route N-S.

**Lauder's cruciform kirk** (right)

B 6362 W over Lauder Common gives a good idea of how the uplands could have looked before division and enclosure; and many traces of pre-improvement cultivation rigs/field systems survive above the present arable limits. From Stow (mid 17th-century pack-horse bridge gives access to ruinous late 15th-century Old Kirk), descend Gala Water by W bank (views of rough hillsides above Bow containing ruinous broch), then S by minor road (fragmentary Torwoodlee Broch/Tower) to Clovenfords and Caddonfoot. Return to Melrose by A 707/B 7060 (The Rink hillfort), and B 6360 to Walter Scott's stately pile at Abbotsford (no. 31).

Hermitage Castle

Selkirk has a fine collection of riverside textile mills and an 1803 Courthouse. A little to the W of the town, off A 708, Bowhill (no. 32) is a later 19th-century country house of distinctive dark whinstone, set in a picturesquely designed, 'natural' landscape (1832) of little lochs and woodlands.

It is an attractive drive up the Yarrow Water, past the brooding, cliff-top bulk of Newark Castle, to the early Christian Yarrow Stone (no. 82), set back from the road on a gentle hill slope. A little beyond, St Mary's Loch is renowned for its beauty and for its 19th-century Tibbie Shiels Inn, whilst a diversion W along minor road to Tweedsmuir runs beside the strikingly attractive Megget Reservoir (1983). Along with the older Talla-Fruid system over the watershed (1895-1905), these reservoirs collect water for Edinburgh; and the hills around provide excellent walking country.

Back on A 708, turn S on B 709 at the Gordon Arms Hotel and take the hill road to the Ettrick Water; thence just a short distance SW along B 709 to Ettrick Kirk (no. 55), a typical post-Reformation country church associated with James Hogg, the literary 'Ettrick Shepherd'. For a complete and startling architectural and cultural contrast, continue S for the Tibetan monastery of Samye Ling, amidst the bleak hills near to Eskdalemuir!

Return along B 7009 past Ettrick Bridge, and take side-road E to the clearly-identifiable lines of Oakwood Roman Fort (no. 88). The narrow hill road close by leads SE by way of Woll Rig and Ashkirk to swing SW up by the Ale Water and over to the Borthwick Water. In the garden of Borthwick Mains farmhouse, close to the road, stands a carved stone (no. 83) inscribed with a single large fish and probably early Christian.

**Bowhill**

At Branxholme Bridgend on A 7, minor roads lead E then S into the undulating and remote hills around Dod. Burgh Hill Stone Setting and prehistoric fortified settlement (no. 109) is an easy short climb from the road. It provides fine views SE in the direction of the Catrail and Tinlee Stone, S to the high hills around Teviotdale and Liddesdale, and W across former cultivation rigs and traces of earlier settlements around the slopes of the Allan Water.

Rejoining the A 7 near Northhouse, either return direct to Hawick or continue S over Teviothead to Fiddleton, then E by a spectacular hill road to the massive, imposing Hermitage Castle (no. 47). The planned village of Newcastleton (no. 21) is a short drive S in Liddesdale, with Ettleton Churchyard and the Millom Cross about 1 km further S on B 6357. N on B 6357, by contrast, lie the remains of Liddel Castle motte and traces of the medieval churchyard of long-lost Castleton; also the moated homestead sites of Kirndean and Florida. Old drove roads are particularly noticeable in this area.

Return by either B 6399 or B 6357 to Hawick Motte (no. 53) and the renovated Drumlanrig Tower, a one-time Douglas stronghold. The route back to Selkirk could maybe take in Denholm (A 698), Lilliesleaf (B 6359) and Midlem (B 6453)—all of them interesting and attractive Border villages. Midlem's rectangular layout still sits within its medieval field system/landscape.

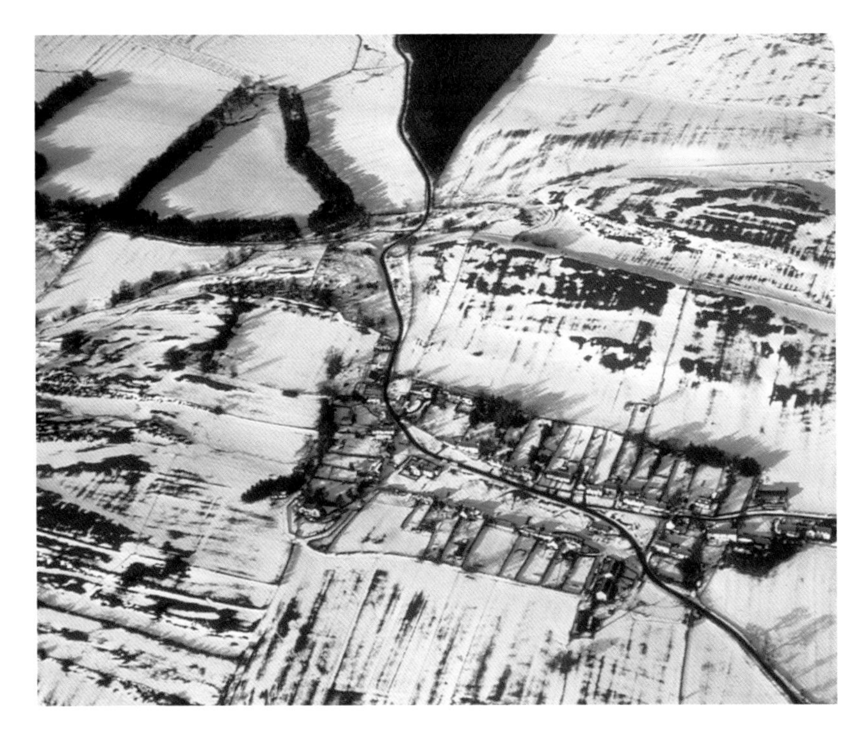

**Midlem village and medieval field system**

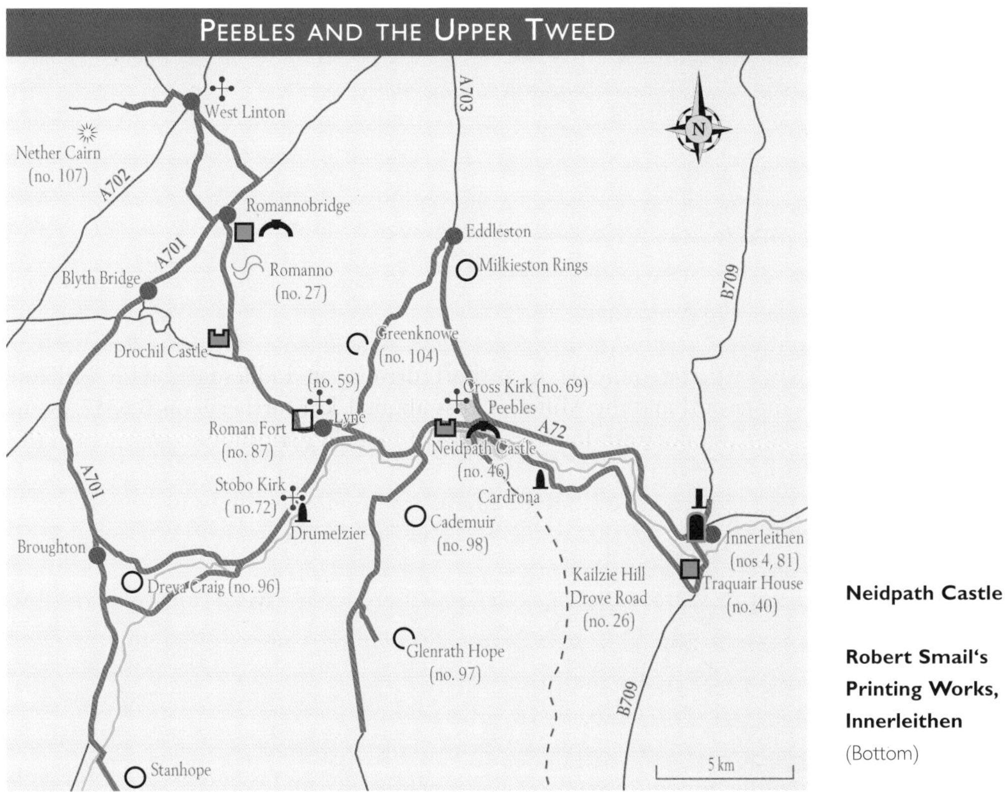


Neidpath Castle

Robert Smail's Printing Works, Innerleithen (Bottom)

Neidpath Castle (no. 46) is a fine, L-shaped tower-house perched rockily above the Tweed just W of Peebles on the A 72. Past single-arch Manor Water Bridge, minor roads lead S to Cademuir Hill Forts (no. 98), Castlehill Farm/tower house stump, and extensive prehistoric Glenrath Hope Settlement and Field Systems (no. 97). There are also largely abandoned, skeletal medieval/later landscapes at Posso and Old Kirkhope, towards the head of the Manor Water.

Return to A 72 and turn SW on B 712 for Stobo Kirk (no. 72). This early church has some fine Norman features and interesting graveslabs/stones. Continue SW to explore Drumelzier's standing stone, ruinous Tinnis fort and castle, and Dawyck Botanic Garden (an outstation of Edinburgh's Royal Botanic Garden); then continue S on A 701 to the remains of a rare but ruinous Border dun standing amongst rough screes at the entrance to Stanhope. Alternatively, from Stobo take minor road N of river direct to attractive Dreva Craig Fort, Settlements and Field Systems (no. 96).

From Broughton (N), drive NE on A 701 to Romanno Bridge and toll-house. A diversion could be made NW to West Linton (no. 57), the bronze-age Nether Cairn (no. 107) and fragments of Roman road around eg Slipperfield; otherwise turn sharply S on B 7059. Romanno Cultivation Terraces (no. 27) are clearly visible to the left, not far from the old Newlands church. Past dilapidated

Drochil Castle near the junction with A 72, thence E to Lyne Roman Fort (no. 87) and Lyne Kirk (no. 59). The 17th-century wooden furnishings are rare; also the Adam and Eve gravestone.

A side road runs N beside the Meldon Burn. Between the two Meldons, a little above the burn on the W side and accessible on foot by a forestry track, lie several unenclosed, bronze-age hut platforms at Green Knowe (no. 104)—a low-key site encouraging fairly strenuous exploration of prehistoric forts, cairns and other settlement sites elsewhere in the vicinity. The White Meldon's fortified hill top and round cairn are particularly enticing on a bright clear day! Near Eddleston, look for the single-storey Milkieston toll-house—the turnpike opened in 1770. The fortified settlement and earthworks of Milkieston Rings lie uphill to the E.

Continue S on A 703 to Peebles and its ruinous Cross Kirk (no. 69). Cattle once crossed the old Tweed Bridge making for the drove road over Kailzie Hill (no. 26), a fine bracing walk. B 7062 SE of the Bridge leads past the Cardrona standing stone to B 709 and Traquair House (no. 40)—one of the most individual and interesting of the south-east's large country houses, complete with its own brewery.

Follow B 709 N. A 9th-century Anglian cross-shaft fragment (no. 81) survives at Innerleithen, where St Ronan's Well has been restored—a medicinal spring with pump room built in 1826. Look out also for Robert Smail's Printing Works on the High Street (no. 4: NTS), a fascinating, largely unaltered Victorian business which only closed in 1986.

These Tweed Valley towns retain a good range of textile mills and associated housing; and the former railway has left interesting bridges and viaducts. Return to Peebles by the A 72.

**Painted ceiling, Traquair House**

# INDUSTRIAL MONUMENTS, BRIDGES AND HARBOURS

**Roxburgh Viaduct**

The classic period of industrial growth in Scotland spanned the late 18th and early 19th century; it was founded on water—to power mills and to carry raw materials and manufactures by sea or along canals. Coal became increasingly important, however, during the 19th century—producing steam to power factories, railways and ships, and to render the horse increasingly redundant as a working animal.

Industrialisation was accompanied by increased urbanisation, mainly in Scotland's lowland belt. Often it was a largely uncontrolled growth based on avaricious enterprise; occasionally a carefully nurtured development sought to minimise the social upheaval caused within a population that almost trebled during the 18th century, and moved en masse from a countryside where agricultural improvements were reducing manpower requirements.

Much evidence of industrialisation survives in the landscape—spoil tips, tall brick chimneys, railway sidings and viaducts, docks and canal basins, massive stone-built factories. Evidence also survives of the 'public' face of Victorian life—schools, hospitals, railway stations, hotels, town halls. There are solidly respectable, stone-built Victorian suburbs, and the sometimes ostentatious neo-Baronial of contemporary country mansions—not infrequently financed by the industrial working classes whose mean, cramped and often unhygienic back-to-back terraces and tenements are frequently set against a neo-Gothic backdrop of multi-denominational spires.

More important industries in south-east Scotland included coal, shale-oil, fire-clay, pottery, glass, paper, flour, textiles, biscuits, brewing, distilling, fish-curing. And though iron-working was more strongly located in the central and western lowlands, the east had not just its foundries but the mills at Cramond (no. 5) which were amongst the first in Scotland to apply water-power to the manufacture of iron goods. Lothian's River Almond, Water of Leith and North Esk, and Berwickshire's Whiteadder were heavily exploited for paper-making—eg at Polton (NT 290649), Balerno (NT 164663) or Chirnside (NT 850562), whilst the good spring water underlying the capital had long been used in brewing. The late 19th and early 20th-century Caledonian Brewery (NT 231730) is largely unchanged: so also is Dunbar's Belhaven Brewery, 1814-87 (NT 665783), and the private brew-house at Traquair (no. 40). Dalkeith retains a most attractive octagonal Victorian water-tower, 1879 (NT 327671: now converted to a private house), with a louvred wooden top; at Portobello two bottle kilns have been preserved at the site of the former Buchan Pottery (NT 304742).

**Dunbar's 19th century Belhaven Brewery retains its distinctive malt-drying kilns**

Lothian had two coalfields—farthest West Lothian's was a continuation of the Lanarkshire and Renfrewshire coalfields; south and east of Edinburgh the monks were working the 'black stanis' as early as the 12th century. With the exception of Monktonhall, all deep mines in Lothian have closed in recent decades, casualties of privatisation and the growth of particularly visually-intrusive open-cast mines; and the visible structural evidence of late 19th and early 20th-century pits is fast disappearing. Good features survive at Newtongrange (no. 1) and Prestongrange (no. 2), and an interesting planned village at Rosewell (NT 288627). Because suitable seams of clay were frequently found in association with coal seams, so brick, tile, fireclay and similar industries were often found close to coal mines—for example at Prestongrange (no. 2), Armadale (Etna Brickworks, Bathville, c 1897-present: NS 944679), Bo'ness/Kinneil (Birkhill Fireclay Mine, c 1916-1980: NS 965579) and Portobello (Thistle Pottery, c 1770-1972: NT 304743).

West of Edinburgh, between the Calders and Kirkliston, most surviving evidence relates not to coal but to shale-oil—a unique industry pioneered by James 'Paraffin' Young from 1850, which supplied fuel oil, later lubricating oils and paraffin wax. It throve for a little over 100 years, evidenced today by shale-miners' villages, for example at Winchburgh (NT 0874), Dalmeny (NT 140779), Broxburn (NT 0772) and Pumpherston (NT 0669), and by its distinctive bings. Little remains of the workings themselves, just a declining handful of spoil heaps, distinguished from their coaly cousins by a reddish- orange colour and distinctive shape. The conical Breich bings (NT 010640) north of West Calder, the Lowlands' 'five sisters', are atypical; most shale-bings, increasingly eroded for road-bottoming, were flat-topped—spatially more economical given the vast amounts of spoil. Those few that remain, moreover, are increasingly grassed over or replanted as nature reserves.

By contrast, the Borders were little touched by the ravages of industrialisation. They were renowned, however, for their textiles. Whilst cotton-spinning was restricted largely to west and central Scotland and flax-weaving was stronger in Fife and the north-east, in the Borders it was wool that was spun and woven or knitted into tweeds or socks. With the exception of the higher Tweed from Walkerburn to Peebles, most mills clustered around the middle Tweed and its tributaries, close to where these merged to run into the Merse—good for communications. Originally a cottage industry, large-scale wool-spinning was pioneered in Scotland at places like Galashiels. As factories became larger, steam supplemented or replaced water-power (tall chimneys rather than large water-wheels) and increasingly single-storey weaving sheds were added to a three or four-storey spinning block—or vice versa! Most surviving mills, generally viewable only from the outside, are mid-late 19th century, notably at Selkirk, Galashiels, Hawick, Walkerburn and Peebles. St Ronan's Mill (NT 335379) at Innerleithen was a typical example dating from 1846, until it was demolished in 1981; Caerlee Mill, c 1788-90 (NT 332368), also at Innerleithen, was the area's first 'modern' woollen mill.

Industrial expansion depended as much on good markets as on good machinery; good markets required good communications, whether overland or over sea. Even close to Edinburgh and between the larger burghs, pre-18th-century roads were fairly basic tracks; riding and pack-

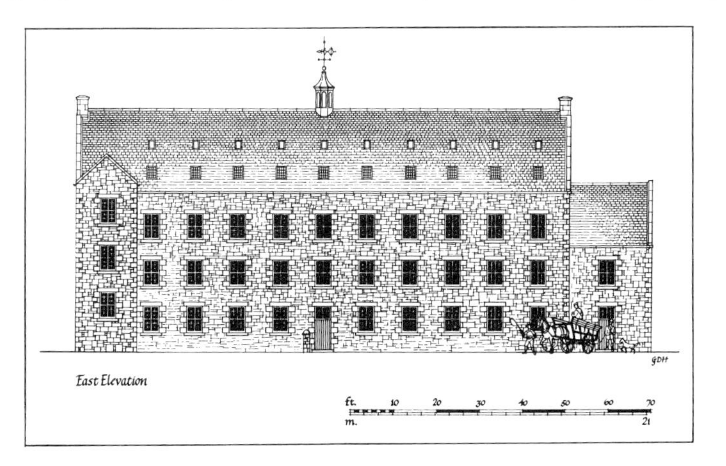

horses, and wheelless sleds and slypes reigned more-or-less supreme. Only after the first Scottish Turnpike Act of 1750 did road-building begin in earnest, so that by the late 18th century new turnpikes ran from Edinburgh to Glasgow, and from Berwick to Dunbar and Edinburgh. The Carter Bar route over the Cheviots was improved, and by 1840 the turnpike from Dalkeith to Greenlaw opened.

Compared to much of Scotland, the south-east had been relatively well-furnished with bridges in medieval times but only at major crossings in long-established settlements. These mainly 16th-century bridges had heavy semi-circular or segmental arches, often ribbed below for further strength and with vast triangular cut-waters to each pier—Abbey Bridge (NT 533745) and Nungate Bridge (NT 519737) in Haddington, Musselburgh's Old Bridge (NT 340725), Newbattle's Maiden Bridge (NT 336665), Canongate Bridge, Jedburgh (NT 652205), Tweed Bridge, Peebles (NT 250402), Cramond Auld Brig (NT 179754) and East Linton Bridge (NT 592771).

The new breed of nationally-renowned civil engineers working on the new turnpikes, with their associated toll-houses, also designed new bridges in the later 18th-early 19th century. They flattened arches, introduced lighter hollow arches and piers and fostered a new elegance—Smeaton's Coldstream Bridge (no. 10), Telford's Lothian Bridge (no. 8) and Dean Bridge in Edinburgh (NT 242739), Rennie's Kelso Bridge (NT 728336)(a model for London's Waterloo Bridge). And other architects built many other less prestigious bridges—the remarkable single-span Ashiestiel Bridge on the Tweed (NT 438350) or the Manor Bridges (NT 229395, 231393). By the early 19th century, new materials were introduced to bridge-building—the forged-iron Union Suspension Bridge (no. 9) at Hutton, 1820, and similar bridges at Kalemouth (NT 709274) and Melrose; and the cast-iron outer girders and steel arches of Edinburgh's North Bridge, 1896-97 (NT 258738).

**Ancrum old bridge, near Jedburgh**

Even more significant for communications was the development of canals and railways. Only the Edinburgh and Glasgow Union Canal (1819-22) touched upon south-east Scotland, crossing West Lothian and into Edinburgh. Its fine hollow-arched masonry aqueducts across the Avon at Woodcockdale (NT 966758), across the Almond at Lin's Mill (no. 11), and across the Water of Leith at Slateford in Edinburgh (no. 3) incorporated cast-iron troughs to carry the water. The life of the canals, however, was overshadowed and cut short by the coming of the railways, whose viaducts (and a handful of stations and hotels) remain prominent and sometimes most spectacular features in the landscape. Fine viaducts are still in use at Dunglass (NT 770721), Kirkliston (NT 112721) and Linlithgow (NS 981769); on lines now closed there are attractive examples at Leaderfoot (no. 7), Roxburgh (NT 702304) and across the Tweed and Lyne Water (eg NT 232401, 209400). That at Leaderfoot, with 19 arches, rises nearly 38 m above the Tweed; the 23 m high Roxburgh viaduct is possibly Scotland's finest—constructed on a curve with each of its arches specially designed. The most magnificent memorial to the age of the train, however, must remain the double-cantilevered Forth Railway Bridge (no. 6).

**Dalkeith Water Tower**

At sea, the 18th and 19th century saw a considerable expansion in fisheries and sea-borne trade. Safety was improved from the late 18th century by the building of such lighthouses as St Abb's Head (no. 16), Barns Ness (NT 723772), the Bass Rock (NT 602872) and Inchkeith (NT 292828)—many bearing a unique pattern of painted rings to avoid misidentification during the day, as well as a unique system of night-time flashes and fog-horn signals. Smaller navigational lights could be associated with piers and harbours—eg Leith (no. 12) and South Queensferry (NT 136784)—and many of these harbours were extended to cope with the developing trade.

Projecting piers, whether straight or curved, were added to provide more effective shelter. These narrowed the entrance and created calmer basins—eg Newhaven (NT 254771), Cockenzie (NT 397756), Port Seton (NT 404759) and Cove (no. 14). Sometimes extensions provided multiple, sometimes inner and outer harbours—eg Granton (NT 2377), St Abbs (NT 920673), Burnmouth (NT 958609). Dunbar (no. 15) is particularly complex; Eyemouth (no. 13) has developed from the simplest of single river-side quays such as still survives at Cramond (NT 189771) and originally lined The Shore at Leith (no. 12)—the only harbour in south-east Scotland to grow sufficiently in size and importance as to merit a wet dock, controlled by lock gates.

**Winding engine house, boiler house and old power station, Lady Victoria Colliery**

### 1* Lady Victoria Colliery, Newtongrange

*Late 19th century AD.*

*NT 333637. W side of A 7 just S of junction with B 703 at S end of Newtongrange village; signposted.*

The Lothian Coal Company began to sink the Lady Victoria shaft in 1890. Originally planned to reach 531 m, uncontrollable flooding caused it to be back-filled to 503 m. The original block of buildings still survives—brick-built furnace house, winding-engine house and ancillary buildings. Seven of the second set of 12 'Lancashire' boilers remain in position, producing steam until 1982 to help power underground machinery as well as the pit-head baths and the winding-engine.

High above the colliery stand the twin symbols of a late 19th to mid 20th-century colliery—the brick-built chimney and the pit-head gantry supporting the pulley wheels over which the winding-ropes passed down to the cages. The winding-engine house was the heart of the colliery. Like the original rope-drum, the present winding-engine was built by Grant Ritchie & Co Ltd of Kilmarnock in 1894. A massive piece of machinery, it hissed and clanked, pistons gradually turning as it began to let out or haul in the thick wire ropes. It survived as a dinosaur into the age of micro- electronics, and has now become extinct, though preserved.

The Lothian Coal Company had been headed by the Marquis of Lothian, descendant of the last abbot of Newbattle, Mark Ker, who secularised his mining interests after the Reformation. To house the miners for his new pit, called after his wife, the Marquis established a company village. Built of brick from the local brickworks, Newtongrange was to became the largest pit village in Scotland. The terraced houses were laid out in a grid pattern and named accordingly—First Street, Second Street . . .; each had its flower garden in front and vegetable garden behind, with outdoor dry closet. The Company also built miners' institutions with reading rooms and libraries, football pitches and bowling greens.

Nearby Rosewell (NT 288627) is one of the most complete pit villages to survive, built even more distinctively in yellow as well as red brick. Its Roman Catholic Church, St Matthew's (1926) is built of the same yellow, industrial brick.

**The hand-operated crane in the power-station was made by J Carrick & Sons**

### 2* Prestongrange Beam-Engine and Brickworks, Prestonpans

*Late 19th century AD.*

*NT 371736. On B 1348 coast road, 3 km E of Musselburgh; signposted.*

The first shaft of what was to become the last mine at Prestongrange was sunk in 1830; the great beam-engine built by Harvey and Company of Hoyle, in Cornwall, was shipped north and erected in 1874 to pump water out of the mine. The water was raised in three stages, with one pump at the Great Seam level (approximately 128 m), one half-way to the surface, and one at the Beggar Seam (approximately 238 m). On average some 2955 litres a minute reached the surface.

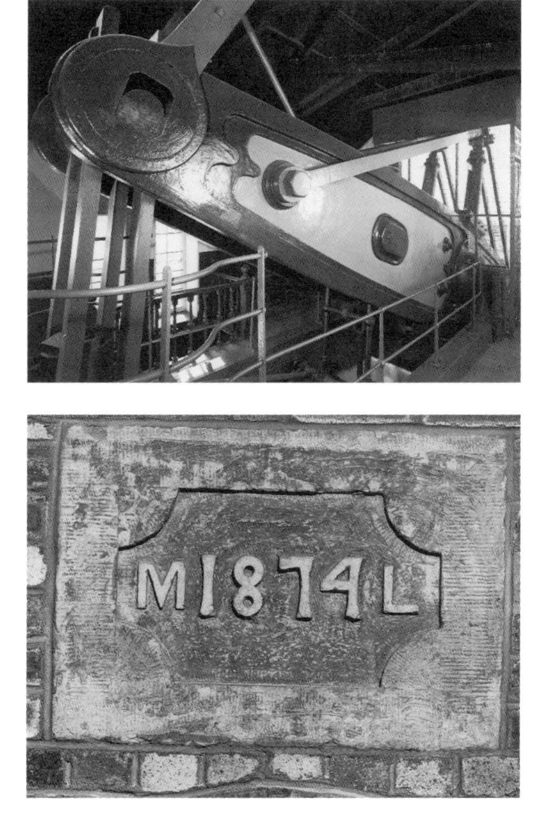


**Part of the beam, Prestongrange Colliery pumping engine** (Left)

**Made by Matthew Loan, 1874, Prestongrange beam engine, Prestonpans** (Left)

The massive cylinder is housed in a tall, narrow, rubble-built engine house. High up, more than 10 m of cast-iron beam protrudes, to which is attached the 102 tonne pump-rod of Oregon pine. The beam pivots on the front wall of the engine-house, which is understandably reinforced! The generating station and the much later pithead baths are the only other surviving original pit buildings on site.

Nearby, however, stands a 24-chamber 'continuous' Hoffmann kiln and its chimney—all that remains of the Prestongrange Brick, Tile and Fireclay Works that was in production c 1760-1970s. (It also had 11 round, downdraught 'intermittent' kilns). It was common for industries that depended on coal for power to cluster near to the colliery and the Brickworks was inherited by the National Coal Board following coal nationalisation in 1947. Brickworks, potteries, chemical works, breweries, saltworks and a flint-mill were all once sited hereabouts, whilst the right to construct a harbour at Prestongrange (the old Acheson's, later Morison's Haven) was granted as early as 1526 to the coal-working monks of Newbattle. A few traces remain. The monks were also involved in salt-working and Prestonpans, so called from the 18th century, was originally Aldhammer but renamed Salt Prieston in the 13th century.

A 'trail' between Prestongrange and Newtongrange (no. 1) could include Prestonpans (17th century lairds' houses and mercat cross); Meadowmill (site of Battle of Prestonpans 1745, and Scotland's first railway 1722); Tranent (coal town from late 15th century; 18th-century parish church with fine gravestones); Birsley Brae (hummocky pits of a medieval coal heugh); Fa'side (restored tower-house; fine view over Lothian Coalfield); Cousland (18th-century smiddy); Dalkeith (old market town and ruinous pre-Reformation Collegiate Church of St Nicholas); Newbattle (18th- and 19th-century mansion of the Marquis of Lothian; remains of 13th-century Cistercian Abbey; Maiden Bridge).

### 3* Caledonian Brewery and the Slateford Bridges, Edinburgh

*Mid 19th century AD.*

*NT 233721. On A 70 Lanark Road (here known as Slateford Road) approx. 3 kms SW of W end of Princes Street, Edinburgh.*

Originally part of the Damhead Estate, the triangular site was a pig farm before George Lorimer (a young brewer) and Robert Clark (formerly head brewer at Alexander Melvin & Co.'s Boroughloch Brewery in Edinburgh) bought the land in 1869. It bordered the main Caledonian Railway line into Edinburgh on one side, and Slateford Road on the other. The Caledonian Brewery was in operation by December 1869, albeit building was not completed until 1870. Two wells were sunk by R Henderson & Co., and a railway siding was added in 1871. During the 1880s and again in the early 1900s, the wells were deepened—the main well reaching some 153 m. Along with such nearby breweries as T&J Bernard and John Jeffrey & Co., however, (and there were over 30 breweries in Edinburgh at this time), Lorimer & Clark experienced regular seepage from the underlying shale oil beds, and by World War I they were using town water for brewing, retaining well water for washing casks.

The largely red-brick buildings divide into 2 main groups. Behind the old offices facing onto Slateford

**Caledonian Brewery, Slateford, Edinburgh**

Road, and across the cobbled yard, the mash house and tun rooms were extended in the early 1960s to give a capacity of 2000 barrels a week. By contrast, the 4-storey maltings was closed in the 1970s (malt being bought in thereafter) and gutted by fire in 1994. Largely rebuilt externally in the original style, with yellowy-white brick around the windows, the pyramidal kiln-vents or 'pagodas' have also been rebuilt (not all in their original position) and continue to dominate the skyline, along with the tall, red-brick, circular-section chimney. In the early 1980s, two of the original coppers were replaced by new coppers manufactured to the original pattern by Abercromby of Alloa (the third is original, made by Archd. McMillan & Co, Coppersmith, Edinburgh, in 1869). Following the miners' strike of 1984-5, however, coal-firing was replaced by gas-firing. Even so, the 4-storey brewhouse is unique—not just in Scotland, but in Britain. For it contains the last working direct-fired, open copper pots for boiling up the malt liquor and hop flowers. The Caledonian Brewery (independent again following a management buy-out in 1987, and specialising in traditional, cask-conditioned ales) exemplifies some of the best in architectural, technological and cultural conservation, where the strength and flavour of tradition is blended with up-to-the-minute systems.

**The original copper tun was made by Archd. McMillan & Co, Coppersmith, Edinburgh**

Almost opposite the Caledonian Brewery, a series of parallel streets (Primrose, Myrtle and Bay Terraces: 1877) reveals one of several housing schemes pioneered by the Edinburgh Cooperative Building Company. Another (1884-5) lies a few hundred metres farther south, where the names Ashley Terrace and Shaftesbury Park commemorate two great, late 19th-century housing reformers. The Company was founded by 6/7 masons with support from the Church and the *Edinburgh Evening News*, and the first 'Colonies' were laid out in 1861 off Glenogle Road, beside the Water of Leith (NT 245749), at no great distance from the Royal Botanic Garden. The designs vary a little, but generally comprised upper and lower flats—sound, stone-built and slated terraces mainly for skilled artisans. Over a period of 15 years, some 10,000 people were housed in such 'Colonies', which complemented the more expensive middle-class tenements of Marchmont, Bruntsfield and Comely Bank.

A kilometre or two farther out, beyond the grass parks and early 20th-century municipal and Cooperative slaughterhouses (in the aptly-named New Market Road), both railway and Union Canal cross the Water of Leith. At Inglis Green Road (NT 220707), an 8-arch aqueduct (1818) stands proudly (partly masked by later development) alongside the later, slender-piered, 14-arch railway viaduct (1847). These solid but graceful stone bridges reflect successive waves of new technology as applied to transport and communications in the 19th century; they also contrast with the dumpy, single-arch reinforced concrete aqueduct over the Lanark Road (1937: NT 222709). (For the Gilmore Park Lifting Bridge and other Lothian aqueducts, see no. 11.)

The composing room, Robert Smail's Printing Works

## 4* Robert Smail's Printing Works, Innerleithen

*18th-19th century AD.*

*NT 334368. On High Street towards E end of Innerleithen. S side; signposted.*

*National Trust for Scotland.*

Robert Smail had been in business from 1857 employing bootmakers and selling footwear; he also sold books and stationery supplied by his brother Thomas, a bookseller and printer in Jedburgh. In 1866, he acquired the present premises for £500 and equipped it as a printing works—a business that coincided with the development of both the town's textile industry and its medicinal springs, and lasted for three generations. The Smails were soon printing for the woollen industry throughout the Borders and as far north as Wick; they also sold fishing tackle, became photographers, started a local newspaper and operated a shipping agency!

The printing works comprised 4 main departments: the composing or case room, the machine room, the paper store and the office. Apart from large wooden type for posters, their many varied type faces were cast from a hard lead tin and antimony alloy. Since they did not invest in new typesetting equipment, the original system of setting type by hand survives—essentially that developed by Johann Gutenberg in Strasbourg in the mid 15th century. By contrast, they introduced new printing presses in the mid/late 19th century: treadle platen machines pioneered in America from 1856, and the flat-bed 'Wharfedale' machine with its revolving cylinder, designed in Yorkshire in 1886. Towards the very end of the 19th century, they added lithography to letter-press technology.

The tiny office, with its acid-etched windows, is filled with stock books and ledgers, cash books, invoices and receipts, the earliest dating from 1865. There are also press-cuttings, bundles of letters relating to the shipping agency, and bound copies of Smail's weekly newspaper, the St. Ronan's Standard and Effective Advertiser (1893-1916). Most important, perhaps, are the 50 large 'guardbooks' containing copies of what they printed from 1876 to 1956—a unique record of the ephemera of social and business life! The whole building simply reeks of dust, inks, oil and the atmosphere of a busy, cluttered Victorian jobbing printer's!

Originally the works were water-powered. Two water wheels fed off a mill-lade tapping the fast-flowing Leithen Water and running under the floor. The wheels were lowered daily into the lade until 1930, when a Crossley gas-powered engine was installed in the paper store (later replaced by electricity). Beyond the back of the premises, moreover, a complex system of lades once led water to power at least 8 different businesses—including Meikle's Saw Mill in a converted 18th-century farm steading, and a turbine generator house. Only the water-wheel and oil engine house now remain of Hogg & Robertson's Engineering Works.

18th-century Innerleithen was a 'kirkton' until the first of the mills was built in 1788 and consisted of a group of thatched houses clustered around the church. Alexander Brodie's 5-storey Caerlee Mill, though not particularly successful in its early years, marked the beginning of the Innerleithen woollen industry—Brodie himself being a successful ironmaster in Shropshire and friend of Thomas Telford, before returning to his native Traquair. It was complemented in 1846 by the 4-storey, 11-bay St Ronan's Mill. A very modern factory in its day, and fed by a 550 m lade from the river, it was used originally for spinning wool by George Roberts & Son, Selkirk. It was demolished in 1981.

In contrast, WH Playfair's St Ronan's Well, 1826, followed publication of Sir Walter Scott's *St. Ronan's Well*. A simple, yet striking building (reconstructed in 1896 and refurbished in 1991), it sits on the slope of Lee Penn at the west end of the town. The Earl of Traquair's pump room housed a library and subscription reading room as well as the 'salubrious mineral spring ... eminently beneficial in cases of scrofulous disorders, inflammations of the eyes, and various diseases originating in impurities of the blood' (*New Statistical Account*). Its waters were also reputed to cure sterility amongst married ladies, and in its early years it was a fashionable haunt of the leisured classes.

## 5 Cramond Iron Mills, Edinburgh

*18th-19th century AD.*

*NT 187765-188769. Side roads N to Cramond from A 90 at Davidson's Mains or Barnton, on W outskirts of Edinburgh.*

Corn and cloth had long been worked in water-mills at Cramond. Industrial iron-working, including nail-making, began a little after 1752 and the Carron Company, later to become internationally renowned, took over in 1759 only to sell out to the Cadell family by 1770.

**Cadell Trademark**

Nothing now remains of the highest mills, Peggie's Mill (1781) and Dowie's Mill (1782), where spades and hoops were made. At Cockle Mill, the lowest mill, there are traces of successive weirs, a fine tidal dock and the former office buildings, now private houses. This was the rolling and slitting mill from c 1752, described by John Rennie in 1782 as having 3 water wheels. The principal forge, however, was at Fair-a-Far, a little upstream; from c 1778 its products included plough socs, girdles and cart axles. The walls still stand a storey high, incorporating the corbels used to support a spur-wheel which operated at the rim of the main water-wheel and presumably drove such small pieces of equipment as a bellows, shears or grindstone. The substantial weir (with modernised fish ladder) was constructed by 1839 to replace another upstream. It helped supply water to two small wheels and to an undershot wheel whose diameter, approximately 4 m, can be gauged from scrape marks on the mill wall.

The present buildings represent the 'west' forge; the 'east' forge has disappeared. Storage sheds for coal and scrap iron were built into the hillside, whilst slag was tipped into the river up to 50 m downstream. Much of it was used to extend and build up the river-bank, laid over large tree-trunks set end-on to the river and occasionally visible through erosion. About 1839 a light tramway linked this mill to the dock at Cockle Mill; the mouth of the river, too, is lined with a substantial stone-built quay where iron was brought in and the finished products exported.

Industrial housing, now modernised and gentrified, survives in Cramond village and at Cockle Mill; above the gorge at Cockle Mill, above the worst of the dirt and smoke and noise, stands the solidly respectable, former manager's house!

Cramond also has a pleasing Auld Brig (NT 179754), the remains of an important Roman fort and bath-house, an interesting churchyard, a mansion house, a tower-house and perhaps the last little river-mouth ferry in Scotland (passengers only).

**Forth Railway Bridge, South Queensferry, built 1882 - 90**

## 6 Forth Railway Bridge, South Queensferry, near Edinburgh

*Late 19th century AD.*

*NT 138781-13805. E end of South Queensferry on B 924, N off A 90; view from below.*

One of the latter-day wonders of the world and a remarkable tribute to Victorian engineering, this bridge—the first really major structure to be made entirely of steel—was built between 1882 and 1890. Over 2.5 km long, and expanding by almost a metre from mid-winter to mid-summer, it incorporates 3 massive double cantilevers, the Queensferry, Inchgarvie and Fife Erections, which support in turn 2 main spans each 518 m long and 110 m high to the top of the main cantilever towers at high water. The approach spans, supported on slender stone piers, are equally dramatic as they reach out across the Forth; they are quite separate, however, from the main cantilevers, and bear none of the weight. Massive 1016 tonne counterpoise weights at either end of the bridge are responsible for this.

After his Tay Bridge collapsed in the winter storm in 1879, Thomas Bouch was stopped from beginning work on the new bridge across the Forth. Finally the crossing was engineered by Sir John Fowler and Benjamin Baker. It owes its massive structure, in part at least, to a deep-seated concern that it, too, should not collapse; and contemporary comment suggests that not every one found it as overtly beautiful as it was strong!

The Railway Bridge cost £3.5 million and 57 lives, and required some 55,000 tonnes of steel, 21,350 tonnes of cement, 49,000 tonnes of concrete and nearly 30,000 cubic metres of granite. It still carries over 1000 trains a week weighing up to 1400 or so tonnes—500 tonnes more than it was designed to carry.

Maintenance is an ongoing necessity—there are some 59 ha of steelwork to be scraped and painted, and maintenance teams use more than 17 tonnes of paint a year if programmes are fully implemented.

It was the equally remarkable road bridge, however, opened in 1964, that finally put an end to the ferry crossing and completed the metamorphosis of Queensferry from ferry-toun to commuter suburb. The first public ferry had been established in 1129 by David I, though Margaret, wife of Malcolm Canmore, had regularly crossed there since 1067, travelling between the abbey at Dunfermline and the castle at Edinburgh. The monks of Dunfermline were given a charter to operate it, and it helped encourage pilgrims from the south to visit the shrine at St Andrews.

The last in a sequence of piers, a straight stone-built sloping jetty built c 1812 by John Rennie in the subsequent shadow of the railway bridge, has been left to the inshore lifeboat and seasonal excursion boat to the 12th-century Augustinian abbey at Inchcolm. A central breakwater bisects it, with a hexagonal lighthouse at its landward end.

**Leaderfoot and Drygrange bridges across the River Tweed**

## 7 Leaderfoot Bridges, near Melrose

*Late 18th-mid 19th century AD.*

*NT 575436-573347. Close to junction of A 68 and B 6361, about 4 km E of Melrose; best seen from B 6361.*

*Historic Scotland (railway viaduct).*

For most of history and prehistory the most important inland north-south route in south-east Scotland lay through Lauderdale; and around the meeting of the Leader Water and the River Tweed it met its most difficult natural barrier. The Tweed, however, was fordable a little to the west, and where the Roman trunk road, later Dere Street, was able to cross the river there grew up perhaps the most important Roman fort in Scotland, Newstead or Trimontium (see section 7).

In more recent times the main road and rail routes have followed the coastal route to the east, but the A 68 is still a key line of communication to north-east England and the most recent 3-span road bridge stands alongside its predecessor, built between 1776 and 1780 and described in 1798 as 'that very substantial and elegant [structure] over Tweed at Drygrange, whose middle arch has a span of 105 feet' (32 m).

This rubble-built bridge has 4 spans. Only the large main arch is segmental; it is flanked by smaller semicircular arches with a sizeable arched recess at the southern end. The cut-waters support piers which terminate in triangular refuges for pedestrians crossing the bridge; and these piers, like the outer walls above the main arch, contain attractive carved decoration. Most prominent are the sculpted urns set within circular panels. From the line of the projecting stone corbels above, it is clear that the parapets have been raised to make for a more level roadway.

A little to the west stands the tall, graceful, single-track Leaderfoot railway viaduct, some 38 m above the Tweed. Built of an attractive pinkish-red sandstone, its 19 semicircular arches rest on slender stone pillars, subsequently reinforced with buttresses. Opened in 1865 for the Berwickshire Railway, and long abandoned (1950s), it linked places such as Earlston, Greenlaw, Duns and Chirnside both with the main east-coast line at Reston and with the Waverley route from Edinburgh to Carlisle, just south of Leaderfoot—a route which for largely industrial reasons (the location of the Midlothian coalfield) passed down the valley of the Gala rather than the Leader Water. Some 130 navvies are said to have died from cholera when the track was being laid through Melrose and Newstead.

## 8 Lothian Bridge, Pathhead, Midlothian

*Early 19th century AD.*

*NT 391645. On A 68, some 200 m NW of Pathhead; best seen from Ford on by-road just to W.*

In the early 17th century, the main road from Edinburgh to the Merse, via Soutra, was described as 'so worne and spoylled as hardlie is thair any journaying on horse or fute . . . botwith haisard and perrell'.

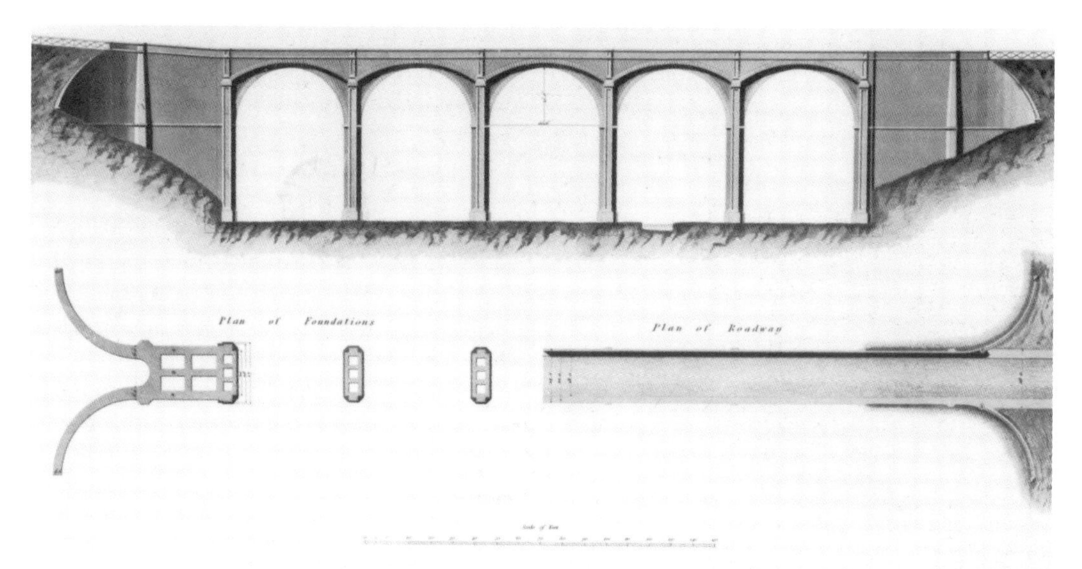


Telford's Lothian Bridge, 1827, Pathhead

And although the first Scottish Turnpike Act was passed in 1780, it was 1840 before Thomas Telford's grand new turnpike between Dalkeith and Greenlaw was finally ready. The modern road is essentially Telford's road, and his graceful Lothian Bridge still carries all its traffic.

Built in 1827-31 of well-dressed stone, it has 5 spans of flattened segmental arches, very similar to those of his Dean Bridge over the Water of Leith in Edinburgh (1829-31). The arches rise some 24 m from the river, to a 15 m span.

In carrying the new road over the peaceful Tyne, the bridge superceded the ford which gave its name to the attractive village in the valley bottom. Pathhead, by contrast, reflects the top of the track which climbed steeply up, south from the ford: it is essentially a mid 18th-century village of one-and two-storeyed houses built in a long line both sides of the curving, uphill A 68. Much renovated, the earlier roofs are pantiled and more steeply-pitched, and on No. 101 a carved stone bears the royal warrant mark of the leather-workers.

Not far to the south of Pathhead a temporary Roman camp has been identified from crop-markings recorded on aerial photographs. It may be that the Roman road, on its way towards Eskbank or Dalkeith, crossed at the ford and continued northward very much along the line of the present impressively straight road through Chesterhill and Edgehead.

Nearby is the linear estate village of Dewartown (NT 378641); also the Dewar family's uncompromisingly massive Victorian mansion house of 1875 at Vogrie (NT 380632). The estate, with its attractive early 19th century Gothic stable-block, is now a country park.

## 9 Union Chain Bridge, Hutton, near Berwick

*Early 19th century AD.*

*NT 934510. Over the Tweed on cross-Border by-road linking B 6461 (Scotland) and A 698 (England), about 6 km W of Berwick-upon-Tweed.*

Union Chain Bridge, Hutton

From c 1810 iron came to be used for bridge-building in Scotland, alongside stone: first of all cast-iron, later steel girders. Iron was also used to manufacture suspension cables or chains; at Hutton the chain links were forged from iron bars, though from mid-century iron plate was used.

The Union Chain Bridge was built in 1820 by Royal Navy Captain Samuel Brown, the first large suspension bridge in Britain and predating the Menai Suspension Bridge in North Wales. It is the largest of three similar bridges in the Borders—the others are at Kalemouth, 1820-39 (NT 708274) and the footbridge at Melrose, 1826 (NT 545346). Strong iron rods connect the 3 sets of iron link chains each side to a light wooden deck, and the chains rise up either end to impressive pylons of well-dressed stone. When the bridge was strengthened in 1902-3, a wire-rope cable and wire-rope suspender linked to steel reinforcements were added each side of the deck—some 112 m long, 5.5 m wide and 8.2 m above the river. The carriageway is flanked by attractive wrought-iron railings.

Before the 4-span Ladykirk-Norham bridge was built in 1885-87, the Union Bridge was the only crossing of the Tweed between Berwick-upon-Tweed and Coldstream, other than by ferry or ford, and it replaced a ford at this, the furthest tidal limit of the river. There are former toll-houses, single-storeyed, on the Scottish side of both bridges.

Just north of the bridge, on the Scottish bank (NT 933510), lies a typical Tweed salmon fishery. Dating from the early 19th century, it had wooden net-drying supports, a single-storey hut with extensions for stowing gear and a stone-built, vaulted ice-house (see no. 37).

## 10 Coldstream Bridge, Coldstream

*Mid 18th century AD.*

*NT 848401. On main A 698 just E of Coldstream, where it crosses Tweed to Cornhill.*

At Coldstream, between 1763 and 1767, John Smeaton built a fine 7-arch bridge across the Tweed, much higher and with flatter arches than the earlier bridges. The 5 main, segmental arches are bounded either side by semi-circular flood arches, and whilst the arches themselves are of well-dressed stone, the spandrels (those areas above and between) are rubble-built. The flood relief holes high in the spandrels have been filled in; above them a line of corbels protrude below the parapet. The bridge was widened in 1962.

Coldstream derived its original importance from its ford—the first of any consequence above Berwick, it is sometimes said, though that at Ladykirk was also significant. On the English side of the border, splendid castles at Wark and Norham respectively commanded access to each ford. Just east of Wark is the site of the battle of Carham where Malcolm II's victory over the Anglian Northumbrians led to the adoption of the Tweed as the national frontier from 1018. A few kilometres south-east, by contrast, the Scots were decimated in 1513 at Flodden Field (NT 890370). This was the route chosen, therefore, by so many armies, Scottish and English. Even today there is no further bridge upstream before John Rennie's magnificent creation at Kelso, built 1800-3 (NT 728336).

Until an Act of Parliament in 1856 forbade clandestine weddings, Coldstream was an eastern equivalent of Gretna Green. Runaway marriages

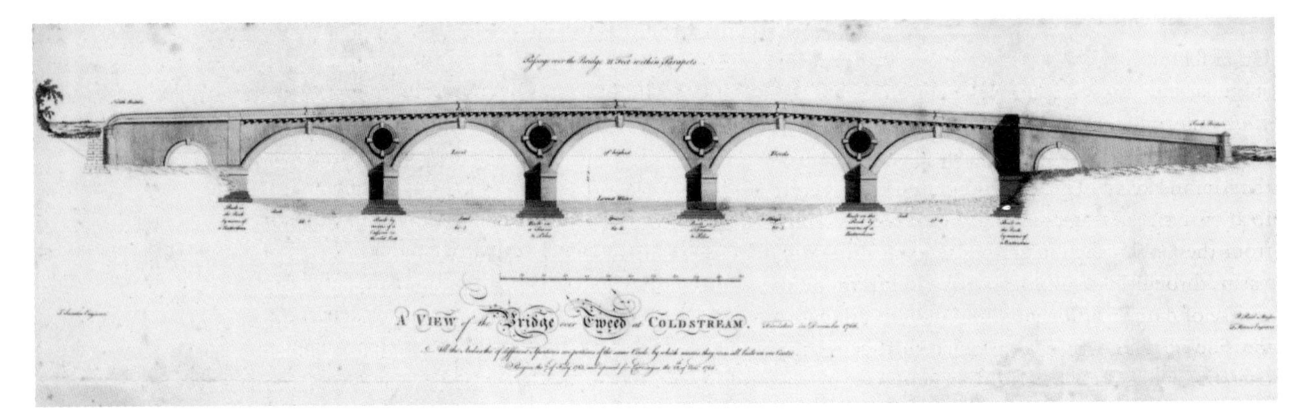


**Engraving of Coldstream Bridge, 1766**

from England were contracted in the toll-house, the one-storey building, with extension, immediately north on the east side of the bridge.

## 11 Lin's Mill Aqueduct, Newbridge, near Edinburgh

*Early 19th century AD.*

*NT 104706. Side road to Newbridge Industrial Estate at M 8/M 9 Newbridge roundabout. Branch immediately left, under both railway bridges turn right, thence past Clifton Hall school. Obscure signpost to Lin's Mill. Also N from A 71, just E of East Calder.*

The 1.5 m deep Edinburgh and Glasgow Canal was begun in 1818 and the first boat sailed through in 1822. It ran for 50 km from the Port Hopetoun Basin in Edinburgh, following the 73 m contour, before linking with the Forth and Clyde Canal at Camelon (lock 16). It was renowned for its tunnel at Callendar and for its fine aqueducts across the Avon, the Almond and the Water of Leith (NT 220707).

The 5-span Lin's Mill aqueduct suffered an early set-back when faulty masonry was detected after construction began in 1819, and the contractors were changed. Like the equally impressive 8-span Slateford aqueduct in Edinburgh, 150 m long by 23 m high (no. 3), and the 247m long by 26 m high Avon aqueduct (NS 966758) with nearby cottages and stables at Woodcockdale (NS 973760), it incorporated progressive concepts in canal-building. Instead of the much heavier channel of puddled clay, a cast-iron trough carried the water across the gorge. This was a system pioneered by Thomas Telford for the Pontcysyllte aqueduct in Wales. The light and slender stonework of the piers and arches would not otherwise have been possible.

Other features are the cobbled tow-paths, the mile-stone at the western end (21 miles to Falkirk; 10½ miles to Edinburgh), and the sluices on the aqueduct itself to let any overflow cascade down to the Almond below. There is a small basin either end to allow barges to wait or turn; also a feeder stream from the Cobbinshaw reservoir enters the eastern basin through a low stone-arched tunnel. The course of part of this feeder can be traced, high on the side of the gorge, 100 m or so further south. Each horse was changed every 8 miles; but to give a top speed of 9 mph, whole teams could be changed every 4 miles.

**Union Canal Aqueduct, Lin's Mill**

North from the aqueduct a remarkable sequence of bridges crosses the Almond: the wafer-thin M 8 road bridge built in 1970; the 8-span Birdsmill viaduct (NT 108712) built for the Edinburgh and Bathgate railway in 1849; and the massive 36-span Kirkliston Viaduct (NT 113722) opened in 1842 for the Edinburgh and Glasgow Railway. Its arches and piers were originally hollow, though filled with concrete in the 1950s to allow for higher speeds.

Elsewhere on the canal there is a pleasing basin at Linlithgow (NT 003769) with a little museum, seasonally, within the former stables. All the original bridges were numbered: a good sequence survives near Hermiston (NT 173703-181705), whilst No. 1 at Viewforth in Edinburgh (NT 243726) incorporates the arms of the cities of Edinburgh and Glasgow on its outer faces. Close by in Edinburgh (NT 244727) stands the distinctive and unusual early 20th-century Gilmore Park/Leamington lifting bridge. (It originally stood on Fountainbridge Road, close to Gardner's Crescent and the Lochrin Basin—a private and still-surving basin built originally for Haig's Distillery.) The bridge has a rivetted steel framework and a short lifting span; the control cabin is incorporated within the framework and when the bridge was lifted, pedestrians could still cross by the lattice girder footbridge. In 1965, however, the Canal was officially closed, and Port Hamilton and Port Hopetoun (named after the Duke of Hamilton and the Earl of Hopetoun) are now filled in.

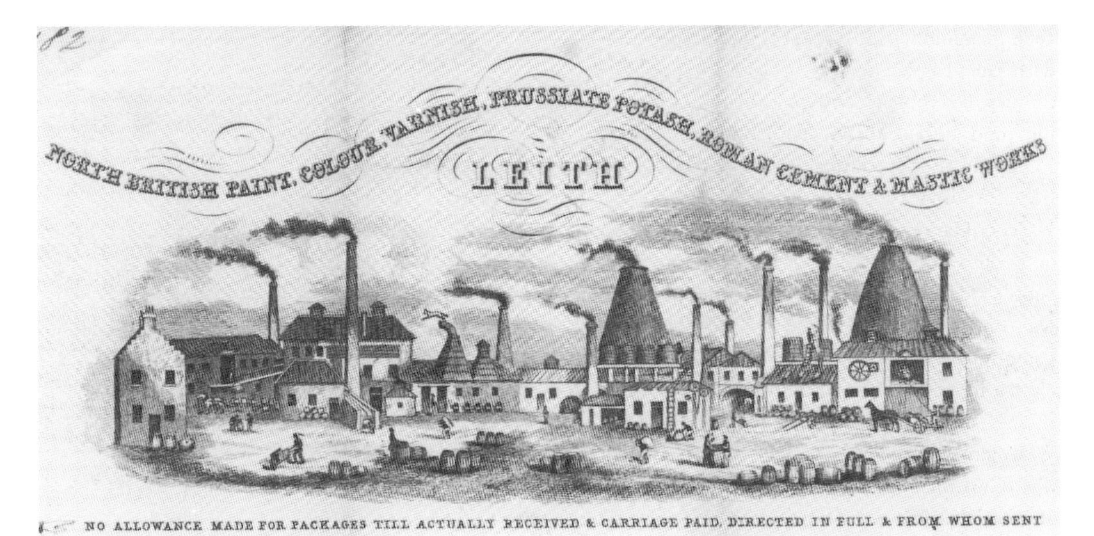


**The industrial port of Leith: engraved billhead**

## 12 Leith Docks, Edinburgh

*16th-19th century AD.*

*NT 270767-275770. From E end of Princes Street in Edinburgh, straight down Leith Walk and Constitution Street: in through main dock gates.*

Most major dock-systems in Scotland were provided with gates to keep the water-level within as high as possible even at low tide. The original harbour, however, first mentioned in the 12th-century Great Charter of Holyrood, simply lined both sides of the Water of Leith along 'The Shore'. Surviving riverside wharfs/quays date from the early 17th century, and the first known dock from the 18th century. It was here that George IV disembarked when he visited Edinburgh in 1822. First these quays were extended and protected by piers, then John Rennie engineered the now filled-in East (1800-6) and West (1810-17) Old Docks. The East Dock entrance gate survives, and the cast-iron swing-bridge (NT 270767) linking both sides of the harbour, across the river. Other docks followed during the second half of the 19th century: Victoria Dock (1847-51), Prince of Wales Graving Dock (1858), Albert Dock (1869), Edinburgh Dock (1877-81: for shipping coal), Imperial Dock (1896-98), Alexandra Graving Dock (1896).

**Victoria swing-bridge, Leith Docks**

Though much modernised and extended, with some docks now filled in, Leith Docks retain parts of their 19th-century layout; they also retain some of its more particular features. A hydraulic crane survives at the western end of Albert Dock; whisky bonds and warehouses (increasingly converted to other uses) still line the edge of the Old Docks on and behind Salamander Street and Commercial Street. Street names such as Baltic Street, Cadiz Street, Coburg Street and Elbe Street betray one-time maritime links; and the elegant buildings on Constitution Street and Bernard Street (former banks and shipping offices; Corn Exchange, 1863; bronze Burns staue, 1848) reflect the prosperity that was once 19th-century Leith.

Evidence for mainly 16th-19th-century Leith survives along and in from the Shore, lining the lowest reaches of the river. Look for the King's Wark (early 18th-century Royal Depot and Stores, restored 1972-78); Robert Mylne's Signal Tower of

1686 (originally a windmill for crushing rape-seed, with later battlements); Timber Bush (early 19th-century warehouses with arched pend); Old Ship Inn (mid 19th century); Trinity House (Kirkgate: 1555 'hospital', remodelled 1816-18). In Water Close, Andrew Lamb's House, 1587, was originally a 'Scots-Hanseatic' merchant's house sandwiched between warehouses above and below (now an old people's day centre); The Vaults in St Giles Street were once a huge warehouse dating from 1682, and containing 16th-century or earlier vaulted cellars for storing and maturing imported wines.

West across the river, Commercial Street boasts a fine Custom House (1810-12); whilst in Dock Street, Leith Citadel Gate is the last surviving fragment of Oliver Cromwell's massive 17th-century fortification. One of only two in Scotland, only Lerwick's Fort Charlotte in Shetland remains virtially intact (see no. 2, *Shetland* volume). By contrast, far out towards the new dock gates stands a largely derelict martello tower, 1809 (NT 268777)—forlorn sentinel and reminder of the Napoleonic Wars, and once isolated on an offshore skerry. It was one of only three in Scotland (see Hackness, no. 5 in *Orkney* volume).

If Leith were the main seagate for Scotland even beyond the Union of 1707, tiny tidal Newhaven was of but local significance—except that the *Great Michael* was built there in 1511. Now tucked in behind Leith's western breakwater, Newhaven harbour was begun in 1812. Its L-shaped pier, ending in an octagonal lighthouse, dates from 1825; the curved breakwater from 1876-78, with further enlargements in 1893-96. Fishermen's tall wooden sheds beside the east pier, gables to the harbour, were demolished in the 1970s; the surviving fishmarket was built c 1850 (now converted to other uses, including Newhaven Heritage Museum). Its slated roof is supported by cast-iron columns and beams; there were no decorative mouldings to collect dust and germs; the sides were formerly open to allow cooling winds to whistle across the boxes of fish; the floor sloped 30 cm from east to west to ease drainage and cleaning; and a raised platform allowed fish storage above vermin level!

**Eyemouth harbour and warehouses**

## 13 Eyemouth Harbour

*Mid 18th-mid 19th century AD.*

*NT 946642. 4.5 km NE of Ayton (A 1) on B 6355 at mouth of Eye Water; 1 km NE A 1107 coast road Burnmouth-Coldingham.*

The simplest kind of harbour was a quay lining a river mouth or inlet. Such was Leith in its earlier days, and Cramond. Eyemouth, a harbour since the 12th century, follows this same pattern with the subsequent addition of two projecting piers. In the mid 18th century, Eyemouth was simply a 'sea tavern' conveniently placed on an otherwise hostile shore to offer succour in the age of sail to vessels foiled by adverse winds.

Change, however, was imminent—triggered by John Smeaton, one of Scotland's engineering giants who had worked on canals and road bridges. The harbour was first built in 1768-70, Smeaton's breakwater being designed to enable ships to lie there even with a rare north or north-east wind—to which it was exposed. Between 1770 and 1841 the harbour was further improved, and it was rebuilt most substantially in 1885-87. Sluices at the inner end allowed the basin to be scoured.

White fisheries had developed around 1750, herring fisheries expanded in the 19th century and so did a coastal trade in corn. As trade increased, more wharves were built; also impressive stone warehouses and granaries, some of them four storeys high (NT 946643). And a rather different trade, in dead bodies, caused a watch-tower to be built in the churchyard! The village too, grew—huddles of houses clustered in the streets at the head of the bay, backing on to the quays; and across the river, the prosperous Gunsgreen House.

On the western promontory of the bay are the remains of a series of fortifications from prehistoric times to the 20th century, occasioned by the good sheltered anchorage. An English fort, said to have been erected by the Protector Somerset, dates to 1547; French defences date to 1557 after the removal of the 60-strong English garrison in 1550. The nearby Corn Fort (NT 940650) and the 'French Camp' at Dunglass (NT 718764) are of the same period. The French withdrew in 1559.

**Tunnel through headland, Cove harbour**

### 14 Cove Harbour, near Cockburnspath

*17th-19th century AD.*

*NT 785718. At N end of A1 Cockburnspath bypass, take minor cul-de-sac E to Cove. Park at clifftop former fishing hamlet; walk down road/track to shore.*

Cove Harbour is one of the delights of the Berwickshire coast. Until the 19th century it was just a tiny fishing station where boats were hauled out on the beach. Others included Bilsdean (just north of the Dunglass Burn), Old Camus, Redheugh and Lumsdaine (west of St. Abbs), as well as Northfield, Coldingham Sands, Eyemouth, Burnmouth and Ross (a little north of Berwick). Only Eyemouth (no. 13) developed into a major 19th-century fishing port; and of the others, only Cove, St. Abbs (no. 16) and Burnmouth were improved sufficiently to offer protection to other than small, open inshore boats. Beaches such as Redheugh Shore (NT 825705) were as renowned for their smuggling as for their white herring and salmon fisheries—though a coastguard station established at Redheugh in the 1820s effectively put paid to the former!

At Cove, the steep, narrow access road is affected by landslips. The surviving harbour dates to 1831, following abortive attempts in the 1750s and 1820s, when storms destroyed the works before their completion. It was built by Sir John Hall of Dunglass (a few kilometres north), and could accommodate boats of up to 60 tons burden.

Because of the steep cliffs and projecting headland, a tunnel was driven through the red sandstone to give easier access to the harbour; and the cliffs are riddled with other tunnels, chambers and caves—said variously to be associated with fish storage and processing, smuggling and howking for coal. A few increasingly dilapidated fishermen's cottages/stores are sited at the head of the north pier, from which an occasional small boat still fishes for lobsters and crabs. The rocks also bear considerable evidence of rock-cut steps and tuskings (projecting ledges, perhaps for bonding in once-planned additions to the harbour wall).

The clifftop fishing hamlet played host in the later 19th century to a 'Glasgow Boys' artists' colony. One kilometre inland, the old village of Cockburnspath retains its distinctive round-towered church (mainly 16th-19th century) and market square. A medieval mercat cross with carved thistle and rose motifs stands on a tiered stone base, and there are attractively pantiled buildings both adjacent to the east side of the church and elsewhere in the village. East of Pease Bay, 2-3 km along the coast, stand the remains of the 12th century St. Helen's or Old Cambus Kirk (NT 803796: west gable rebuilt c 1400). Well-weathered in its graveyard, 10th to 12th-century hogbacked tombstones are characteristic of a Northumbrian Christianity, heavily influenced by the incoming Scandinavians.

**Dunbar harbours and castle**
(Top left)

**Barometer plinth, 1856: Dunbar old harbour**

### 15 Dunbar Harbour, East Lothian

*18th-mid 19th century AD.*

*NT 679793-681792. A 1087 loops off A 1: go N along High Street in centre of town and bear right, down to harbours.*

In the 18th century Dunbar ranked as Scotland's major herring port; as late as 1788 Leith and Dunbar between them headed Scotland's whaling ports. In earlier times, however, the harbour (dating at least from 1574) comprised but a simple pier on a muddy shore. It could hold only a few small ships, and little seems to have been done until Cromwell spent £300 on pier works following his defeat of the Covenanters at Dunbar in 1650. The older part of the present harbour dates to c 1710-30; 2.4 m of solid rock were removed, and a basin formed of a curved rubble pier and a shorter straight pier, with some of the stonework laid vertically for greater stability. Stone steps giving access to the boats survive on the inner wall. In 1761, inside the curved pier, a coal import quay was built. The Old Harbour also includes an unusual stilling basin—an outer basin facing the harbour entrance, with a sloping end on which the waves break and weaken.

The new Victoria Harbour is altogether larger. Government assistance had been secured in 1842 as the town sought to expand its trade, a wall was built linking rocky outcrops to seaward, and a parallel quay constructed along the shore. This harbour had two entrances—that to the north is open; the other links to the old channel and is spanned by an interesting little hand-operated, wrought-iron bascule bridge, a kind of drawbridge balanced by a counterpoise as it is raised or lowered.

Around Dunbar's harbours are 18th- and 19th-century warehouses, granaries and maltings, most now sympathetically converted to other uses. Many of them are 3 or 4 storeys high. There are good examples of 17th- and 18th-century houses at the Shore, by the old harbour, and a fine inscribed stone pedestal dated 1856 bears a sculptured relief of a fisherman leaving his family. It once held a barometer.

A third harbour, and the smallest, based on the old channel, is Broadhaven. It is formed by a causeway to Lamer Island and the 18th-century D-shaped blockhouse. Dunbar Castle, by contrast, originally a courtyard castle, was ruined by order of Parliament in 1567; it was further damaged when the Victoria Harbour was built, and is now subject to very considerable erosion by the sea. Here also are the remains of a 16th-century battery, probably built by the Duke of Albany c 1522-36 and an important survival of early fortification.

The lifeboat shed houses a small, seasonal 'lifeboat' museum; whilst in the town there is a fine 17th-century steepled tolbooth or Town House in the middle of the High Street—blocked at its northern end by Robert Adam's handsome Lauderdale House.

**St Abb's Head lighthouse, foghorn and former keepers' cottage**

**Fisherman's hut, Sea View Terrace, St Abbs**
(Top right)

## 16 St Abb's Head Lighthouse, St Abbs

*Mid 19th century AD.*

*NT 917674-915692. B 6438 NE to St. Abbs from Coldingham (A 1107). Park at Northfield Farm Steading (NTS/SWT visitor centre), thence 2 km walk N by minor road/tracks or clifftop. Disabled may be able to drive up; ask at visitor centre; signposted.*

The original inner harbour at St. Abbs (from 1833) huddles below low cliffs, with houses and sheds terraced up the slopes. Together with later breakwaters, it provided shelter for fishermen who had once pulled up their boats on Coldingham Sands. Along Sea View Terrace, look for surviving examples of tiny, pantiled fishermen's huts.

David and Thomas Stevenson's short, stubby lighthouse on St. Abb's Head can be approached on foot either from the harbour or from the visitor centre—whether coastally along the spectacular clifftop (hordes of nesting seabirds in spring), or inland partly through farmland and skirting the thin ribbon of a reservoir. The Stevensons were sons of Robert Stevenson (1772-1850), who had built 23 Scottish lighthouses in 47 years. Thomas's son was the novelist Robert Louis Stevenson. The lighthouse complex includes water and fuel tanks, pump house, stores and keepers' house. The foghorn stands a little lower than the lighthouse itself (94 m), and between the two lie the batteries of rivetted steel air receivers used to store air for the foghorn. The foghorn engine house latterly contained Kelvin diesel engines, a driving alley and Maclellan air compressors.

Along with Barns Ness, the Bass Rock, Leith and Inchkeith (and the Longstone light on the Farne Islands to the S), St. Abb's Head is one of the major lighthouses on the south-east coast of Scotland. Their number and frequency emphasise the treacherous nature of these cliff-girt shores and skerry-strewn inshore waters. St. Abb's has a white flashing light visible every 10 seconds over 21 miles, and the foghorn or siren blasted out every 45 seconds. (At Port Seton harbour it was a Fog Hand Bell that was rung when boats were expected!) As a result of automation and increasingly sophisticated satellite navigational systems, air-operated foghorns have been discontinued in Scotland. The remaining operational horns are now electric and powered either by battery or by solar heat. Minor lights (in addition to those at harbour entrances and on the Forth Bridges) stand on eg St. Baldred's Boat (a skerry just off Tantallon Castle), on Fidra, the Oxcars, Inchcolm, Inch Garvie and the Beamer Rock—all helping mark the channel up the Firth of Forth.

Along the clifftop south of the Lighthouse, look for a promontory rampart; west of the Lighthouse lie the remains of a monastery believed to have housed both monks and nuns in two separate locations 1 km apart. Caer Golud was the original name for the British (Celtic) fortress on St. Abb's Head. The incoming Anglians called it Coludesburh, and the nearby (perhaps 7th century) settlement Coldingham—the settlement of the people of Coludesburh. The name St Abbs, meanwhile, recalls the female saint Abba, associated with the nunnery. The clifftops and moorland north-west of St Abb's Head are littered with old settlements and prehistoric hillforts, including Earn's Heugh Forts (no. 99). And the promontory ruins of 16th-century Fast Castle are but 6 kms away as the gannet flies.

# 2 MERCAT CROSSES, RURAL BUILDINGS AND AGRICULTURE

**Late 16th-early 17th century town houses, Linlithgow**

In the days before improved communications and transport, localised opportunities for trade were vital. Markets might be held on a particular day each week in the smaller centres; more frequently and of a more specialised nature perhaps in larger towns such as Kelso, Haddington or Dalkeith. The market was designed to service the small-scale but frequent and regular needs of a local hinterland, as well as the needs of the market-burgh itself; and much of the trade was in lower-value goods and foodstuffs, particularly grain. Such periodic markets were distinct from seasonal or annual fairs which might last one or two days; seven or eight days in the larger towns. These dealt in higher-value merchandise, livestock, textiles, manufactured goods—the Martinmas Fair in Edinburgh, stock fairs at West Linton, Newtown St Boswells, Hawick, Kelso and elsewhere. Up to the mid 17th century the distribution of markets and fairs was primarily medieval; from the early 18th century, however, numbers increased dramatically, not only to provide for poorly-served areas, but also to cope with an expanding trade with the south, further evidenced by the expansion of droving (Kailzie Hill, no. 26).

Market places might take the form of a square or a particularly wide street in towns like Peebles, Melrose, Jedburgh, Duns and Linlithgow. In a town like Lauder, the main street splits either side of the Tolbooth or Town House, where business was conducted and prisoners incarcerated; otherwise, tolbooths or court houses might simply face on to the widened street or market place—eg Dunbar, Musselburgh, Selkirk.

**Lauder: a classic medieval burgh**

But if the tolbooth were one symbol of a burgh, the mercat cross was the other, always afforded a prominent position which, in smaller places, might be on or near a village green—eg Ancrum (no. 18), Oldhamstocks (NT 739706). Surviving mercat crosses are of stone but very few incorporate actual crosses; rather a shield, a sundial or some other appropriate carving. Very occasionally, a more elaborate structure survives, such as the remarkable rotunda supporting the cross at Preston (no. 17) east of Musselburgh, almost unique in Scotland. Other than a 15th-century example at Peebles, virtually all surviving crosses, some rather mutilated, are post-Reformation—Cockburnspath (NT 774711), Aberlady (NT 464799), Wester Pencaitland (NT 440689), Gifford (NT 533680), Bowden (NT 554305), Galashiels (NT 492357). One of Stenton's 'greens' (NT 621742), though it cannot boast a mercat cross, does have a reconstructed tron or public weigh-beam; there is also a conically-roofed, cylindrical rood-well a little further east at the end of the village.

With the exception of Ormiston (no. 19), mercat crosses are restricted to pre-improvement burghs. Otherwise, prior to the mid 18th century, most settlement was scattered, with joint-tenant farmers and their families living in fermtouns. These were loose assemblages of dwellings, barns, byres and associated buildings surrounded by open fields divided in some kind of run-rig (strips of land that were reallocated periodically between the

**Reconstructed tron or weighbeam, Stenton, East Lothian**

**Teind barn and church, Whitekirk, East Lothian**

tenants). Beyond the township dyke, muirs and hills were grazed in common, and though seasonally-occupied summer-touns or shielings were discontinued in parts of the Lammermuirs as early as the 12th-13th centuries, as the great abbeys developed large-scale hill-grazing, evidence survives in names like Penshiel, Mayshiel and Gamelshiel, high up the Whiteadder Water.

As for the old nucleated fermtouns, the main period of change in East Lothian for example was 1730-90, with some enclosures begun in the 1690s. The Merse was equally forward, though in upland areas improvement, particularly underground drainage, might not be completed until well into the 19th century—thus it should not be assumed that surviving rigs representing ridge and furrow cultivation, the mainstay of the old system, are necessarily very old. Straight, fairly low, fairly narrow and parallel rigs, worked with improved ploughs and neatly parcelled into individual fields are most frequently post-1800. Many can be seen on lower moorland south of the Lammermuirs, around Castle Law hillfort (no. 84) in the Pentland Hills, and on Edinburgh's Braid Hills (NT 2469-2569). Only the sinuous, broader and higher-crowned rigs are older, eg above Ellemford (NT 718614) near Cranshaws; and these may reflect more of a fossilised landscape, evidence of higher-level cultivation with older cumbersome ploughs in a more advantageous climate—perhaps by tenants of the Border Abbeys, and abandoned by 1600. In Southdean parish (no. 29), these settlements are surrounded by a head dyke or assart bank, and represent agricultural holdings carved out of the medieval Royal hunting forest of Jedburgh.

Could the distinctive cultivation terraces at Romanno (no. 27) and Braemore Knowe (no. 28) also have connections with the great monastic houses? Or do they relate rather to areas of Anglian influence? They are almost impossible to date and may range from the 7th-17th centuries! It may be that subsequent cultivation has destroyed the evidence in more fertile, lowland areas of Lothian and Berwickshire; as they are recorded, however, terraces cluster around the Cheviot parishes of Yetholm, Morebattle, Hownam and Oxnam. Elsewhere they are found mainly around the middle and upper Tweed and its tributaries and across to the upper Clyde—with outliers, as it were, on Edinburgh's Arthur's Seat and a little further west and north. There are numerous other good examples—at Headshaw Law (NT 7918), Stotfield Hill (NT 693121-698117), Countridge Knowe (NT 822254-826251), Calroust (NT 824193-824196), Glenternie (NT 206363-209368), Goseland Hill (NT 078350, 070355), Woodhousehill (NT 212375) and The Wham (NT 234388). They might be assumed in some cases alternatives to rigs on steeper ground; on occasion the two types blend into each other. At Glenrath Hope (no. 97), by contrast, they overlie earlier, small, square, 'Celtic' fields; and not infrequently around the Manor Water they lie close to the remains of iron-age forts and settlements. Their dating, however, must remain unproven.

With the exception of certain late/post medieval townships and field systems at sites such as Old Thornylee (NT 4136, 4137), Lour (NT 179356) and Posso (NT 200322) in Peeblesshire, virtually nothing appears to survive of the earlier traditional pattern of farming in south-east Scotland; the present landscape of neat, rectangular fields enclosed with dykes (hedges, where insufficient stone was available) is man-made—streaked with lines of matured planted trees or fuller shelter belts. It has changed little over 150-250 years, but it is no older.

The buildings too are no older. Improved farmhouses, increasingly set aside from the steading, were based on 18th- century manses or minor lairds' houses, symmetrical to a plain, four-square, two-storey block with central staircase. Farm cottages too, estate- or farm-built, tended to be symmetrical, neat and functional in pairs or terraces. A row of such tied cottages, flower garden in front, vegetable garden behind, is still a distinctive landscape feature particularly in East and Midlothian and Berwickshire which, with 6-8 farm servants to a farm, had the largest labour teams in Scotland. The adjacent districts generally had 4-5. The cottages were occupied by married farmworkers, descendants in many

**Lour tower and late/ post medieval settlement and field system near Stobo**

areas of the previously dispossessed joint-tenant farmers; unmarried males were generally housed collectively in single-room bothies built into the steading.

Steadings were normally set about a courtyard and incorporated byres, cattle-sheds, stable, dairy and barns. Arches indicate former cart-sheds and are a guide to the number of working Clydesdale horses kept on the farm. Cart-sheds are now tractor or implement sheds; grain silos have taken the

**Easter Happrew farmhouse, near Lyne, Peebles**

**Farm windmill stump, Swinton**

place of barns; the combine has dispossessed the threshing barn. A handful of mainly 18th-century windmill stumps set into steadings, on exposed sites generally not too far from the east coast, reflect one form of power used to drive barn threshing mills—eg West Barns/Bielside (NT 654783; later turned into a dovecote), Balgone Barns (NT 553827), Rumbletonlaw (NT 676453), Swinton (NT 8347) and Gunsgreenhill at Eyemouth (NT 948629).

Much more common, however, were horses treading round an octagonal or circular, covered horse-gang set against the outer wall of the barn. As coal became more widely available by the mid 19th century, horses were replaced quite widely on the larger lowland farms by small engines, clearly indicated in the landscape by brick-built chimneys towering over the steading.

Water-power also was once used in places to drive barn threshing mills; moreover it was widely used to power grain mills and saw mills. Scores yet remain, eg Kirkton Manor Mill (NT 221379), though in increasingly dilapidated condition. Preston Mill (no. 24) and Livingston Mill (NT 033668), have been restored; others such as Nether Liberton in Edinburgh (NT 273706), Tyninghame (no. 22) and Blythe Mill (NT 132453) have survived by virtue of conversion to houses or inns.

A further distinctive feature of the lowland landscape is the dovecote (doocot or pigeon house). The oldest are tapering and beeskep-shaped, circular in plan and once home to perhaps 600 birds—probably 15th-17th century. Rectangular, lectern-type dovecotes with nest boxes for maybe 1000 birds (occasionally over 2000) are generally 17th-19th century, as are cylindrical examples. There are good examples of beehive dovecotes at Phantassie (no. 24), Prestonpans (no. 2), Craigmillar Castle (no. 48), Corstorphine (NT 200725), Chirnside (NT 870562) and Merton, 1576 (NT 620319); rectangular dovecotes at Preston Tower (no. 2), Hermitage of Braid (NT 248703), Nether Liberton (NT 273706) and Tantallon Castle (no. 49); cylindrical dovecotes at Marchmont House, 1749 (NT 760498), Dryburgh Abbey House, 1828 (NT 591314) and Burnhouse near Channelkirk, early 19th century (NT 439491).

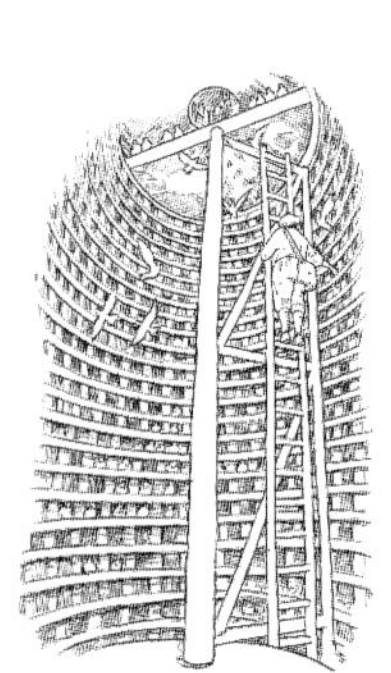

**Doocot interior, Dirleton Castle**

Where present, a sloping landing platform on the roof generally faces south to give the birds a warm sunny roost, and the north wall often projects upwards to give better shelter from the north wind (though cylindrical dovecotes frequently have a domed roof with a small, circular domed cap or access 'turret'). String courses around the building were not merely decorative, but helped deter rats from climbing and entering through the flight holes; whilst within, the walls were lined with stack upon stack of stone-built nesting/roosting boxes, reached from a (sometimes revolving) ladder or pole.

For these were the intensive farming techniques of late medieval and somewhat later times, when lairds and the more substantial farmers sought to provide themselves with fresh young pigeon meat, in season, at the expense of their (sub-)tenants' and neighbours' crops! They were common in many parts of eastern Scotland, and remarkably high numbers have survived—perhaps on account of the old belief that if a doocot were demolished, the wife of the owner would die within the year!

Increased yields of grain and the cultivation of otherwise marginal lands were made possible, in part at least, by liming and improved field drainage. It was clay tiles that truly revolutionised field drainage from the early 19th century, and enabled the switch from narrow rigs with open drains alongside, to large and flat rectangular fields. A landowner or farmer could simply open up a convenient clay dub and begin manufacturing, with the result that, in comparison to most brick-making, tile-making was more of a rural activity. Paxton's kilns, for instance (NT 937539: no. 37), were operational from the 1830s to c 1900, and produced roofing pantiles as well as drainage tiles. It was a seasonal occupation. The clay was dug in the autumn and left over the winter to weather and saturate; in spring it was dug over with spades, moistened and covered in straw; at the beginning of summer it was milled—softened, with varying quantities of sand added. The tiles were then moulded and dried carefully to prevent distortion prior to firing. Temporary 'clamps' or Scottish updraught kilns were later replaced by more sophisticated and permanent 'intermittent' updraught, downdraught and Newcastle kilns, before new brick-making machinery and such 'continuous' kilns as the Hoffman were introduced to the larger enterprises in the late 19th century.

Lime was also important for the new agriculture. It was particularly valuable in reducing soil acidity, and Lothian was particularly fortunate in having extensive workable limestones to the east, west and south of Edinburgh and south of Dunbar. The Borders were less fortunate—a reason why so much higher land there, bedded on old red sandstone, was not reclaimed as quickly as in Lothian. To prepare lime for agriculture and other uses, the quarried limestone was mixed with coal and burnt, originally in horizontal clamps but from the later 18th century in massive stone-built vertical draw-kilns. As well as one restored at Cat Craig (no. 23), many more-or-less complete but partially overgrown examples feature in the countryside—notably at Landridge (NT 457754), Burdiehouse

**Builder's premises in The Bow, Coldingham**

(NT 277673), Raw Camps (NT 096683), Macbiehill (NT 183520), Carham (NT 789369), Ballencrieff (NS 978704) and Wairdlaw (NS 995730). A more fully industrial complex stands abandoned at Esperston (NT 3457), not far from the surviving lime works at Middleton in Midlothian.

If the tide of change in mid 18th-century Scotland began to sweep away the old system, in addition to new farm complexes (which in themselves may have housed communities as large as those once living in the old townships!), it also brought a rash of new, planned villages. These were not as common in south-east Scotland as in many other parts of the country, but a number were built, inspired as much as anything perhaps by Cockburn's early success at Ormiston (no. 19). Athelstaneford (NT 5377) was wholly agricultural, with an emphasis on craftsmen and smallholders; Tyninghame (no. 22) housed workers pensioned off from the Earl of Haddington's estates; Gavinton (NT 7652) and Gifford (NT 5368) were rebuilt. In creating such villages as Newcastleton (no. 21; known locally as Copshawholm), private landowners were seeking to help the national economy by channelling surplus agricultural labour into cottage textile industries. Thus Carlops (NT 1655–1656), an interesting linear village, was founded originally in 1784 for cotton-weaving and adapted in 1800 for woollen manufactories. The stocking-weaving village of Denholm (NT 5618) built, by contrast, around a large rectangular green, is also 18th century—though Westgate Hall at the southern corner is 17th century.

**Preston doocot, Prestonpans**

**Preston mercat cross, restored 1980** (Left)

## 17 Preston Mercat Cross, East Lothian

*Early 17th century AD.*

*NT 391740. Just N of A 198 Musselburgh-North Berwick road, close to link road N to Prestonpans; signposted.*

*Historic Scotland.*

In medieval times the mercat cross indicated burgh status—a community established either as a royal burgh by the king or as a burgh of barony by secular or ecclesiastical vassals. Only stone crosses survive, though wood would also once have been used. The term 'cross' is less than accurate, however; most simply tapered to a simple head, often decorated, but not cruciform.

Preston cross, of yellow sandstone, has been described as the most handsome in Scotland. Dating to the early 17th century, probably to just after 1617 when Preston was granted a weekly market and annual fair, it is one of only two of its type surviving in Scotland and the only one in its original position.

The central shaft ends in a rectangular capital topped with a unicorn supporting a tablet carved with a lion rampant. Below, the column is set in the rare and distinctive circular 'rotunda', some 4.3 m diameter by 3.7 m high. Six of the compartments, separated vertically by pilasters, have niches fitted with seats and semi-circular scallop-shell heads. The other two contain doorways, one leading to a small vaulted chamber and the other taking a narrow winding stair to the upper, crier's platform.

Preston, like the once separate coastal settlement of Salt Prieston/Prestonpans, was associated with the monks of Newbattle and Holyrood. From the later 14th century it belonged to a branch of the Hamilton family. Of interest nearby: the mainly 15th-century Preston Tower with 17th-century, rectangular, 1000 bird, lectern-type dovecote; a fragment of the 17th-century Preston House; the 17th-century two-storey Hamilton House with its courtyard. A beehive-shaped 600 bird dovecote not far from the mercat cross is probably 16th-17th century; it was associated with the late 16th-early 17th-century Northfield House, an unfortified tower-house with turreted stairs (exteriors viewable). The Parish Church (Kirk Street), 1596, is one of Scotland's very first post-Reformation churches—with an interesting ?18th-century naval painting, 17th-18th-century mortification panels, gravestones and monuments.

## 18 Ancrum Mercat Cross, near Jedburgh

*Late 16th century AD.*

*NT 628245. On B 6400 just W of A 68 between St Boswells and Jedburgh.*

This cross, like the remnants of that of Bowden (NT 554305), dates from the late 16th century. It is complete other than for its cross-head and stands on the triangular village green, close to its original position. The shaft is about 3.5 m high, set in a socket-stone about a metre square which is boldly decorated with leaf-like carving.

The manor of Ancrum belonged to the Bishop of Glasgow from before the time of David I, and Bishop Robert 'Blacader' received a charter from James IV in 1490 confirming its status as a barony. Most of the houses around the green are 19th century or later, though a few two-storeyed late 18th-century examples survive at Causewayend. At least one was originally thatched.

The 'old' Ancrum bridge (NT 638237) is probably that standing in 1794—two arches, with a third to

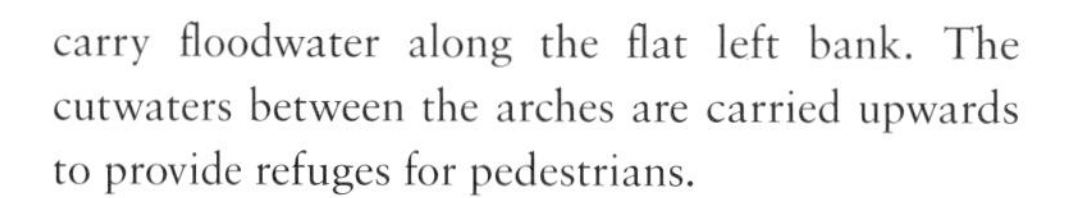

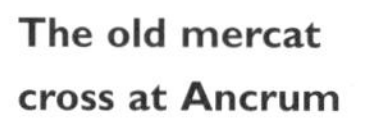

**The old mercat cross at Ancrum**

**Ormiston cross**
(Far right)

carry floodwater along the flat left bank. The cutwaters between the arches are carried upwards to provide refuges for pedestrians.

Just south of the ruins of the mid 18th-century parish church (NT 621248), a 10th-12th-century hogbacked tombstone was found with ridged top, shingle-/tile-patterned sloping sides and end gables (see section 7); and just across the A 68, Peniel Heugh (NT 653263) offers a good sequence of hillforts spanning the early iron-age to sub-Roman period (see section 8). The hill, a fine vantage point, is crowned by the splendid Wellington Pillar, a commanding tower commemorating the battle of Waterloo (1815).

## 19 Ormiston Mercat Cross and Planned Village, East Lothian

*15th and mid 18th century AD.*

*NT 414692. On B 6371 S of Tranent, and just N of A 6093 Pencaitland-Haddington road; signposted.*

*Historic Scotland (Cross).*

The mining settlement at Ormiston dates from 1903 when John Clark founded the Ormiston Coal Company. Previously the settlement, set on higher ground a little back from the north bank of the Tyne Water, was essentially rural; and the old part of the village owes much of its character to a former land-owner, John Cockburn.

Cockburn was a member of the last Scots Parliament; he subsequently sat in the English Parliament from 1707-41, and during his time in the south familiarised himself with new agricultural practices. In 1736 he founded an agricultural society at Ormiston which met monthly in the village inn to discuss agricultural practices. He sent the sons of his tenants to England to learn new methods; he also founded a brewery and distillery to provide a market for local barley, and laid out a bleach field to support a linen industry, bringing skilled flax workers from Ireland and Holland. A flax-spinning school followed. The enterprise was insufficiently profitable at the time, however, and in 1747 he was obliged to sell the village to the Earl of Hopetoun (see no. 38).

Cockburn's principal architectural legacy is his estate village, begun c 1736, a little to the east of the older mill-toun. The wide, tree-lined High Street, 'closed' at both ends by 90° turns in the road, was to be a market centre; the new housing accommodated local craftsmen and the cottage textile workers. He provided the building materials himself, and expected high standards: 'I can give my consent to no houses being built in the Main Street of the town but what are two storeys high'.

The fine mercat cross stands in the middle of the High Street. It dates to the 15th century, a rare survival of a truly cruciform, pre-Reformation 'cross'! It may have been associated with a chapel standing across the present street, or it may have come from elsewhere, revitalised as a focus to the new village. The old base is octagonal, set above modern steps. The square-sectioned shaft carries a shield on its western side; the cross-head stands above the moulded 'neck'.

**The old fermtoun of Swanston, Edinburgh**

## 20 Swanston Village, Edinburgh

*18th-19th century AD.*

*NT 240673. City by-pass to Lothianburn Junction, then A 702 Biggar Road citywards to traffic lights at Fairmilehead, and W 1 km along Oxgangs Road (A 720). S on Swanston Road to public car park at foot of village, beside entrance to Golf Club. (Please do not drive beyond this carpark.)*

Swanston has long been the only identifiably rural village to survive within Edinburgh. Ironically, its situation—nestling amongst the northern slopes of the Pentland Hills—has prevented virtually any modern development and left its character almost uniquely protected (albeit gentrified).

It comprises several different elements, sited around the farm. The classic reddish stone-built 19th-century steading (now partly converted into housing) is arranged symmetrically around a courtyard, with fine arched entrance and steep gables. To the west, Swanston Cottage was built in 1761 by the Edinburgh Burgh Council, at the same time as the square water house in the field north-east below the carpark. The land had been bought by the City Magistrates so as to tap natural springs and pipe the water to the Castlehill Reservoir, just below the Castle Esplanade (a supplement to wells established at Comiston from 1681, feeding stone fountains in the High Street).

The single-storey Cottage was built in the shelter of a low ridge, overlooking the hills—an attractive, secluded spot where important visitors might be entertained. It incorporates gargoyles and other stone features from the old kirk of St Giles which was being renovated at the time. The cottage was heightened in 1620, bow windows added in 1867, and further alterations made by Lorimer in 1908 for Lord Guthrie. As a part (albeit a highly atypical part) of the public housing stock, it was bought for the proverbial 'song' in the 1980s, when central government required local authorities to sell off council-owned property to interested sitting tenants at a discounted price. It was at Swanston Cottage that Robert Louis Stevenson spent his summers from 1867 to 1880.

Above the car park lies the tall, 18th century, L-plan, crow-step-gabled farmhouse (now converted into several individual houses); beyond, the mid 18th-century schoolhouse (the 'White House') adjoins a row of simple, probably 17th-century, single-storey thatched cottages, which were part of the old Swanston village and a fairly typical, rare example of an old-style fermtoun. All are now whitewashed. The cottages were restored by the City Council in 1964, but, although their roofs are still thatched, this is now secured with netting and concrete ridging, rather than ropes and and a ridge of thatch. Close by, a half-square of stone-built and slated farm-workers' cottages is more-or-less contemporary with the 19th-century farm steading. Typical of their type across the Lowlands, they have been much extended at the rear with a motley collection of annexes and outshots, often in brick and harled.

Hill access from Swanston climbs past the so-called T-wood (a cross-shaped shelter belt), to Hillend hillfort (NT 245662: above the ski slope) and steeply upwards to the much-eroded bronze-age burial cairn on top of Caerketton (NT 237662).

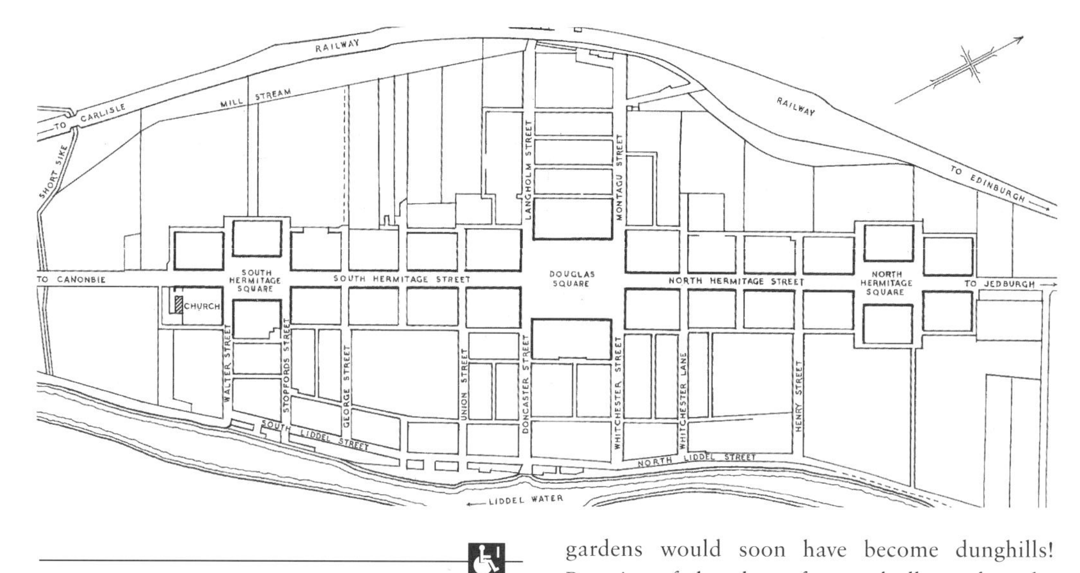


**The hand-loom weavers' village of Newcastleton, founded 1793**

## 21 Newcastleton Well and Planned Village

*Late 18th century AD.*

*NY 483875. On B 6357 in Liddesdale, 2 km S of junction with B 6399.*

A 'pant' is a public well or fountain generally covered with a stone or metal lid. The Newcastleton well in Douglas Square is a small stone structure with a domed top—a type uncommon in Scotland, though reminiscent of the larger well-heads in Edinburgh's Royal Mile and Grassmarket and the village pump at Oldhamstocks (NT 739705).

Newcastleton (Copshawholm) is an attractive, classic estate village, founded in 1793 by the third Duke of Buccleuch to house hand-loom weavers. It consists of a long main street, with Douglas Square as its modest centrepiece. Here, in addition to the well, are two-storey houses and the war-memorial. At each end of the street are two smaller squares—North and South Hermitage Square—with mainly one and one-and-a-half storey houses; and a parallel street, built up on one side only, faces the Liddel Water. The first house to be finished (44 North Hermitage Street) is dated 1793, with the initials of Francis Ballantyne carved into the entrance lintel. A characteristic feature of many of the houses was a large front window to light the loom. That the houses face directly on to the street is also characteristic—typical of many (if not most) Scottish planned villages and medieval burghs, where it seems that landowners feared that front gardens would soon have become dunghills! Remains of the plots of ground allocated to the settlers can yet be seen a little down the valley, south of the village. For it had proved impractical to link them directly to the rear of the houses, given the river to one side and the steep slope to the other.

A kilometre or two south of Newcastleton, Milnholm or Millom Cross (NY 476861) is said, traditionally, to have been erected c 1320 following the murder of Alexander Armstrong of Mangerton at Hermitage Castle. It is said that those bearing his body rested there on the way to Ettleton Churchyard—at the top of the side road beside the cross. The churchyard (NY 472863) contains interesting early tombstones and cross-shaft fragments, as well as a curious mid 19th-century memorial to William Armstrong of Sorbytrees 'shot without challenge or warning in 1851 by the Revd. Joseph Smith, incumbent of Walton, Cumberland'. There is a fine outlook along and across the Liddel Water.

A few kilometres north-east of Newcastleton, by contrast, along B 6357, Liddel Castle (NY 510900) is what is left of the de Soulis motte, abandoned by the 14th century in favour of Hermitage Castle (no. 47). Ridge and furrow cultivation strips survive the other side of the Liddel Water; adjacent to the castle, a churchyard (NY 509898) and the base of a medieval cross (NY 511898) are all that remain of the medieval settlement of Castleton. The cross (its shaft is modern) perhaps marks the site of Castleton's weekly markets and three annual fairs, granted to the Duke of Buccleuch in 1672. Further up the valley are two moated homesteads (see no. 52). Florida (NY 517908) is just a little north of the farm; Kirndean (NY 532909) lies 0.5 m along a track east from near Florida Farm. It is a small, square earthwork, c 30 m across, with a 5 m wide by 50 cm high bank, and a likely entrance on the west side. The rigs around the moat are of a later date, perhaps early 19th century when much marginal land was cultivated on account of high grain prices during the Napoleonic Wars.

## 22 Tyninghame Sawmill and Estate Village, East Lothian

*First half 19th century AD.*

*NT 610790. Close to junction of A 198 North Berwick to A 1 road and B 1407 from East Linton.*

Whilst Cockburn was busy improving his estates and rebuilding the village at Ormiston, Thomas Hamilton, sixth Earl of Haddington, was equally immersed in agricultural experimentation, notably in forestry. He planted Tyninghame and Binning Woods which are still prominent landscape features. It was a later generation, however, a century on, that built the estate village—still a very model of its kind, though gradually changing hands.

The harled factor's house, c 1800, stands on the east side of the A 198, as do the lodge and arched gateway to the main house, c 1880. The estate sawmill opposite, now converted to a private house, was built in 1828 by Thomas Hannan, mason, and George Sked, engineer. It is an attractive, single-storey building with diamond-paned windows and crow-stepped gables. The machinery was driven by a six-spoke undershot (more accurately, low breast-shot wheel) of wood and iron, some 4.3 m in diameter by 1.2 m wide.

The main part of the village, on the side road, is largely 19th century, mostly by the same Thomas Hannan. Of rose-pink sandstone, the houses blend in varied relationships with each other and with the line of the road—a little clinical perhaps, but attractively so! The restored village pump, encased in wood, stands below the smiddy—note the windows—near to the Post Office.

'Tyninghame' signifies the farm on the river Tyne; it is one of three names in south-east Scotland (also Whittinghame, Coldingham) that reflect the earliest stratum of Anglian (Northumbrian) settlement. And within the grounds of Tyninghame House stand the remains of the old parish church of St Baldred (NT 619796), an anchorite who died in AD 756 or 757. The 9th-century monastery on the site was sacked by the later, Anglo-Danish Northumbrians in AD 941; the mid 12th-century parish church remained intact until the old village was 'cleared' in 1761. The surviving Norman carving on the arches to its chancel and apse suggest, however, a church at least as spectacular as that at Dalmeny (no. 74).

## 23 Cat Craig Lime Kilns, East Lothian

*Mid 19th century AD.*

*NT 715772. Some 4 km SE of Dunbar; side road E off A 1 to Barns Ness Lighthouse; turn left at shore and walk along to kiln.*

There are considerable deposits of carboniferous limestone in Midlothian, East Lothian and parts of West Lothian—though relatively little in the Borders where the farmers of the Merse, for instance, sent their carts 30-40 kms to collect lime from Skateraw. These deposits contain many fossil shells and corals, laid down long ago in deep clear waters. The proximity of a reliable, developing, nearby coal industry able to power the reduction of limestone to quicklime became increasingly important by the mid 18th century when agricultural improvers looked to lime to counteract

**Cat Craig limekiln**

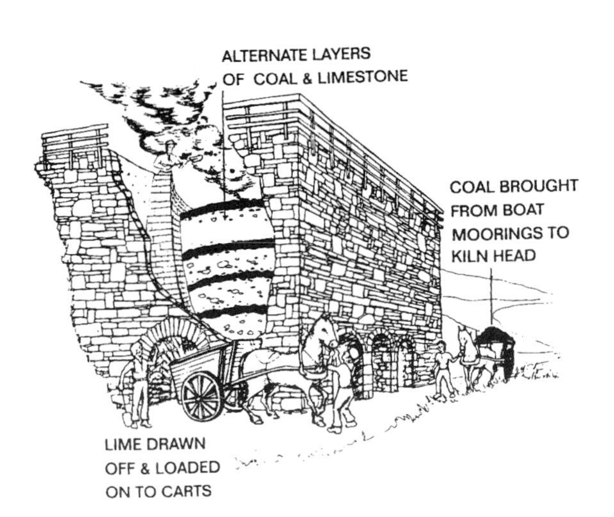


**Cat Craig limekiln**

natural acidity in the soil. It became equally important for such new urban building programmes as Edinburgh's New Town, 1767-1825, and for industrial use (eg gasworks, iron-working and potteries).

Lime burning, therefore, came to take on an industrial character of its own, though generally in rural surroundings. And the principle was much the same in the larger as in the smaller kilns, once vertical draw-kilns came to replace horizontal horse-shoe shaped clamp kilns in the later 18th century.

Small rural draw-kilns as at Cat Craig were generally egg-shaped and built with a stone-facing and brick lining (brick retains and reflects heat better, hence the brick facings to walled gardens attached to country mansions). The kiln was packed with alternate layers of coal and lime—one part coal to four parts quarried limestone seems about average—and set alight. Lime burning continued all summer; it was a hot, dry and dusty occupation, and beer was often provided as part of the daily wages. When burnt, the lime was taken out through the draw-hole at the base and more coal and limestone added through the opening at the top. To see a kiln at full power at night must have been a remarkable sight; in 1810 two ships mistook that at Skateraw for the coal-fired beacon on May Island, with disastrous results!

At Cat Craig there is a pair of mid 19th-century kilns, one a 2-draw kiln, the other a 3-draw kiln. The centre arch in the face of the bank gives access to draw-holes for both kilns. The kilns were associated with extensive quarries, a power-house and a track leading to a landing place on the rocks, before their closure in 1921. At low tide, on the foreshore, nine different limestones can be identified from their different fossils. (For nearby Barns Ness lighthouse, see no. 16.)

## 24* Preston Mill and Phantassie Doocot, East Linton, East Lothian

*17th-18th century AD.*

*NT 594778, 596774. 500 m along B 1407 from East Linton to Tyninghame, just past church; signposted. Dovecote can also be approached by track from Phantassie Farm, off A 1, 500 m E of East Linton.*

*National Trust for Scotland.*

In 1835 Preston Mill was one of 7 water-mills in Prestonkirk parish—4 oatmeal and barley mills, 1 exclusively barley mill, 1 flour mill and 1 associated with a distillery. In 1854, some 73 are recorded for rural East Lothian, 34 of them corn mills and 14 on the River Tyne. The Preston Mill complex seems to betray at least four phases, and dates in part to the 17th century. It is not as typically Scottish as Livingston Mill in West Lothian (NT 033668), for its polygonal-roofed, circular kiln with conical ventilator suggests something of the Low Countries and parallels with hop-country oast-houses in south-east England. Originally, access to the kiln was restricted to the stone staircase outside. At first-floor level the grain was spread about 13 cm-16 cm thick on 30 cm square, cast iron plates (formerly 30 cm square perforated clay tiles), marked Standley Bros. Ltd., Nuneaton. It was dried by the fire below.

The mill itself is on two levels—the upper floor housing the stones and hoppers (the stone beds are probably the oldest surviving part of the machinery). First the grain was cleaned, through the cockler (from Bury St. Edmonds in England, late 19th-early 20th century); then fed into the shelling stones to separate the husks, removed by the fanners below. Upstairs once again, and the kernels were ready for grinding into meal. All this machinery is powered by an undershot water wheel and wooden cog wheels and gearing, the flow of

**Fire-clay kiln-floor tile, Preston Mill: by Standley Bros. Ltd., Nuneaton, England** (Top left)

**Phantassie doocot, East Linton before restoration and harling** (left)

water to which is controlled by a sluice operated from within the mill. The water-wheel is likely mid-late 19th century, probably by Alex. Mather, Fountainbridge, Edinburgh.

The mill building is likely to be 18th century; the kiln may be somewhat earlier. That mill and kiln are offset may be the legacy of a major rebuilding of the mill, perhaps because the original kiln could have resembled small farm kilns in design and materials—where drying floors were of wood and straw. Because of fire risk, such kilns were kept separate from the relatively expensive mill machinery, much of which was also formerly of wood. (A detached kiln with circular floor set into a circular-plan building survives at Luffness Mains, Aberlady: NT 479809.) The whole complex is attractively built of orange sandstone rubble and roofed in traditional east coast pantiles.

A ten minute stroll south of the mill lies Phantassie Farm, where the engineer John Rennie was born in 1761 and where a wind-powered threshing machine was introduced in 1799. The farmhouse is 18th-19th century; the long two-storey steading is mid 19th century—as is the single-storey half-square block of farm cottages. The lime kiln, however, is late 18th century and the distinctive dovecote probably 16th-17th century. Access to almost 600 nesting boxes is by way of a ladder fixed to the cross-beam.

## 25 Foulden Teind Barn, near Chirnside

*18th-19th century AD.*

*NT 931557. On A 6105 Berwick-upon-Tweed to Chirnside road, just E of Foulden Village; signposted.*

*Historic Scotland (exterior only).*

Foulden is a small, linear village lining the north side of the road and looking south across the Merse to the Cheviots. To the west, Foulden West Mains (NT 911558) boasts a typical mid 19th-century brick-built farm chimney attached to a small single-storey steam-engine house once used for threshing. To the east stands the church with its associated graveyard (18th-19th-century stones) and the teind or tithe barn.

Considerably altered in the 18th-19th century, the barn stored the produce collected each year by the church as teinds or tithes. It is an attractive two-storey stone building with crowstepped gables, approached by an outside stair. On the north side,

**Foulden teind barn**

**Ventilation slab, Foulden teind barn**

beside the road, the joists of the main floor reach through to the outside of the wall; below is a basement level approached directly by doors in the south wall.

An equally interesting and large teind barn survives at Whitekirk (NT 596816) in East Lothian, the west end being a mid 16th-century tower-house built with stone from the hostels used by medieval pilgrims visiting a nearby healing well; it was subsequently extended in the 17th century to give a large, three-storey barn with crowstepped gables and an outside stone stair to the first floor.

These two teind barns are the only ones known to survive in Scotland.

**Kailzie Hill drove road**

## 26 Kailzie Hill Drove Road, near Peebles

*17th-19th century AD.*

*NT 2736. Road to Cademuir, branching just S of Peebles Bridge, off B 7062; bear left at junction and continue SE beyond built-up area; climb hill and ridge ahead on foot.*

The droving of cattle from the Highlands, and thence south from the trysts at Crieff or Falkirk, was a serious business from at least the early 17th century. It reached its height during the second quarter of the 19th century but had almost disappeared by 1900.

The route lay through the Cauldstane Slap (NT 1158) in the Pentland Hills, and down to West Linton: 'a much frequented pass, through which the periodical droves of black cattle are transported into England' (1775).

Through the Baddinsgill enclosures (NT 1255) the way is marked by roughly parallel stone dykes up to 13.7 m apart, continuing lower down as turf dykes. On to Romanno Bridge and through the hills east of the Lyne Water, it crossed the Tweed by Peebles Bridge.

After following the approximate line of what are now the Springhill and Glen roads, double dykes reappear, carrying the road to a ford on the Haystoun Burn. The rise through Camp Law Plantation is so steep as to be negotiable only by pedestrians or animals; but subsequently the way is fairly gentle, following the contours or ridge. The dyked trackway varies in width between about 12 m and 50 m, and where the road emerges on to the open ground of Kailzie Hill, traces of animal tracks can yet be seen.

The road, increasingly indistinct, avoids the actual summits of the hills, keeping a little to the west, reaching a height of about 637 m. It then makes south for the Yarrow and Ettrick Waters and on across the Border. Though this is generally considered to be the main drove road south, the area is criss-crossed with sections of other north-south routes, and not a few that travel roughly east-west. Many would be local routes, feeding local markets.

## 27 Romanno Cultivation Terraces, near Romanno Bridge

*Middle Ages.*

*NT 161481-163482. 1.5 km S on B 7059 from its junction with A 701 at Romanno Bridge.*

In 1726 Alexander Gordon wrote that these terraces extended 'for a whole mile, not unlike a large amphitheatre'; and one cannot but wonder whether the fragments at Romanno Bridge (NT 162482-163483) and at Whiteside Hill (NT 163457) were not originally part of the same system.

The present group of west-facing terraces is one of the best-known in Scotland. Fourteen are still well preserved, saved from later cultivation by the steepness of the slope. They lie between 222 m and 268 m, the longest now measuring 140 m. Generally the terraces are narrow (0.9 m-3 m) and the risers steep (0.6 m-6.7 m high). But though they appear as steps, they rise towards the centre, falling away towards each end. The sandy subsoil is similar to that on the adjacent hillside; excavation showed it to be covered, however, with a loam built up through intensive cultivation.

Though unproven, the suggestion has been made that the terraces originated with the canons of Holyrood who, in the mid 12th century, were granted a carucate of land (roughly the land worked by a team of 8 oxen during a year) together with pasturage for 1000 sheep at 'Rothmaneic'—Ràth Manach, the monks' rath or farm. Certainly they are similar to the terraces on the slopes of Arthur's Seat near to the Abbey in Edinburgh. Perhaps the Romanno name and terraces relate, however, to an earlier religious settlement of the Celtic church? The terraces themselves are notoriously difficult to date, and in general terms could be anything from 300-1300 or so years old.

Nearby is the old Romanno Bridge (NT 159479) of 1774, and the former toll-house (NT 160480) built either in 1830 when the turnpike was constructed, or shortly after. In 1832, over half the revenue came from cattle droves.

**Romanno cultivation terraces, Romanno Bridge** (Top)

**Braemore Knowe cultivation terrraces**

## 28 Braemoor Knowe Cultivation Terraces, Kale Water, near Kelso

*Middle Ages.*

*NT 784213-785203. On E bank of Kale Water 2 km short of Hownam on minor road S from Morebattle. Take track from Hownam Mains up hillside and follow contours.*

The spectacular terraces on the lower westerly slopes of Braemoor Knowe cover some 18 ha. They stretch from about 130 m to 210 m up the hillside. Seen from the road there are no less than 23 terraces, one above the other, on the bluff north-west of the little plantation.

Elsewhere, the hillside is cut through by two gullies, so that the terraces lie on different axes and vary in depth and steepness. The most prominent are six lying below and to the west of the plantation; others, running on to the steep east side of the north gully, have curved points. Many of the wider terraces, and those on the gentler slopes, incorporate the longitudinal rigs of later/post-medieval cultivation.

## 29 Martinlee Sike Settlements and Field Systems, Southdean

*Last millennium BC - c 18th century AD.*

*NT 655076/658075. On S side of A 6088, running down to Carter Burn, roughly half-way between the ruins of Southdean Church and the Border crossing (A 68) at Carter Bar.*

The Southdean landscape contains many prehistoric sites, including ramparted hillforts, homesteads (less than three houses) and enclosed settlements (more than three houses). They generally date to the last millennium BC, many to the last centuries BC, some into the Roman/Romano-British period. At Martinlee Sike there are four homesteads and one enclosed settlement within 500 m of each other (NT 657080/659079). The homesteads comprise a roughly oval yard, 11.5 m-21 m across, slightly scooped into the slope and enclosed within a stone wall. Roughly circular house platforms, 6 m-7 m in diameter, lie to one side of the yard.

There is also a medieval landscape, remarkable in its survival. The area retains the ruins of numerous pele towers, which were defensive structures for local farmers to take refuge in during the once-frequent cross-Border raids (Slack's Tower and its associated settlement is a good example: NT 644098). Although there is no such pele at Martinlee Sike, two medieval farmsteads and an extensive area of broad rig cultivation (7 ha in all), are enclosed by a clearly-defined head dyke or assart bank—a dyke or bank with outer ditch. Certainly there are later features, including an earthen-banked stock enclosure at the west end of the site, and an additional and larger 2 ha enclosure on the west side containing once-cultivated ground and rough pasture. Otherwise the site seems to have been largely undisturbed since settlement was abandoned—perhaps in the 18th century.

The rigs at Martinlee/Southdean (NT 655076) range from 3 m-10 m wide by 50 m-300 m long. They would have been cultivated with the Old Scots Plough. This was a heavy, cumbersome implement with an iron ploughshare and flat mouldboard, drawn by a team of maybe 4, 6 or 8 small oxen or horses. Arranged in furlongs of adjoining ridges, the hollows between served as open drains in those times before technology designed underground drainage. The houses were round-ended, presumably thatched buildings, each farmstead consisting of a main house and subsidiary buildings, within an enclosing yard.

The closest parallel for the Southdean head dyke seems to be at Alnhamsheles in Northumberland (presumably established on an earlier *shiel* or pasture). There, a dyke enclosed the cultivated ground of a late 13th-early 16th-century township and its successor desmesne farms—abandoned in the 18th century. The key factor seems to be its 'forest' location, the enclosure marking an assart (land reclaimed for agriculture from a designated 'forest'). On the edge of Dartmoor, for example, in south-west England, 12th-century Forest Laws required enclosure of assarts in order to prevent incursions by deer.

Many parts of Scotland, particularly southern Scotland, were also designated hunting forest (see no. 47). Few assarts are recorded in Scottish documents, however, and what 12th to 14th-century references there are, do not relate to Jedburgh Forest (of which this was a part). Nonetheless, ditched boundaries are recorded for Ettrick Forest, and it is quite possible that agriculture and settlement in the Royal Forest of Jedburgh (held subsequently by the Douglases) was strictly controlled until the relaxation of the Forest Laws in late/post-medieval times.

The medieval/post-medieval landscape of Southdean is quite special, determined in part by its location within the former Forest, in part by its proximity to the English Border. In the light of 20th-century changes in land-use, in particular the planting of extensive coniferous forests, such a fossilised landscape continues to be under considerable threat.

Nearby are the ruins of a Norman church, with unusually large but rough and simple 17th-century gravestones (NT 631091); and a ruinous tower stands to the south of the Jed Water (NT 629091).

# 3 STATELY HOMES AND COUNTRY MANSIONS

**The stair hall, Stobo Castle, near Peebles**

If planned villages, solidly square farm steadings, well-built farmhouses and planted woodlands are one face of change over the past 250 or so years; if fine turnpikes and graceful bridges, railway viaducts, canal aqueducts and revitalised harbours are another (even allowing that labourers' housing, rural and urban, was always more than a step behind), then the improvement landscape was completed by the remarkable scatter of immense country mansions built by established landed proprietors and successful entrepreneurial merchants and manufacturers alike.

Royal palaces, massive castles and vast abbeys apart, nothing highlights so eloquently perhaps the power and privilege of Scotland's ruling castes—in this case from the late 16th to early 20th centuries. They most certainly do add what Millman terms 'a final note of dignity to a unique and richly various cultural landscape that is amongst the finest in Europe'!

Though set against green or purple hills or against the undulating patchwork of regularly enclosed farms and woodlands, the newly-built mansions did not deliberately explore the most extensive and elevated vistas. Fine views there are, but as well as seeking to escape from the defensive cliff top, promontory or riverside crag that had drawn their ancestors, landowners also sought shelter and protection from the elements. A view was not everything!

Though improvement generally began with the house, frequently domestic offices, stables and granaries were built or remodelled at roughly the same time; also the gardens and policies. Formal schemes continued to be significant throughout the period 1600-1850, though in the late 18th century most of the larger policies were laid out in the more fashionable informal manner, as at Hopetoun (no. 38). Only around this time, too, were significant parts of the policies reserved exclusively for ornamentation or recreation. Up until then, and afterwards in many cases, proprietors used their policies (often the earliest parts of an estate to have been enclosed) for sylviculture and for agriculture. Stock would graze close to the house, hence the ha-ha, a stepped dyke invisible from the house to provide an illusion of unrestricted grassland; and nearby mains farms (Old French *demeine*, English demesne: manor, head or home farm) were used as examples of good practice to tenants.

**Hamilton House, Prestonpans, East Lothian**

The new classical mansions, like palaces and castles, sometimes incorporated earlier tower-houses or other structures (see section 4), so that a seemingly unitary exterior can belie internal complexity. Thus, just as Bruce's reconstruction of the royal palace of Holyroodhouse, begun in 1671, incorporated an early 16th-century tower, so his Thirlestane Castle (no. 39), 1670-76, enlarged one of the late 16th century, and in 1673 he drew up a scheme for extending Lennoxlove's mainly 15th-century tower (NT 514721) near Haddington. Bruce also built such fine new houses as Mertoun, formerly Harden, near St Boswells, 1703-09 (NT 618318) and Craigiehall west of Edinburgh, 1698-99. In turn, however, his Hopetoun House, 1699-1703, was later converted and incorporated by William Adam. Elsewhere, at Traquair (no. 40), late 17th-century rebuilding involved James Smith, overseer of the Royal Works in Scotland, who also worked for the

Duke of Buccleuch refashioning Dalkeith House in 1702-11 (NT 333679) and contributed to Yester House (NT 543671). It was a fairly close-knit circle at work on the 'top' houses—and many a King's craftsman was engaged, whether master-masons like the Mylnes or woodcarvers like Alexander Eizat.

**The Turret House, Kelso: a later 17th-century town house**

Some of the very finest houses are those in the early classical tradition, peaking in the first half of the 18th century. The pace was set by the Scottish nobility who had begun to take notice of English styles and architects on their journeys south to Court and to Parliament after the Union of the Parliaments in 1707. Those who identified with the New Britain built a fine new country house in the English fashion; those who identified with the Old Europe remained with their old castle. Since it was politically naive, if not downright dangerous, to stick with the Old Europe, most built a new classical house on their estate, often located so as to give a romantic perspective of the new ruin. For many of Scotland's leading families, it took perhaps 70 or more years fully to come to terms architecturally with the Union, but this was less so in south-east Scotland, closer to the seat of power, than many other areas. Lothian, indeed, was particularly well-endowed with such houses even before the Union, and provided a model and stimulus for other parts of Lowland Scotland, including the Borders. Moreover, just as later architects such as Burn, Bryce and Lorimer were sought after as much in England as in Scotland, the Adam family was equally popular. The Adams were involved in the design of such contrasting, complementary houses as Paxton (no. 37) and Marchmont (NT 742484), Mellerstain (no. 36), Floors (no. 33) and Hopetoun (no. 38).

The architectural genius lay mainly with the sons. Yet without the father, it seems unlikely that much would have been achieved in the earlier 18th century, subsequent to the reign of such as William Bruce. For William

**Sundial dated 1679 at Lennoxlove, near Haddington (originally from North Barr, Renfrewshire)**

Adam had few good contemporaries. As to his own designs, he was best perhaps as a collaborator, drawing together ideas originated by others and those featured in contemporary source-books and pattern-books.

The classical house presented a main central block, flanked by pavilions often distanced somewhat and linked to the main house by colonades (the 'palace' fronts of Edinburgh's New Town are a flattened, urban version). In many respects such a design was a more formal, 'wide angle' version of the house-and-forecourt 'enclosure' style of earlier Scottish houses—as in the earlier phase of The Binns (no. 35). Many classical houses, especially in the later phases, retain a certain feeling of enclosure, whilst at Whittingeham, 1817, the classical style itself became so severely and abstractly geometrical as to be more properly termed neo-classical than early classical.

Other fine, albeit more modest, Georgian country seats survive at The Haining, 1784 and 1819 (NT 469280), at Yair, 1788 (NT 453329), and at Torwoodlee, 1783 (NT 472300)—where the later house replaced a tower of 1601, itself a replacement for an earlier tower. The smaller Georgian house, moreover, became the model for so many improved 18th-19th-century farmhouses and manses that these too are a lasting reminder of the genre.

**The Haining, near Selkirk**

In the later 18th century, alongside neo-classicism, a more predominantly romantic approach began to develop—an emergent neo-Gothic extravaganza whether 'picturesque' or 'castellated'. Robert Adam designed the new house of Mellerstain (no. 36), recast Oxenfoord Castle, 1780-82 (NT 388655) and created a forceful Seton House (NT 417751) in 1789. He also designed the now-considerably altered Gosford House (NT 453787); and with James Adam, the castle-style Wedderburn House (NT 809529: see no. 37). James Playfair created a three-storey 'toy-fort' at Melville Castle, 1786-91 (NT 301669); The Binns (no. 35) was 're-fortified' from c 1810 after the style of Gillespie Graham who designed Ayton Castle (NT 929614) in Berwickshire for William-Innes, Governor of the Bank of Scotland. And at Stobo Castle, 1805-11 (NT 172366), designed by Archibald and James Elliot, the main symmetrical rectangular block with angle turrets and a high central tower betrays strong influence from both Inveraray Castle in Argyll and the more grandiose Taymouth Castle in Perthshire. A different form, however, was to emerge at Dalmeny House, 1814-17 and Scotland's first Gothic Revival house (no. 34), where William Wilkins incorporated English Tudor in such a way as to devise a curious marriage of McWilliam's 'cloister-like Gothic galleries which . . . lead to simple Grecian rooms', all within a turretted and embattled, highly 'mechanical' exterior.

These later country houses were increasingly sumptuous in their display of worldly wealth—a reflection both of industrial/manufacturing affluence and of imperial grandeur. The old-established landed proprietors were as settled and prosperous as their new neighbours, the industrial tycoons and businessmen who sought to emulate their rural estates and imposing mansions; and where the 19th century's 'barons' led, the lesser lairds, lawyers, merchants and factory-owners followed. Old classical mansions were considered outdated, both in style and convenience, and new architects were being commissioned to prepare elaborate designs which also took account of improved plumbing and lighting. Two of the most renowned, William Burn and David Bryce, were based in Edinburgh, and between them built or remodelled over 300 country houses, the bulk of them in Scotland. Indeed, Bryce effectively succeeded Burn when the latter moved to London in 1844—a succession seen clearly at Bowhill (no. 32), which began life in 1708 as a simple, small country house.

If the romantic approach was primarily neo-Gothic from the 1770s to the 1820s, from then until the end of the century it became predominantly neo-Baronial—turrets and battlements, crowsteps and corbelling. And if forerunners might be identified at an Oxenfoord or a Stobo Castle, the trigger might rather have been the conscious, deliberate romanticism of Walter Scott's Abbotsford, 1816-23 (no. 31). It was a movement that culminated with Queen Victoria at Balmoral in the 1850s, but continued apace. Tyninghame (NT 619798) had been re-cast and extended in 1829 by Burn as a bold, asymmetrical structure; Bryce's Clifton Hall, 1850 (NT 109709) maybe provides a fuller flowering where, in the original model at least, form had always reflected function—a fundamental of the Scottish Baronial. By 1875, however, the style had become increasingly austere, witness the stark simplification of design and stonework at Vogrie (NT 380632)—whose stables, c 1825 and all that remains of the earlier house, are pure Gothic revival (NT 381633). By way of contrast, however, the 1881 Victorian re-build of Barnbougle Castle, beside the Forth (NT 169785: no. 34), intended mainly as a private library for the 5th Earl of Roseberry whose main house was now Dalmeny, harks back to the stylistic simplicity of the 16th-century tower-house. It does not, in effect, aspire to being a real 'country house' in the Baronial style.

By the turn of the century the days of widespread building of rural mansions were over. A few were still to appear, notably Manderston near Duns (no. 30), an elaborate and stately pile re-modelled and extended between 1903 and 1905 to provide a unique and atypical mix of the neo-Classical and Edwardian. Its neo-Baronial outbuildings merely add to its individuality! Otherwise, though architects like Charles Rennie Mackintosh and Robert Lorimer were building fine houses early in the present century, they were primarily concerned with the 'villa'. And whilst Lorimer is noted for his re-working of Scots vernacular tradition, many of his contemporaries sought inspiration rather in English half-timbering, cottage and manor house traditions—influences particularly evident along those desirable parts of the East Lothian and Berwickshire coasts made accessible by the railways—at Gullane, North Berwick and Coldingham.

**Engraving of Tyninghame House, East Lothian, 1839**

### 30* Manderston, near Duns

*Late 18th-early 20th century AD.*

*NT 810543. About 2.5 km E of Duns on side road to Edrom continuing E from A 6105; signposted.*

Manderston was rebuilt between 1903 and 1905—an outstanding country house designed by John Kinross, restorer of Falkland Palace in Fife and the Franciscan Friary in Elgin. Sir James Miller, whose family had made a fortune trading with Russia in hemp and herring, spared no expense—'it simply doesn't matter'!

To the original Georgian House, built in the 1790s, a north front portico and rather inept French Renaissance roof had been added in the later 19th century. These were removed when the house was deepened, and a new wing and service area added along with a full-height entrance portico. Like the earlier house, however, the present exterior betrays a somewhat severe front—though the Lion's head bell-pushes in the entrance colonade indicate a continuing flair for the idiosyncratic!

Inside, the house also continues to show a neo-Georgian face, in particular the influence of Robert Adam who had designed Kedleston Hall in Derbyshire, the house of Sir James Miller's wife, sister to Lord Curzon, viceroy of India. The hall, dining room, library and ballroom are all early 20th century, their fine stuccoed ceilings specially commissioned from French and Italian craftsmen. That it is difficult to distinguish them stylistically from the drawing room, morning room and tea room—all along the garden front and all part of the original late 18th-century house—is a tribute to the skill of John Kinross. The first-floor corridor, imposingly wide and with columnar screens, is reached by a staircase modelled on that in the Petit Trianon at Versailles and fitted with a silver-plated balustrade topped with brass rails.

Below stairs at Manderston, and true to its Edwardian sophistication, are the atmospheric kitchens, housekeeper's room and manservant's room. They are complemented outside, at a discreet distance, by a remarkable set of courtyard stables, 1895, with teak stalls and marble floors; also by the elegant, vaulted, marble dairy in the style of a Roman cloister set around a fountain, and by a neo-Scots Baronial head gardener's house. Such historical and theatrical eclecticism is echoed nearby in a mock Border tower-house—an aristocratic retreat in the manner of Marie Antoinette's rustic hideaway at Versailles. It even has a hidden staircase for the maids.

### 31* Abbotsford, near Melrose

*Early-mid 19th century AD.*

*NT 508342. About 3.5 km W of Melrose, on B 6360 to Selkirk, a little SW of junction with A 7; signposted.*

The old farmhouse of Cartleyhole, bought by Sir Walter Scott in 1811 along with some 44.5 ha of riverside haugh-land and rough hillside, was pulled down in 1822—replaced by 1824 by the present main block of entrance hall, study, library and Chinese drawing room. The first phase of Scott's improvements, which included the change of name, was completed in 1818—dining room, conservatory, study and armouries. The remaining buildings are later 19th century.

The house is essentially Scots Baronial, designed by Edward Blore and William Patterson; but Abbotsford is more than simply a neo-Baronial fantasy. Scott had a strong interest in Scotland, and a remarkable aspect of Abbotsford is the way in which medieval architectural features have been incorporated: 'I have selected for the hall-chimney piece one of the cloister arches of Melrose. . . . I have transferr'd almost all the masques from Melrose to my roofs and they really look delightfully . . . you never saw such delightful grinners. . . . The Stirling Heads will be admirably disposed in the glass of the Armoury window. . . .'

Outside there are parapets and gargoyles; the main entrance is based on the entrance porch to Linlithgow Palace (no. 41); the screen wall in the garden reflects the Melrose Abbey cloister (no. 76). Elsewhere, set against the north-east wall of the garden is a fine period greenhouse, each bay surmounted by a triangular-headed arch.

Built into the house and garden walls are numerous carved or inscribed stones 'rescued' from sites across south-eastern Scotland—16th-century door and 15th-century niche from Edinburgh's Tolbooth, and parts of her original mercat cross;

17th-century panel from the Guild House of the Soutars of Selkirk; medieval gable-cross from Lindean Church. And from Old Penrith in Cumbria come five Roman deities, Mercury, Jupiter, Venus, Apollo and Mars—part of a series representing the days of the week.

It was at Abbotsford that Scott wrote most of his Waverley Novels; the building itself reflects the eclectic creativity of an endlessly curious romantic: 'It is a kind of conundrum castle to be sure, and I have great pleasure in it, for while it pleases a fantastic person in style and manner of its architecture it has all the comforts of a commodious habitation'.

**Bowhill: the post-1812 house**

### 32* Bowhill, near Selkirk

*Mid 19th century AD.*

*NT 425278. About 5 km W of Selkirk on A 708; cross Yarrow Water to B 7039; signposted.*

A characteristic feature of Bowhill, and in contrast to so many other large country mansions, is its dark whinstone. Though more easily dressed sandstone has been used, for example, at the corners of the building, most is of small-sized dusty-grey rubble worked into regular courses, at a distance almost like bricks. The facade is generally simple, with mainly single, regularly-set windows; between the second and third floors of the central block there is a cornice which follows round the line of the wall-head of the wings, and which belongs to the earlier two-storey building. The tower, seemingly added at the same time as the further storey, gives light to galleries surrounding the hall, with their pictures and tapestries.

Bowhill is the work of several architects. Between 1874 and 1876, David Bryce added to the enlargements created by William Burn between 1830 and 1833. It was Burn who raised the central block an extra storey, who added the porch and built the eastern wing which provided the 'Duchess suite' on the principal floor. He also made many internal changes. This was not the first remodelling, however. The original, modest, early 18th-century country house with its hipped roof and small flanking wings soon disappeared c 1812-19, when William Atkinson provided designs which added a substantial facade to the central block and added both a west wing and a separate stable block, subsequently joined to the house.

Although all traces of the pre-1812 house have gone, the existing buildings retain the principle at least of a central block and wings. The 19th-century kitchen has been restored, but Bowhill's primary glory (house apart) is its superb collection of paintings—Van Dyke, Raeburn, Wilkie, Naesmyth, Reynolds, Canaletto, Gainsborough, Claud Lorrain and others.

So carefully landscaped and 'natural' is the estate that the landscaping is all-but invisible. Designed by Thomas Gilpin in 1832, with access over the Faulshope Bridge, 1834, it features small lochs and woodlands—with Newark Castle incorporated as a romantic and picturesque ruin.

### 33* Floors Castle, near Kelso

*Early 18th-mid 19th century AD.*

*NT 711345. About 2.5 km NW of Kelso just off A 6089; signposted.*

The present imposing and well-grouped buildings appear at the same time both solidly four-square and flamboyantly embattled! W H Playfair (1789-1857) began his romantic remodelling in 1838 for the sixth Duke of Roxburghe; he was also engaged in restoring Heriot's Hospital at the time, and building the new Donaldson's Hospital—both of them in Edinburgh and both of them an influence on Floors. He started with the east Pavilion or stables, continued with the west Pavilion in 1841, and completed the main block about 1849. Hood-moulds were added above all the windows, corbelling, castellated parapets and ornate water-spouts to the wall-heads, and pepper-pot turrets to the corners of the towers. He built further turrets in the re-entrant angles (the inward-looking angles made by two adjoining walls); and, at the north-west front entrance, the porch admitted a carriage below it—a *porte-cochère*. Bay windows within the angles either side helped break up the solid mass of masonry.

This wealth of extravagant architectural detail quite transformed the plain Georgian mansion designed for the first duke in 1718—a design once attributed to Sir John Vanburg and added to by the time of its completion in 1721 by William Adam, but more likely all the work of Adam. This earlier house consisted of a rectangular main block with a tower at each corner, two pavilions and a forecourt. Much of the stone was brought to Fleurs (the 18th-century name) from Cessford Castle (no. 44); it was Adam who also master-minded much of the 18th-century landscaping.

Playfair's house is much more in tune with the site, however—a superb location on a terrace overlooking the Tweed, Kelso Abbey and the remains of Roxburgh Castle. Far beyond lie the Cheviots.

**Floors Castle, after its mid-19th century remodelling** (Top)

**Dalmeny House c 1820: engraving by JP Neale**

## 34* Dalmeny House, South Queensferry

*Early 19th century AD.*

*NT 168780. A 90 Edinburgh-Forth Road Bridge road, then along old Edinburgh-South Queensferry road (B 924), and into Dalmeny Estate at Chapel Gate. Alternatively, walk from Cramond/South Queensferry along coastal track. Signposted.*

Dalmeny's predecessor was Barnbougle Castle (NT 168785), originally a 13th-century tower house down by the shore, and largely refashioned by Wardrop & Reid in 1881 as a library for the 5th Earl of Rosebery, then Prime Minister. A navigational aid for shipping in the Forth, it was to become a realistic imitation of a 3-storey 16th century tower house, with a corbelled stair turret in the angle—far removed from R & J Adam's proposals (1774-93) for a large triangular castle projecting into the Firth.

The Dalmeny Estate was acquired by Sir Archibald Primrose of Carrington in 1662, and the family continued to live in the old tower until the 3rd Earl—drenched at dinner, it is said, by a huge wave—agreed to rebuild at a safer location. From 1817 until 1881, therefore, Barnbougle lay largely ruinous.

Its successor is a remarkable Tudor Gothic mansion by William Wilkins, the first such Gothic Revival house in Scotland. It stands on a terrace overlooking the Forth, with fine views north and east. The L-plan house is bedecked with gables, battlements, turrets, chimneys and mullioned windows, and has a tall projecting porch. The triangular gables have no roofs behind them; they are simply architectural features intended to make the 'skyline' more interesting. Most of the house is in a fine yellow-grey stone, but carved panels, chimneys and other details were made from synthetic stone ('Coade') brought from London by sea at considerable cost (£5000).

Internally, the house is a mix of Gothic and Classical, with a large Gothic stairwell and fan-vaulted Gallery, and Classical public rooms. These include the untouched Napoleon room (formerly the billiard room). The furnishings include much of the Rothschild Collection of 18th-century French furniture, porcelain and tapestries, brought north after the sale in 1977 of Mentmore, the Roseberys' former Buckinghamshire mansion.

The estate policies include a landscaped pond and tree-lined driveways, the Home Farm and former salmon-fisher cottages at Long Green (traces of stakes in the sands indicate where nets were once set). There are seven Lodges, probably also by Wilkins, each with its name inscribed upon it—Coble Cott, beside the mouth of the Almond, being the ferryman's house. The single-oared river-mouth pedestrian ferry (the last of its kind in Scotland) gives access to the gentle and pleasing shore walk between Cramond and South Queensferry—which also passes Hound Point Oil Tanker Terminal and the 'Eagle' Stone (see section 10; check locally if/when the ferry is running before setting out.)

### 35* The House of the Binns, West Lothian

*Early 17th—early 19th century AD.*

*NT 050785. About half-way between South Queensferry and Linlithgow on A 904, just E of B 9109 N to Blackness; signposted.*

*National Trust for Scotland.*

**The 'toy-town' House of the Binns, remodelled in the early 19th century**

In 1612 an Edinburgh merchant, Thomas Dalyell, acquired the small properties of Mannerstoun, East Scotstoun, Fludders and Merrilies. He was living in Mannerstoun in 1614, but began to build a new house on the western shoulder of Binns Hill a little before 1621. It was completed by 1630.

The present exterior reflects a remodelling begun c 1810. The east and west ranges were enlarged, the south side was extended into the forecourt, square corbelled turrets were added to all of the major gables, and everywhere imitation battlements gave it the appearance of a caricature fort—compare the grandiose and romantic Tudor Gothic turrets and battlements of William Wilkins' Dalmeny House, 1814-17 (no. 34).

The original west wing had been built to match an earlier east wing shortly after 1665 when the notable royalist General Sir Tam Dalyell was recalled from Russia by Charles II. It made the house into a hollow square around a courtyard, open to the south and entered from there. The General is said to have responded to the Devil's threat to blow down the house, with the words 'I will build me a turret at every corner to pin down my walls'. Not all of them, therefore, are 19th century!

The original house would seem to have been the north-west part of the present main block—three storeys and a garret, with two turnpike turrets set symmetrically on the north side. Each floor had four unvaulted chambers. The ground-floor rooms are mainly 19th century, except for the vaulted kitchen or bakehouse with its wide-arched fireplace and two ovens in the eastern, originally detached wing.

On the first floor are the major early rooms, the High Hall or 'Chamber of Desse', the King's Room and the Vault Chamber—three state rooms which might be said to 'embody the theory if not the actual functions, of feudal loyalty'. They all have interesting ceilings, reflecting a move to Elizabethan-type modelled plaster-work in parts of Scotland following the Union of the Crowns in 1603. Most notable is that in the King's Room where rose, thistle, harp and fleur-de-lys feature in some compartments, low relief heads of King Alexander or King David in others. The elaborate

The High Hall at The Binns

frieze contains finely-modelled fruit, and above the fireplace a late 18th-century royal coat-of-arms echoes the thistle and rose theme to reinforce a Unionist flavour.

Northwards lies Blackness Castle (mid 15th-late 19th century, NT 055802), to which tradition attributes an underground passage leading from the base of the east stair turret at the Binns. On the hill west of the house a round, crenellated tower was built in 1826; and south towards the road, the remains of a modest pack-horse bridge survive in the middle of a meadow.

### 36* Mellerstain, near Gordon

*Mid 18th century AD.*

*NT 647390. On a side road about 1.5 km SW of Whitehill on A 6089 Gordon-Kelso road; or 2 km NE of Covehouse on B 6397 Earlston-Kelso road; signposted.*

The south or 'garden' front, Mellerstain

The estate of Mellerstain is mentioned as early as 1451—owned by the Haliburtons, later by the Haitlies. In 1642 it passed into the hands of the Baillies. George Baillie of Jerviswood was the son of a wealthy Edinburgh merchant and though the estates were forfeited in 1684 on account of the Covenanting zeal of his son Robert, they were restored in 1691. Robert's son George married Grizell Hume, renowned for her 'Household Book' in which, as mistress and manager of the household, she recorded what has survived as a unique social document of the time. They began the new house of Mellerstain in 1725 to replace 'ane old melancholick hous that had had great buildings about it' in 1639, and only the two wings were completed to the design of William Adam.

The present house, linked to Adam's wings, is largely the creation of the next George Baillie. After his Grand Tour of Europe in 1740-44, he returned fired with enthusiasm for a truly classical dimension to Mellerstain, and in addition to commissioning Robert Adam he seems to have worked on many of the plans himself. The house exhibits a strong central projection to the north; it is contrastingly flat to the south where it overlooks the Italian-style terraced gardens laid out in 1909 by Sir Reginald Blomfield. It is one of the earlier 'Adam castles' seen by some as 'rather lifeless and box-like'.

If Hopetoun's interiors (no. 38) are amongst the most palatial and ornate of 18th-century Scotland, those at Mellerstain (and Paxton: no. 37) are perhaps the most beautiful and refined, with particularly attractive ceilings and friezes in the library, music room and drawing room. The latter, decorated with griffins and vases, is dated 1778 and must be one of the last completed; the first, dated 1770, incorporates a circular oil-painting of Minerva, flanked by representations of 'Teaching' and 'Learning'. Preserved in the original colours they could be mistaken for pieces of Wedgewood porcelain! The ceiling in the Great Gallery, by contrast, was never completed, though the architect's drawings of 1775 along with the end colonnades, friezes, tracery and (plain) barrel roof, give an idea at least of what might have been.

In 1717 the Baillies were linked in marriage to the Earls of Haddington. The estates remain linked and Mellerstain has become the residence of the 13th Earl.

**Paxton House**

### 37* Paxton House, near Berwick

*Mid 18th Century AD.*

*NT 931520. At junction of B 6460 and B 6461 Kelso-Berwick road, just S of Paxton village, turn in through Lion Gates and follow estate road to House; signposted.*

Paxton House was built for Patrick Home of Billie mainly between 1756 and 1766 in anticipation of his marriage (which never took place) with 'Miss de Brandt', illegitimate daughter of Frederick the Great of Prussia. Probably designed by John and James Adam, the work was supervised by James Nisbet. When he did eventually marry, for his new bride he built castellated Wedderburn around an earlier-tower house (NT 809529: also designed by James Adam and supervised by Nisbet).

Standing close to the Tweed, this very fine Scottish Palladian mansion is U-plan, with a central red sandstone house with 4-column portico, flanked by pavilions with associated courtyards behind (stable court and kitchen court). The house retains a considerable collection of Thomas Chippendale mahogany furniture in the entrance hall, breakfast parlour, certain bedrooms and above all in the dining room and principal bedchamber.

Particularly delicate plaster ceilings are probably the work of Robert Adam c 1773. Several bedrooms have been restored to their 1820s style, and some wallpapers have been specially re-made either from surviving fragments or from surviving contemporary designs.

The library and picture gallery were designed by Robert Reid (1812-13); with richly-styled rosewood furniture by William Trotter of Edinburgh, Scotland's leading cabint-maker at that time. The Greek temple-style gallery, established privately and pre-dating any public gallery in Scotland, was reconstructed in 1876 and has been restored to provide a peaceful outstation for the National Galleries of Scotland (1993, with fine Italian marble and a carpet re-made to the original design). This follows the transfer of the house and 70 acres of policies by the Labour MP John Hume Robertson to the Paxton Trust in 1988.

The approach to the house is as impressive as the House itself—between a pair of classical lodges and Lion Gates set into the estate walls, thence over a fine estate bridge, c 1770. Though planned rotundas and obelisks were never built, the grounds were laid out from 1767 by Robert Robertson, an assistant of 'Capability' Brown.

They extend as far as Paxton village—a fairly typical Borders village whose pantiles were made in the estate's brick, tile and drain works. The remains of a 3-chamber, stone-built 'Newcastle' kiln still lie in the middle of a field (NT 937539), consisting of barrel-vaulted, brick-lined tunnels with fireboxes at one end and chimneys built into the wall at the other end. Paxton also boasts a well-known net fishery for salmon, where bothies, icehouse, boathouse and towpath, as well as timber watch towers, provided an interesting architectural contrast to the House.

## 38* Hopetoun House, near South Queensferry

*Late 17th-mid 18th century AD.*

*NT 088790. B 924 into South Queensferry, then about 4 km along minor shore road W from beneath Forth Road Bridge: also from A 904 at Woodend, W of Newton; signposted.*

**Hopetoun House, the earlier west gardens revealed by cropmarks**

The Hopes came to West Lothian in 1657 to extend silver- and lead-mining interests acquired by marriage a little earlier. They acquired land at Abercorn in 1678, transferring the name of 'Hopetoun', formerly associated with the village of Leadhills. Mining, linked increasingly with progressive approaches to agricultural improvements on their many estates across southern Scotland, provided the wealth to build one of the most palatial mansions in Scotland.

Sir William Bruce (c 1630-1710) was the founder of the classical school in Scotland and a pioneer in garden design and planting. He worked on the reconstruction of the Palace of Holyroodhouse in 1671-79, and Hopetoun House (1698-1702; extended 1706-?10) represents his grandest country house. The Bruce house consisted of a centrally-planned main block (most of which survives); angle pavilions linked to office wings by convex colonnades (which do not survive, and the colonnades may never have been built). The formal gardens associated with this period, laid out with the help of Alexander Edward, can be picked out from the roof in a dry summer as 'crop-marks' in the green lawns sweeping down to the fountain.

In 1721, the then inexperienced William Adam (1689-1748) was invited to enlarge the house and to

**Hopetoun House, the richly-panelled octagonal staircase**

provide a palace for the Earl. The work was completed in the 1750s, reputedly by both his sons, John and Robert Adam, but in practice by John.

The marriage of the two great houses, however, is uneasy. The new attic floor and balustrade simply stops when it reaches the older west front; and some of the blind or false windows suggest a strain in blending new interiors to a partly-existing exterior. A 'reluctant centrepiece' the Bruce house has been called, in the later, elongated, west elevation. Moreover the new colonnades, without the imposing central portico and double curving staircase planned for the east front but never built, hardly measure up to the elegant steeple-topped pavilions (one with a clock, the other a weather-vane), or to the magnificent facade. This elevation incorporates massive Corinthian pilasters, a rash of horizontal string-courses drawing it all together, and a rich variety of rustication breaking up the solid front of large angular masonry.

Internally the relationships between the houses are much happier. The elaborately ornate and formal state-rooms fitted out by the Adam brothers after 1752 are far removed from and contrast with the relative simplicity and domesticity of the Bruce rooms—which include a tiny vaulted strongroom. The octagonal Bruce stone staircase incorporates oak panelling richly carved by Alexander Eizat (who also workd at Holyroodhouse).

Elsewhere the wide range of ancillary buildings and servants' quarters emphasises the symbiotic relationship of an intensive labour force required to maintain an aristocratic life-style—whilst gradations of quality and expense in the the laying-out of stables and stable courts reflect a strict hierarchy as much amongst horses as amongst humans!

**Thirlestane Castle from the north-west**

### 39* Thirlestane Castle, near Lauder

*Late 16th-mid 19th century AD.*

*NT 533479. Just S of Lauder A 697 branches E from A 68; 700 m turn left into Castle grounds; signposted.*

Old Thirlestane Castle (NT 564473) stands beside the Boondreigh Water 4 km east of Lauder. An L-shaped tower, it was the main residence of the Maitland family until around the end of the 16th century.

In the late 16th century John Maitland became Chancellor of Scotland; it was he who commissioned the 'new' castle, an unusual rectangular block with a large round tower at each corner. In 1670-76, however, the Duke of Lauderdale considerably enlarged and improved the castle. Close friend of Charles II, a member of the Cabal Cabinet and effectively ruler of Scotland from 1660 to 1680, he commissioned William Bruce, a royalist 'gentleman architect', who engaged in turn Robert Mylne, the King's Master-Mason. Bruce rebuilt the tower-house to provide a central six-storey block with projecting angles flanked by circular turrets. The disposition of towers and staircases is unique in Scotland—three semi-circular towers on each long wall, the central pair giving direct access from basement to upper floors. Separate access to bedrooms on these floors was then provided by means of stairs in many of the turrets. Parapet walks run the length of both walls, supported by arches differently arranged on each side. A celebration of the Scots Baronial!

It was Bruce who introduced the symmetrical forecourt to Thirlestane with a flight of steps leading to a balustraded terrace at first-floor level, flanked by projecting pavilion-topped, three-storey wings. These wings were extended by David Bryce in 1841, thereby giving a more pronounced 'bar' to the 'T'.

Internally, Lauderdale, Bruce and Mylne between them brought plasterers from Holyroodhouse to redecorate the state rooms, and Dutch joiners and painters from Ham House in Surrey. It was they who created the rich garlands, coronets and crests (including the 'Lauderdale Eagle') that feature in the ceilings of The Duke's Room and the Large Drawing Room, the latter ceiling taking more than five years to complete.

There was a stronghold on this site long before the Maitland family took over, however. The old Lauder Fort had been occupied and strengthened in 1548 by the Protector Somerset whose English troops were removed two years later with the help of the French. But 200 years earlier it had also been occupied by the English, rebuilt in 1324 by Edward II. 'The Row', formerly 'Rotten Row', on the east side of Lauder's main street, reputedly originates in 'rue du Roi'—Edward's direct route to the fort. As a name, however, Rotten Row is common. It may instead immortalize the dunghills and rotting rubbish accumulated at the rear of the main street properties (see no. 21).

### 40* Traquair House, near Innerleithen

*Late 15th-early 16th century AD.*

*NT 330354. On B 709 to St Mary's Loch about 2 km S of Innerleithen; signposted.*

'Traquair' means 'the village on the winding stream'. It reflects a settlement of Cumbric- or British-speaking people prior to the arrival of the English-speaking Northumbrians. The earliest building known, however, is that referred to in a 1512 charter, 'turris et fortalicium de Trakware', presumably that of James Stewart, 1st of Traquair, who inherited from his father, the 1st Earl of Buchan, in 1492. It was within the one-time Royal Forest of Ettrick.

The original tower-house, three storeys high with an attic, occupies the northern end of the present main block. A new wing was added directly to its south wall about the middle of the 16th century, with further southwards extensions and angle turrets later that century when most of the new wing was four storeys high. By the mid 17th century the tower itself had been raised to the same height and an angle turret added to the north-west corner.

It was at this time that there had been a rise in stature of the family. John, 7th of Traquair, actively supported Charles I; he was made 1st Earl of Traquair in 1633 and Lord High Treasurer of Scotland in 1636. To preserve the house

**Traquair House**

foundations he made the New Water, by re-routing the course of the Tweed (c 1640). Under his son, another John, the family became Roman Catholic, so that the upper storey of the old tower came to house secret masses and a concealed staircase.

At the very end of the 17th century, plans were drawn up for further extensions by the Edinburgh architect, James Smith, overseer of the Royal Works in Scotland. The formal forecourt was built, along with the two service wings which were remodelled in the late 18th-early 19th century. The present north wing includes stables and a working brew house; the chapel dates only from the mid 19th century following the Roman Catholic Emancipation Act of 1829.

**The still-room, Traquair House brewery**

The Stewarts' Catholic and Jacobite sympathies did not generate great wealth in the 18th century; and a substantial classical mansion, therefore, did not replace the old house—which simply became ever more complex. As well as being the oldest inhabited house in Scotland, therefore, it retains many early features—the early-mid 16th-century carved oak Passion and Nativity panels from 'Queen Mary's Chapell in Leith'; a remarkable mid 16th-century mural; parts of a late 16th to early 17th-century painted ceiling; a 17th-century close-garderobe in the Old Chapel; Smith's late 17th-century panelling in the High Drawing Room; wrought-iron door furniture including the knocker-plate for the main entrance dated 1795.

In the grounds, the Bear Gates (1737-38, with George Jamesone's bears added in 1745) were closed in 1796 after the death of the 7th Earl's wife. Elsewhere, the restored summer-house—a blending of hazel twigs, heather and reeds—was built in 1834 for the last Earl of Traquair. Original fittings include a curved arcade bench and pedestal table. Such 'moss houses' are illustrated in Charles McIntosh's Book of the Garden (1853). Though it was expected to last no more than 40 years, estate workers collected heather annually until the last thatchers died out. The exterior was restored in 1990.

Traquair is arguably the best and most interesting country house in south-east Scotland!

# 4 PALACES, CASTLES AND FORTIFIED HOUSES

Slezer's late 17th-century view of the Bass Rock. The castle dates from the 16th century, with a chapel higher up the slope. A lighthouse was built over part of the castle walls in 1902

Palaces such as Linlithgow (no. 41) and Holyroodhouse (NT 269739) belong as much to the period of the stately home as of the fortified castle; they were very much courtyard palaces. Holyrood was remodelled in the 1670s by Sir William Bruce, incorporating the early 16th-century Great Tower and main quadrangle; at Linlithgow the double-pile north range, constructed just after James VI's visit in 1617, was added to a courtyard laid out a century earlier; the great hall lining one side of Edinburgh Castle's Crown Square was completed c 1500, and the King's Lodgings built just before James VI's visit.

Here, then, was an age of transition, with initiatives taken first by the Scottish Crown but after the Union of the Crowns, mainly by the nobility—changes triggered largely by the search for greater space and comfort at a time when military defence had become less pressing. The north range of Crichton Castle (no. 45), rebuilt in the 1580s, and the Regent Morton's Drochil Castle (NT 161434), c 1578, reflect forceful foreign influences, Italian and French; but more generally, later 16th-century castle architecture is strongly Scottish vernacular. This is the period when Scottish castles reach their optimum. Craigmillar (no. 48) is a case in point, where massive 15th- and 16th-century courtyard extensions and encircling curtain-walls in no way destroy the earlier keep. What do appear, however, are gun-loops for cannon or for small arms; and more specifically artillery fortifications appear at Dunbar (no. 15), and Eyemouth (no. 13), built by the English in the mid 16th century to consolidate their gains—sometimes with complementary French defences of the same period (eg Eyemouth), reflecting the ebb and flow of military success. Leith's Citadel Gate, moreover, 1656-57 (no. 12) is the last surviving fragment of Cromwell's fortifications.

Many of the later castles in the Lothians and the Borders originated as tower-houses, a type of defensible house particularly characteristic of late medieval Scotland (and Ireland). Indeed the landscape of south-east Scotland is littered with the remains of 14th-17th-century towers. This is particularly so in the Borders—a frontier zone as effectively outwith the control of Scotland's government as the Highlands until well into the 17th century. The most basic was a single square or rectangular vertical keep, several storeys high with strong barrel-vaults tying together massive outer walls—instance Newark (NT 420293), Smailholm (no. 43), Liberton (NT 265696) and the well-preserved and inhabited Cranshaws (NT 681618). The late 16th-century main block at Ferniehurst (NT 652179) is unusually long. Early towers often had overlapping stone slab roofs, often with a parapet walk and an entrance frequently at first-floor level giving direct access to the first-floor hall. A stout wooden door was generally protected by an iron yett or gate.

How to create more space continually taxed the minds of their owners and designers. At its simplest, development might take the form of a projecting circular stair-tower at one corner, as at Cramond (NT 190769). At Darnick (NT 532343), by contrast, such a stair-wing protrudes from the middle of one side to give a T-shaped structure, whilst the mid 16th-century D-shaped Littledean Tower (NT 632313), is clearly a maverick! Considerably more convenient, however, was the addition of a more spacious wing, generally as high as the main tower and containing further accommodation, as well as a stair. The result most commonly was an L-shaped tower: Greenknowe (no. 42), Neidpath (no. 46), Cessford (no. 44), Hillslap (NT 513393) and the Black Tower of Drumlanrig in Hawick (converted by Anne Duchess of

**Borthwick Castle, Midlothian, a double tower-house**

Monmouth, 1701-2, into a comfortable town house). The massive double L as at Borthwick (NT 369597) is atypical and outstanding. Z-plan towers, popular in the later 16th century, are much less common in the south-east than in other parts of Scotland. At dilapidated Drochil (NT 161434) and at Branxholme (NT 464116), rebuilt in the 1570s, flanking towers project from one pair of opposite corners—circular and rectangular respectively.

**Drochil Castle, near Romanno Bridge, 19th-century engraving by Billings**

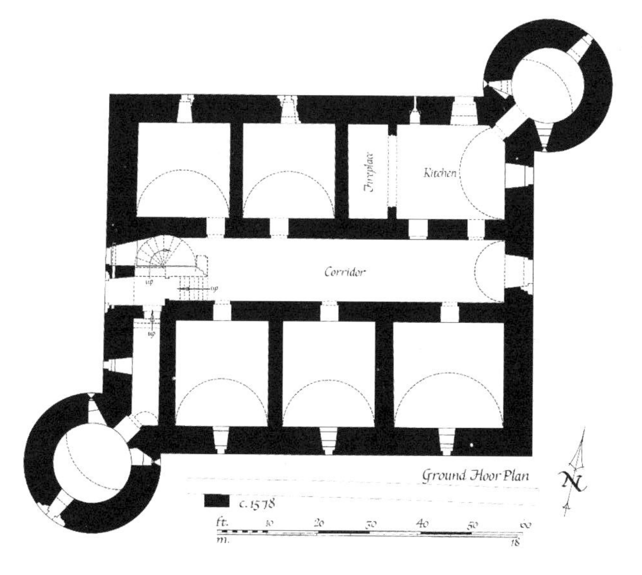


**Drochil Castle, ground-floor plan**

Such wings could also be useful in defence. With an L-plan, cover could be given to the entrance in the inner corner of the walls; with the Z-plan, each tower commanded two walls, which in turn covered the towers. The modest scatter of small gun-loops at Drochil or Smailholm, as in the 15th- and 16th-century curtain walls of mighty Craigmillar, reveals that after their introduction into Scotland, firearms, particularly hand guns, might be used to defend a laird's house. But it may be supposed that this was a secondary purpose, for by this time raiding was diminishing, and after 1603 the Borders, by and large, were pacified. Excepting the period of the English Civil Wars in the 1640s and 1650s, times were generally more settled, and landowners were more inclined to use the law than the raid as a means of settling differences.

**Drochil Castle: corbelling, gun-loop and window**

'The world may change agayn', however, Sir Robert Kerr warned his son in 1632, so houses remained 'strong in the outsyde'. In more gentle Lothian, houses such as Pinkie House (NT 348726), Winton House (NT 438694), Fountainhall (NT 426677), Northfield House (NT 389739) and The Binns (no. 35) were spreading horizontally, and defensive features withering away; in the Borders, however, they did not entirely forego defence. Larger rooms with bigger windows and better services were adopted maybe, but ground floors often remained windowless, with stout doors and gun-loops. And the transitional late 17th-century remodelling at Neidpath (no. 46) shows that naturally defensive sites were not immediately abandoned; indeed courtyard accommodation within the enclosing wall was also remodelled at this time.

Barmkins were a further means of defence, found on a much larger scale as the curtain walls of Craigmillar (no. 48) or Hailes (no. 50). Of stone and lime, occasionally earth and timber, modest versions survive in part at Smailholm (no. 43), Newark and Tinnis (NT 141344).

Barmkins provided additional space, however, not just protection. The higher and lesser nobility and the gentry, each at their respective levels, had large households; and they needed space to entertain.The extra space was not found only in extensions to the tower-house itself, but within the courtyard created by the barmkin. In other words, whilst livestock and people could certainly be brought within at times of unrest, it was not simply a matter of a tower-house dwelling surrounded by miscellaneous farmyard buildings. Whilst the tower-house remained the chief residential unit and the most secure, additional buildings within the courtyard increasingly formed an integral part of the residential unit—and as much at the likes of modest Smailholm as at mighty Craigmillar or Crichton.

Smaller and less substantial peles, resembling the simplest square tower-houses but generally lacking the strength of vaulted chambers, were common amongst the Border hills. Two-storeyed, the living accommodation on the upper floor was reached by a removable ladder, whilst the lower floor was used for livestock and storage. They were more by way of temporary refuges for local farmers, developed in the second half of the 16th century. A rather different but similarly less substantial structure was the fortified house or bastle (French *bastille*) which, although having a vaulted basement like a proper tower-house, was not so high and usually gable-ended, for instance Queen Mary's House (NT 651206) in Jedburgh. There were also a number of moated homesteads—notably Muirhouselaw (no. 52), Dykeheads (NT 582073), Bloomfield (NT 588234), Florida (NY 517908) and Kirndean (NY 532909). Their oval or rectangular water-filled ditches date broadly from the 12th to 16th centuries.

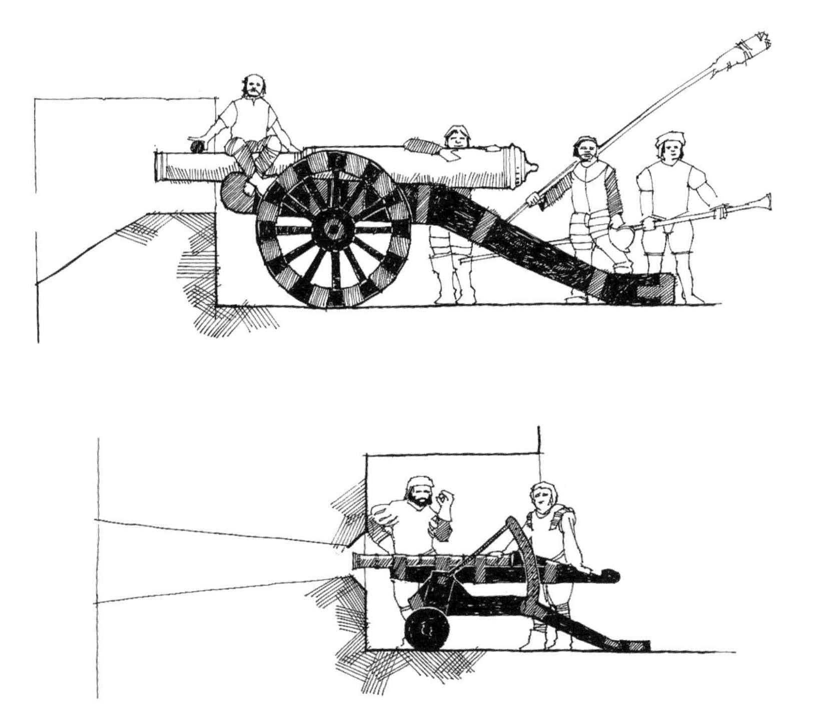

**Cannon on heavy carriages could be used from the tops of the main towers**

**Smaller breech-loaded guns served the oval gun-loops**

Quite distinct from the relatively humble tower-house (some of which, like Aikwood and Kirkhope on the Ettrick Water, have been converted to modern dwellings), the south-east possesses some of the finest 13th to 14th-century baronial castles in Scotland in Dirleton (no. 51), Hailes (no. 50), Yester (NT 556667), Tantallon (no. 49) and Hermitage (no. 47)—massive keeps of varying forms, with large towers flanking curtain walls enclosing courtyards. And although Roxburgh Castle (NT 713337) is now little but a scatter of irregular grassy mounds on its promontory between Teviot and

Tweed, just west of Kelso, it was more critical for the security of medieval Scotland than any castle other than Edinburgh and Stirling. (Along with Berwick, their associated settlements comprised Scotland's four Royal Burghs.) A key fortress, Roxburgh changed hands several times between 1296 and 1346, and was largely demolished by the Scots in 1460 after more than a century's occupation by the English. It was finally destroyed in 1550. By contrast, 13th-century Hume Castle, which was also wasted, was replaced between 1790 and 1796 by today's hilltop 'folly'!

These, then, were the castles of the truly powerful and wealthy Anglo-Norman families introduced to Scotland in the 12th century, in large part by David I, but also by Malcolm IV and William the Lion. Their first strongholds had been timber castles set on top of a large earthen mound, often with an additional palisaded courtyard protecting associated buildings. The archetypal feudal castle, such mottes and baileys were the first 'modern' castles and almost the only kind in 12th-century Scotland. Barely identifiable in Lothian, there are however a number of sites in the Borders—at Hawick (no. 53), The Mount (no. 54), Riddell (NT 520248), Selkirk (NT 470281), Howden (NT 458268), Phenzhopehaugh (NT 318127) and Liddel Castle (NY 510909) for instance. A likely motte at Bedrule (NT 595182) probably reflects a transitional 13th-century form.

**Queen Mary's House, Jedburgh, a fortified house or bastle**

**Linlithgow Palace and St Michael's Church**

## 41* Linlithgow Palace, West Lothian

*Early 16th-17th century AD.*

*NT 002773. A 9 to centre of Linlithgow; turn N at square; signposted.*

*Historic Scotland.*

Linlithgow Loch was once more extensive and the promontory more conspicuously secure than it is today. Fragments of Roman pottery have been found on the site; there too stood the 12th-century parish church, and the royal manor house incorporated in Edward I's peel in 1301-2. Nothing clearly identifiable, however, predates the fire of 1424.

The earlier 16th-century gatehouse (copied by Scott at Abbotsford, no. 31) contains modern replica panels bearing the insignia of the Orders of the Garter, Thistle, Fleece and St Michael. Within, an early 16th-century stair tower rises at each corner of the central courtyard with its elaborate fountain (c 1535); and the stairs are linked by a series of mainly 16th-century wings. This strikingly simple, symmetrical plan, unique in Scotland in the Middle Ages though echoed in Edinburgh's 17th-century Heriot's Hospital, seems to derive from late 14th-century north-east English fortified manor-houses. Given Linlithgow's elaborate domestic provision, combined with a high degree of defensibility, 'fortified palace' may indeed be a more appropriate description!

At first-floor level, the south wing held the chapel and what appears to have been 'My Lord's Hall' of 1633; the west wing the 'King's Hall' and the 'Presence Chamber' (1629); the north wing, rebuilt 1618-20, a whole series of 'chalmers' evidenced by multiple marooned fireplaces and chimney-stacks in the now-ruinous walls. The east wing, as well as housing the court kitchen with its surviving 'beehive' ovens, also contained the 'Great Hall' or 'Lion Chalmer' with its fine great window, remarkable triple fireplace and battery of upper-storey windows.

**Reconstruction drawing of Linlithgow Palace**

**The 1530s fountain in the courtyard, Linlithgow Palace**

The north-west stair tower was known locally as the Queen's turnpike, surmounted by 'Queen Margaret's Bower'—an octagonal rib-vaulted chamber with fine views to the surrounding countryside. To the east the way opens out towards Edinburgh; westwards, the railway, canal and motorway all follow the inland route that the Palace commands north of the Torphichen Hills.

Below the palace, in the town, the High Street retains a few late 16th-17th-century houses; also an interesting well-head '1720/Saint Michael is Kinde to Strangers', and an 1807 replica of the 1628 Cross Well (no mercat cross survives).

St Michael's parish church dates from the later 15th century and was completed towards the mid 16th century, just in time to be 'cleansed' in 1559, at the 'Reformation'. Along with St Mary's Haddington (no. 68), it reflects burgh wealth and status as no other in this part of Scotland. The present 'open' spire, added in 1964, is influenced by the medieval crown steeple (cf St Giles in Edinburgh) taken down c 1821.

## 42* Greenknowe Tower, near Gordon

*Late 16th century AD.*

*NT 639428. Close to A 6105 Earlston-Greenlaw road, 1 km W of Gordon; signposted.*

*Historic Scotland.*

'Green knowe' or 'green hill' was once surrounded by marshy ground—an important feature in its defence. Built in the late 16th century, it is a classic, 3-storey L-shaped tower-house consisting of a main rectangular block with a shorter wing. The entrance is found at the 're-entrant' angle, its usual

**Greenknowe Tower**

**Artist's impression of Greenknowe Tower as built in 1581** (Left)

**Iron yett and inscribed marriage lintel, Greenknowe Tower** (Left)

position, where the two wings meet in a right-angle. It was thus easily defended or covered from the tower.

The turnpike stair just beyond the entrance leads down to the vaulted kitchen with its large arched fireplace. It also leads up to the main hall, whence the usual turret stair corbelled out from the re-entrant corner rises to the upper floors of both the main tower and the wing. Some of the wall plaster survives in the hall; the fireplace is decorated with ornate side pilasters; the kitchen flue is carried up the north wall with small closets built in either side. The westward one may have been a garderobe or toilet. Along the gable-edges the crowsteps are typical, whilst three circular angle turrets spring from corbels at third-floor level.

The entrance comprises a stout timber door with a strong iron yett immediately behind—difficult to batter or burn down. Above, the lintel incorporates a finely-sculptured panel dated 1581, with two sets of initials and two shields. The Seton family acquired the property by marriage in the early 15th century and the tower was apparently built by James Seton of Touch (I.S.) in 1581, with his wife Jane Edmonstone (I.E.). It was held by the Pringles of Stichel in the 17th century.

## 43* Smailholm Tower, near Earlston

*15-17th century AD.*

*NT 637346. Half way along side road to Smailholm, N off B 6404 St Boswells-Kelso road; SW along track and through Sandyknowe farm; signposted.*

*Historic Scotland.*

'Smallam-tower' (Old English *smææl hām*, small village), is recorded in 1546 when a Sir John Ellerker attacked it. It is a simple rectangular tower now set beside a one-time mill pond and rising some 17.3 m from the highest of a series of rocky outcrops. The hill gives a fine panorama to the Cheviots, the Lammermuirs, east to the Eildon Hills and west down the Merse.

Five storeys high, with walls over 2 m thick, and all its windows small, the tower was primarily defensive. Both the ground and uppermost compartments are barrel-vaulted. There are only two gun-loops—one oval and one keyhole-shaped; the chutes opening out of the north wall served the closets or toilets at first and second-floor level. The top floor had been reconstructed either in the late 16th or more probably 17th century; earlier the parapet walk presumably overhung the walls on all sides. 'Everie man that hath a castle or towre of stone shall, upon everie fray raysed in the night, give warning to the countrie by fire in the topps of the castle or towre'. (*Laws of the Marches*).

Such was required c 1570 and the structure of the present north parapet wall doubtless relates to this law—it has a watchman's seat and a recess for his lantern.

**Smailholm Tower**

**Impression of Smailholm Tower in the 17th-century**

From the 15th century until 1645, the tower was occupied by the Pringles/Hopringles, squires to the Earls of Douglas; given the absence of additional architectural detail, it could as easily be 15th as 16th century! In essence it is a very much smaller, humbler and less costly version of the Douglases' massive 5-storey Newark Castle, c 1400, on the Yarrow Water (NT 420293); and since the Douglas estates were forfeited c 1455, it is not unreasonable to think that Smailholm dates from roughly this period. For the Pringles (well-to-do landed gentry with holdings in many parts of the Borders) acquired sound title to their estates c 1455-59.

Like Newark, Smailholm is enclosed by a barmkin. Parts of the enclosing wall survive on the west side where a bar-hole marks the entrance; and, whilst the courtyard to the east seems always to have been open ground, the west courtyard housed a second residential unit, complementary to the tower itself. A hall and chamber lay adjacent to the tower on the north side, with a free-standing kitchen and other service buildings close by. Far from enclosing simply low-status buildings, therefore, excavation has shown this courtyard to have provided 88 m square residential space and 37 m square services (125 m square in total)—compared to 130 m square and 79 m square in the tower itself (209 m square). Whilst the tower house remained the heart of the complex, therefore, the courtyard allowed for considerable elaboration of the facilities.

**Seal of John Hopringle of Smailholm**

## 44 Cessford Castle, near Kelso

*Mid 15th-16th century AD.*

*NT 738238. 1.5 km W of Morebattle, minor road leads SW off B 6401 to Cessford and Jedburgh; castle stands E of road, just N of Cessford village/farm.*

This massive L-shaped tower, 1446, overlooks the valley of the Kale Water. It was surrounded by an earth and stone rampart, now no more than 1.5 m high, and formerly bounded by a deep ditch or moat.

The English attacked Cessford in 1519 and again in 1523 when the Earl of Surrey, with eleven cannon, considered it the third strongest castle in Scotland. It was taken and dismantled only when its absent owner, Sir Andrew Ker, Warden of the Marches, returned and simply handed it over. In further English invasions in 1543 and 1544 it was burnt; it remains, however, one of the few castles in this area to have escaped entire destruction (Hermitage is another: no. 47).

The tower had two entrances. A ground-level doorway in the east wall of the main block was sheltered by a 'false' barbican enclosing the re-entrant angle of the L, and was covered by two gun-loops in the north wall of the wing (the 'real' defensive barbican ran between the two ruinous outbuildings adjoining the rampart north-east of the tower). Almost directly above, but in the wing, a second entrance must have been reached by a wooden ladder to a projecting landing. It was protected by an iron yett opening inward and a thick wooden outer door opening on to the landing. The lowest parts of the wing contained a vaulted prison with a vaulted and ventilated but unlit pit prison below; at first-floor level was the kitchen, adjacent to the main hall with a 15th (possibly 14th) century fireplace and intra-mural chambers once safely reached by a turnpike stair within the wall at the re-entrant angle.

The main tower rose three storeys to the wall-head; the wing, four storeys within the same height (cf Neidpath: no. 46) with a further two storeys above, both of which may have been built (or rebuilt) in the 16th century. The comparatively thin walls of these upper storeys, now fallen, were raised on the inner faces of massive 4.3 m thick lower walls, so that the sloping roof dropped over the upper wall-head to the outer edges of the thicker wall below—a most unusual feature. Another distinctive feature are the many huge, finely-jointed corner stones up to 1.5 m by 0.6 m by 0.3 m.

## 45* Crichton Castle, Midlothian

*Late 14th-late 16th century AD.*

*NT 380611. 3.5 km S of Pathhead on main A 68 Edinburgh-Lauder road; follow B 6367 to Crichton village, then side-road to church; signposted.*

*Historic Scotland.*

Crichton is one of two castles commanding the Middleton Gap and the route south to the Gala Water. Borthwick (NT 369597) on the Gore Water, is still inhabited and remains an outstandingly complete, large 15th-century tower-house with two wings and the remains of a curtain wall; Crichton, on the Tyne, is an equally interesting example of a late 14th-century tower, probably built by John de Crichton but subsequently extended and enveloped. The central, protruding section of the east wall is the east wall of the tower; the south and west courtyard sections were added in the 15th century; the present northern range dates from 1581-91.

From without, Crichton is a stark and forbidding shell standing on a projecting terrace sharply above the still marshy river-side haugh. Internally, the original tower-house, some 14 m by 11 m, had a high pointed barrel vault to the first-floor hall. There is a mezzanine floor; also a small prison (2 m by 2.6 m) entered through a tiny entrance but 0.6 m

**Crighton Castle's 16th century stables with horseshoe entrance arch**

**Cessford Castle** (Top)

broad by 0.8 m high and once secured by a strong, heavily-barred door.

It is the facing wall of the later north range, however, that provides a most remarkable contrast to the bleak exterior. For this wall, with its large, rectangular, precisely-positioned windows, is ornamented in a way virtually unique in Scotland. Above an arcade of seven bays (and an extra 'return' bay on the west side), a distinctive diamond rustication covers the surface of the stone. Such embellishment reflects Continental Renaissance architecture, influenced more specifically here perhaps by Italian palaces of the period. It was commissioned by the 5th Earl of Bothwell (nephew of Mary, Queen of Scots' consort), who returned from Italy in 1581.

Bothwell also built the nearby stable, one of numerous ancillary buildings once standing on the plateau to the south. The stable was entered beneath a horseshoe-shaped opening decorated with a 'thong' patterning. Its vaulted roof set up stresses that later required external buttressing. Above was the hayloft, maybe heightened and made habitable, with crow-stepped gables.

Crichton Village has an interesting church to St Mary and St Kentigern, restored in 1896 but parish church by decree in 1661 (NT 380616). Formerly collegiate (see section 6), it is cruciform, aisleless and tunnel-vaulted, with a barely evident nave. There are three iron headstones in the churchyard, the first dated 1841 to George Douglas of the Broughton Foundry in Edinburgh.

### 46* Neidpath Castle, near Peebles

*Late 14th-late 17th century AD.*

*NT 235404. 2 km W of Peebles on A 72, on S side of road; signposted.*

Until the 16th century, the lands of Neidpath seem to have been called 'Jedderfield'. They were acquired by the Hays of Yester from the Frasers of Oliver about 1310, and the castle was probably begun in the late 14th century. It tops a steep rocky crag towering above the Tweed, and commands the river near to where it emerges from a wooded gorge. Given the shape of the site, the main block takes the form of a parallelogram rather than a rectangle.

But essentially Neidpath is an L-shaped tower-house, where the extra wing on each floor made for more flexible use. Though sub-divided overall into five-storeys, structurally the tower was divided into just three high compartments, each barrel-vaulted in stone. The great hall characteristically occupied

**Part of the arcade or piazza, with diamond rustication above: Crichton Castle courtyard**

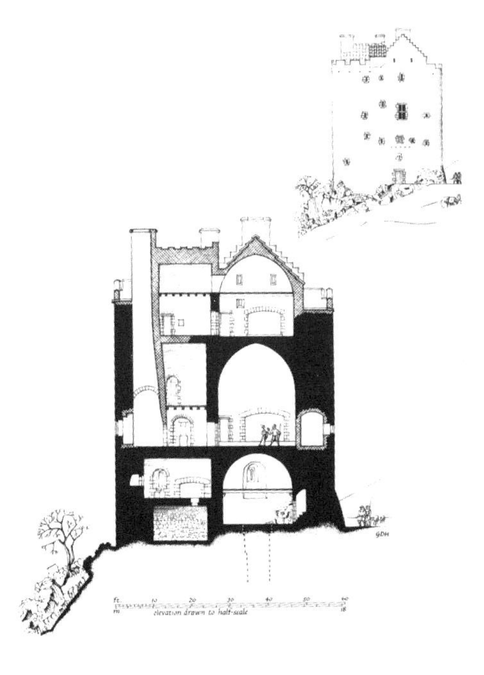

**Neidpath Castle, Tweeddale: reconstruction drawing by GD Hay** (Far right)

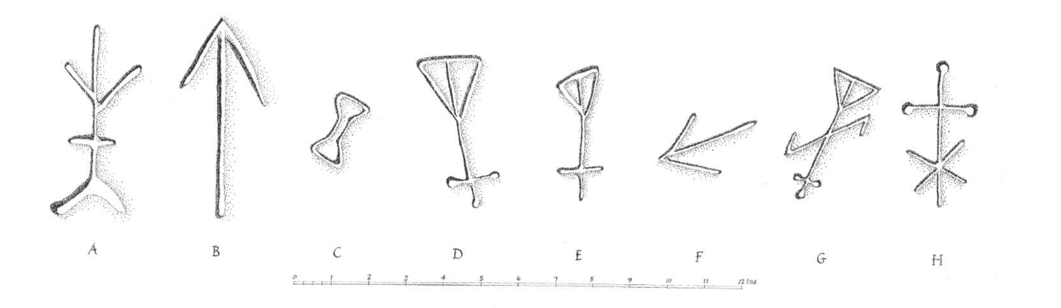


**Masons' marks, Neidpath Castle**

the entire first floor; its attendant kitchen and services filled the first-floor wing, whilst smaller rooms were built ingeniously into the thickness of the walls. At basement level, the main block was available for storage; the wing contained a pit-prison. A number of stones in the tower, up to first-floor level, bear the marks—a kind of signature—of the masons who worked them.

Few alterations seem to have been made for some 300 or so years, until the upper parts were remodelled in the late 16th-early 17th century; major internal reconstruction, however, was carried out in the second half of the 17th century and parts of the older 16th-century courtyard buildings remodelled. The keystone of the 17th-century forecourt gateway incorporates the crest of the Hays, Earls of Tweeddale—a goat's head upon a coronet.

The 'gairdene of neidpeth' is recorded in 1581, and the surviving parallel terraces may date from this or a slightly earlier period. Although their retaining walls are ruinous, considerable traces survive to the east of the castle running down towards the river—and the approach road itself keeps to one. The gardens went out of use around the end of the 18th century.

## 47* Hermitage Castle, near Newcastleton

*Late 14th-16th century AD.*

*NY 496960. About 9 km N of Newcastleton on side road linking B 6399 and A 7; signposted.*

*Historic Scotland.*

Hermitage is associated with many families—de Bolbeck, de Soulis, Dacre, Douglas, Bothwell. It is the most perfect of the medieval Border castles, even though heavily restored early in the 19th century. Standing amongst high hills, on the banks of the Hermitage Water, it was described in the mid 16th century as 'a oulde house not stronng, but ewill to be wyn by reasone of the strate grounde aboute the same'—the then broken, marshy ground difficult to negotiate in any but the driest weather.

Of a 13th-century structure, nothing survives. The 14th-century castle was rectangular and enclosed the small central courtyard; its entrance was in the south wall; and a turnpike stair opposite rose no higher than first-floor level. This phase in the castle's evolution is associated with the Dacres (1358 to at least 1365) and reflects the style of some 14th-century, northern English fortified manor-houses. Some of the surviving, well-dressed red sandstone masonry bears masons' marks—distinctively large, well-cut and Gothic in the 14th-century manner.

Towards the end of the 14th century a rectangular tower-house incorporated the earlier features, and subsequently massive rectangular towers were added to all but the south-east corner of the keep. This latter succumbed in due course, when a further massive tower enveloped the short wing or 'jamb' of the late 14th-century keep—traces of whose entrance and protective portcullises, above ground-level, survive internally. The 'new', four-storey castle was topped by a projecting battlement below which, to the outside, ran a continuous wooden hoarding supported on corbels and accessible through rectangular openings easily visible high up in the walls. In the 16th century, when firearms came to be used for defence, a few wide-mouthed, oblong gun-loops were added to the outer walls.

**Hermitage Castle, near Newcastleton**

Hermitage is a magnificently solid, gaunt castle where Mary, Queen of Scots, visited the seriously injured Bothwell in 1566. About 370 m west lie the ruins of a small chapel, probably 14th century and set within a graveyard, amidst a series of earthworks. Enclosed fields and a hollow track lie up the hillside; the churchyard more or less fills one set of enclosures; further earthworks lie to the west. Could the churchyard be the site of the first castle recorded in 1242-44, with a western outer bailey? Or do the earthworks reflect a moated homestead possibly of c 1300? Between the burial ground dyke and the river stands the low mound 'Cout o' Kielder's Grave'— traditionally the grave of Sir Richart Knout (or Knut/Cout) of Kielder, in Northumbrian Tynedale. Knout, who died between 1289 and 1291, was an enemy of Lord de Soulis. He was reputedly killed here—driven into the river and held under by the lances of his attackers.

At about 350 m, some 130 m uphill from the Castle, on the slopes of Hermitage Hill, the White Dyke stretches for over 1 km (NY 486973-NY 495972). Still nearly 2 m high by 1.5 m thick in places, this limestone dyke formed part of the boundary of the Hermitage Deer Park. As population and settlement margins expanded in medieval times, first it was the new farms that had to be enclosed (see no. 29). As pressure mounted, however, what remained of the one-time royal hunting forests (not necessarily afforested!) were themselves enclosed, so as to protect the deer.

## 48* Craigmillar Castle, Edinburgh

*Early 15th-mid 17th century AD.*

*NT 288708. 4 km SE of centre of Edinburgh by A 68; side road NE. Or S from traffic lights in centre of Craigmillar (A 6095); signposted.*

*Historic Scotland.*

By the 17th century, Craigmillar Castle had more or less achieved its final form. In 1661 the west wings within the courtyard were reconstructed for Sir John Gilmour who had just bought the barony from the Prestons—its owners since 1374 and recalled not only in numerous armorial tablets but also in the P-shaped hollow of a pond outwith the southern walls, a pond once stocked to provide fresh fish for those within.

The east side of the courtyard, by contrast, had been rebuilt following the burning of the castle in 1544 by English forces under Hertford—they 'gatt great spoyle' since Edinburgh folk had 'sowght to saif thare movables thairin'. The outermost precinct wall was built then too, furnished with gun-loops in the corner towers, but not with battlements. A dovecote was incorporated in its north-east corner, presumably to supplement or replace that in the equivalent tower of the inner curtain wall.

These reconstructions and extensions did not conflict with earlier principles of fortification,

however. The castle had continued to develop on a medieval pattern; and the massive L-shaped tower-house continued to play a central role.

Built above a rocky 9 m precipice, the original early 15th-century entrance faced west, protected by a shelving pitfall (now filled in) spanned in peace-time by a timber bridge. Stout wooden doors, an outer iron yett, narrow passages and spiral turnpike stair with a midway 'fighting platform' added to an attacker's problems. Above, the Great Hall occupied the entire first floor of the main block, fitted with a massive stone, probably 15th-century fireplace, hooded and elaborately moulded. The original kitchen, at the same level, later converted into a bedroom, is sometimes known as Queen Mary's Room. She stayed in the Castle in 1563 (when she received Queen Elizabeth's ambassador, Thomas Randolph); and again in 1566 after the murder of Rizzio in Holyroodhouse and the birth of her son, the future James VI/I. It was here at Craigmillar that the plot was hatched to murder her ailing husband Darnley.

In 1427, the massive enceinte or curtain wall had been built around the original tower to create the present inner courtyard. Its walls are remarkably complete, with towers at each corner and parapet walks to the north, east, and part of the south. And whilst the tower-house carries a parapet rising flush from the wall, that of the curtain-wall projects—with openings in the floor through which unpleasant gifts could be dropped on to the attackers. This kind of projecting paprapet (contrasting with the wooden hoardings that would have been set on joists on the outside of the original tower-house parapet), though known earlier south of the Tweed, spread northwards only after about 1400. Furthermore, the north-east tower has openings perhaps for hand-guns, but equally perhaps for cannon to defend the main approach to the castle—amongst the first such batteries in Scotland.

**Craigmillar Castle and fish-pond, Edinburgh**

**The original early 15th century towerhouse**
(Top left)

**Preston family heraldic panel, with a rebus making play with a 'press' and a 'tun'**
(Left)

Craigmillar is probably the best example of a medieval castle surviving in Scotland, built according to 15th- and 16th-century principles of fortification, and it affords spectacular views of Edinburgh's Old Town skyline, Arthur's Seat, the East Lothian coastline and the Pentland Hills.

The Gilmours finally abandoned Craigmillar at some date prior to 1775. They moved a kilometre westwards to the elegant Inch House, sheltered beside the Braid Burn, and built originally for James Winram, Keeper of the Great Seal of Scotland, in 1617.

### 49* Tantallon Castle, East Lothian

*Late 14th—mid 17th century AD.*

*NT 596850. A 198 North Berwick to Dunbar coast road, some 6 km E of North Berwick; signposted.*

*Historic Scotland.*

**Impression of Tantallon Castle during James V's seige, 1528-9**

**Tantallon Castle and Doocot, near North Berwick** (Bottom)

Tantallon's situation is spectacular, perched on a small but lofty sea-girt promontory. Though there may have been some kind of castle before 1300, the earliest reference to 'Temptaloun' comes in 1374 from the 1st Earl of Douglas and Mar, who held the barony of North Berwick as a tenant of the Earls of Fife. With virtually unscaleable 30 m high sea-cliffs on three sides, Tantallon's curtain wall comprises a single, huge linear barrier of reddish sandstone, thrown across the landward side. Over 15 m high and 3.6 m thick, it is flanked by a D-shaped East Tower and a circular Douglas Tower with pit-prison.

In 1529 James V laid siege and battered the castle with cannons and other artillery. Surrender was finally agreed by negotiation rather than destruction, however, as the besiegers had run out of gunpowder (with further supplies apparently available only from France!). Then, in reinforcing the walls, James subsequently enlarged the Mid-Tower, thereby concealing the earlier drawbridge, portcullis and barbican.

Beyond the ditch, extensive earthworks represent defences thrown up against the King's cannon; but others farther out date from the mid 17th century. For here at Tantallon, during the English Civil War, 30 horsemen established themselves to harry Cromwell's lines of communication. General Monk attacked with cannon for 12 days in 1651 and very much reduced the flanking towers.

The main block of domestic buildings—hall, kitchen, bakehouse—lies north of the courtyard; also the remains of a sea-gate and probably of a landing stage in the bay immediately north-west of the castle. Outside the curtain wall, the 17th-century rectangular dovecote contains two chambers.

Offshore lie the ruins of the 15th-century St. Baldred's Chapel and Bass Castle (NT 601872), a largely ruinous structure dating in its present form from the 16th century. The lighthouse buildings are built on top of the governor's house. The Bass can be visited seasonally from North Berwick, and its innumerable breeding colonies of sea-birds—gannets, guillemots, puffins, gulls—make early summer a particularly interesting time: similarly the cliffs around St Abbs Head (NT 9169: see no. 16).

## 50* Hailes Castle, East Lothian

*13th-15th century AD.*

*NT 574757. Side road S of River Tyne from East Linton to Haddington, about 4 km SW of East Linton; signposted.*

*Historic Scotland.*

A strange place to build a castle, perhaps, low down beside a lazy river, particularly with Traprain Law (no. 92), fortified so much earlier, rising up the south. But it is an attractive site—a steep, rocky outcrop above the river, bounded to the west by a small ravine; and not far to the east the river cuts through and falls more rapidly around East Linton. A site of some strategic importance, therefore.

The earliest parts of the castle pre-date the Wars of Independence and may suggest, rather, a fortified manor-house comparable to Aydon Castle in Northumberland. In essence, however, it is a 13th to 14th-century castle of enclosure, comprising two towers (both with pit-prisons) and a curtain wall. A stone stair led through the earlier part of the riverside wall to a well; and possibly extended across a drawbridge, thence by way of a ladder, to the river itself. The main gateway survives in the south curtain wall; a little postern or 'back gate' to the east. The north range of buildings, between the towers, is mainly 15th century and includes a chapel with tunnel-vaulted basement below.

The castle was heavily involved in the 'Rough Wooing', 1544-45, when the English under Hertford attempted to force through by invasion the marriage of young Mary, Queen of Scots, to the boy prince Edward, later Edward VI. In 1547 Hertford, now Duke of Somerset, writing an account of his Scottish expedition speaks of 'a proper house and of sum strengthe bylyke they call it Hayles Castle, and pertayneth to the Erle Bothwell'. It was taken by the English in the following year and held for them, with 50 men, by Hugh Douglas (of Longniddry?). Cromwell finally demolished it a century later, in 1650.

**Dirleton Castle: reconstruction by Alan Sorrell**

**Hailes Castle, beside the River Tyne, below Traprain Law, East Lothian** (Top)

## 51* Dirleton Castle, East Lothian

*12th-16th century AD.*

*NT 516839. In village of Dirleton on A 198 coastal road, about 6.5 km W of North Berwick; signposted.*

*Historic Scotland.*

Dirleton was described as a 'castellum' c 1225. Sited on a rocky, igneous outcrop at the east end of a gentle ridge and commanding the east-west coastal route, its principal structures were built by the de Vaux, an Anglo-Norman family granted the barony of Dirleton in the 12th century. In 1298, however, the castle was taken by Edward I.

There are three main periods of construction. Most recent are the 16th-century additions of the Ruthvens enclosing the inner court or close at the south-west corner. During the preceding two centuries, 14th and 15th, the Halyburtons had raised most of the east block—including cellars, bakery, kitchens and chapel. Below the chapel is a prison; below this, a pit-prison which, like others of the lower chambers, has been hewn out of the natural rock. The outer wall of this block was built against parts of the earlier curtain wall—re-used to provide further support for the new tunnel-vaulting. And the imposing main entrance and drawbridge also date to this period.

In its original form, however, Dirleton consisted of an enclosing wall or enceinte following very much the line of the present wall. Circular towers, now overlaid by later building, once occupied the south-east and north-north-west angles; in the south-west corner stood the main block, very much as it still is. Off the triangular inner court a semi-circular and a rectangular tower both project outwards; also the principal 'drum' tower of well-dressed masonry, with 3 m thick walls to an overall diameter of some 11 m. At first-floor level it contains the roughly hexagonal Lord's Chamber, with stone seats—three of them in window openings (cf Craigmillar: no. 48).

There is a 16th-century beehive-shaped dovecote in the grounds, and a 17th-century bowling green whose surviving yew trees are a reminder of an earlier, formal planting within the 'garth'.

Dirleton is one of south-east Scotland's most attractive villages, and its present form can be traced back with certainty to the early 16th century. Set around a village green, it predates the 18th and 19th-century estate or planned villages. It may perhaps have a medieval origin after the manner of some northern English villages laid out around a green; or it may echo such 'green' villages as Ancrum, Bowden and Maxton in the Borders, which were granted charters as market centres in the 16th-17th centuries.

## 52 Muirhouselaw Moated Homestead, near St Boswells

*13th-15th century AD.*

*NT 631283. 2.3 km along side road SE off A 699 at Maxton, some 3 km W of St Boswells; just SSE of farm, beyond trees flanking road.*

Little is known of the medieval Scottish homestead, for most seem to have been swept away by the plough or overlaid by later buildings on the same site. The fortified, moated homestead was more likely to survive, and at least three are recorded in Roxburghshire.

Dykeheads (NT 582073) and Bloomfield (NT 588234) are both roughly rectangular earthworks consisting of a wide ditch with modestly raised earthen banks either side, while Muirhouselaw (or Morhus) is also rectangular but consists of two contiguous enclosures sharing a common outer ditch and separated by a common transverse ditch. Only the south-west end of the north-west enclosure survives; it was perhaps half the size of a still-complete main enclosure some 67 m square. The ditch is steep-sided and still marshy, about 6 m to 9 m wide at the top, and 2 m to 3 m wide at the bottom. As it stands, it is up to 1.5 m deep, and is bounded by small banks of upcast on either side, spreading up to 3.7 m across but only about 0.5 m high. The original entrance seems to have been in the north-east side, close to the east corner, where a causeway across the ditch matches a 3.7 m gap in the inner 'rampart'.

Between the disturbed ground immediately inside this corner and the slope leading down to a former pond, are the remains of two possibly contemporary structures: the larger was a rectangular, two-roomed building, with double walls; the other, a square structure within a mound, may rather have been a tower. The pond may also be an original feature, feeding the moat—though certainly a later feeder channel has been cut to it destroying evidence of a ditch on the north-east side. Not all such moated homesteads, however, had wet ditches; and ditches were not only intended as defence against invaders— whether men or wild animals. They would also have served as an open drain for dwelling house, byre and barn.

As to date, none in England has proved to be earlier than the Norman conquest; most are probably 13th-15th century and associated with the late medieval settlement of woodland areas. In Scotland, they may reflect a form of defence used by smaller landowners before tower houses became more general. Other examples are found at Florida (NY 517908) and Kirndean (NY 532909).

## 53 Hawick Motte

*12th century AD.*

*NT 499140. A 7 in Hawick, W side of Slitrig Water: side road SW for 500 m.*

The site of Hawick Motte forms the extremity of the watershed about 500 m south-south-west of the meeting of the River Teviot and the Slitrig Water. The ditch surrounding the motte is now almost obliterated, but the mound itself is still a high, truncated cone apparently artificial in its construction. When excavated in 1912, the ditch yielded objects which included a bone needle, a coin of Henry II and numerous sherds of pottery, all pointing to a likely 12th-century date. In the time of William the Lion, Richard Lovel of the Somersetshire Lovels was granted Hawick and Branxholm. This was doubtless his castle!

Some 10 or so km due north lies Riddell Motte (NT 520248)—an oval motte formed by trimming the tail of a natural ridge and surrounded by a rectangular bailey which was defended on one, and probably on three sides, by a wide, steep-sided ditch flanked by two ramparts. And to the south, in Liddesdale, between Hobkirk and Newcastleton, the de Soulis Motte at Liddel Castle (NY 510900) is an equally impressive survivor.

## 54 'The Mount' Motte, Castle Law, near Coldstream

*12th century AD.*

*NT 814418. A 697 Greenlaw-Coldstream road, 2.5 km N of River Tweed, take minor road E, then N towards Castlelaw.*

The earthen mound at Castle Law is a 7 m-8 m high cone with a flattened, somewhat oval summit up to 21 m across, which would have been surmounted by a strong palisade protecting a wooden tower. Such towers may have been crenellated, possibly with external hoardings or fighting platforms.

The motte stands on top of a steep bank rising from the Leet Water. It is surrounded by a ditch some 9 m wide and up to 3 m deep, with further defences probably extending westwards along the edge of the ravine, which would doubtless have included a bailey or larger enclosure housing a wider range of domestic buildings. These ditches may have been spanned by a high-flying bridge, or by a lower bridge and steps up the side of the motte hill. Given that mottes were occupied for 50-200 years, the original mound may well have grown over time as improvements and developments took place.

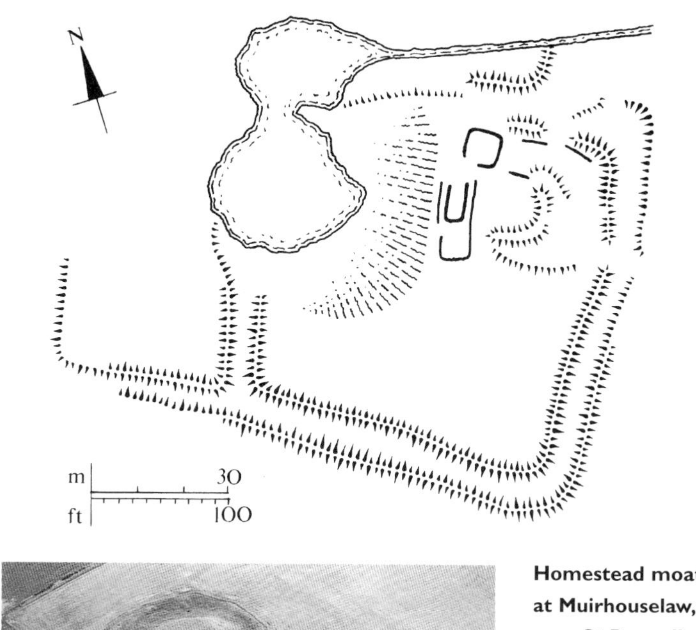


**Homestead moat at Muirhouselaw, near St Boswells**

**Motte and bailey: The Mount, Castle Law, near Coldstream** (Left)

# 5 POST-REFORMATION CHURCHES AND GRAVEYARDS

**Prestonpans church tower, 1596**

Like the tower-houses of late medieval times, the churches of Victorian Scotland lie increasingly derelict; visible symbols of a spiritually troubled age, many have been forsaken in more settled, apathetic or disillusioned times. Yet the disruption of 1843 and other breakaways brought about a wealth of church building unknown since the Middle Ages—by Presbyterian, Free Church and numerous other seceding sects. Many of the supporters of the new churches, as well as Episcopalians and Roman Catholics, were as wealthy as they were overtly religious; many sought prestigious buildings in neo-Gothic or sometimes Baronial forms, complete with stair towers and spires, competing for height and ostentation. Glencorse Church, 1883 (NT 246626) and Penicuik South Church, 1862 (NT 235595) are appropriate examples—a contrast to the oftimes architectural simplicity of Baptist and other Non-Conformist Churches, particularly in the smaller towns and villages.

At the Reformation, however, with the break-up of the monastic monopolies, the Scottish church had been left almost without endowment—rather like the Church of Ireland after the establishment of the Irish Free State in 1921. And provision by the local land-owning heritors and magistrates was usually minimal. Consequently there had been no sudden wave of new building at that time; rather a change of emphasis in interior layout in those churches that were retained, determined by the new theology. No longer was it necessary to face east; rather had the minister to be seen, heard and followed by all. In the 'preaching kirk', therefore, the pulpit was sited halfway along the main wall with the baptismal vessel alongside in full public view. The penitent's stool was equally prominent! There was now no need for an east-end altar; instead, a long communion table would be set out east-west the length of the church when required—no difficult task when so many churches were bereft of fixed seating for long after the break.

**T-plan kirk at Kirkurd, near Broughton, 17th century**

Where buildings were reconstructed in the late 16th or early 17th century as at Cockburnspath (NT 774710: with truncated round tower) and Pencaitland (NT 443690), or newly-built as at Lyne, 1640-45 (no. 59), the Gothic style tended to persist and they were generally narrowly rectangular after the medieval pattern. They had, however, only one compartment—naves, chancels, transepts and chapels were seen merely as barriers to full participation. The plain, square tower of the earliest post-Reformation church in Lothian, 1596, still stands at Prestonpans (NT 388745). Increasingly, however, to provide more accommodation, a cross-aisle was built centrally, facing the pulpit, to provide the T-plan of Kirkurd (NT 127442), Ettrick (no. 55), Newton (NT 334690) or Torphichen (NS 968725). A tower projecting from the opposite fourth wall features at Gifford (NT 534681) and Carrington (NT 318605). Within, 'Daskes and Lofts', seats and galleries, were added from before the mid 17th century to provide a second, sometimes a third tier of seating.

By the early 19th century, however, the T-plan had gone; new churches were built to a wider rectangular format, appropriately lined on all but the south (pulpit) side with galleries. At Channelkirk, 1841 (NT 481545), it was nonetheless still felt necessary to set the gallery stair in a stubby outshot on the north long wall. Gone too, by now, were the more centrally-planned churches, whether the cruciform church at Lauder, 1673 (no. 61) in the form of a Greek cross, or the octagonal church of 1773 at Kelso (NT 729339)—a shape advocated by John Wesley as the most suitable for preaching, whilst maximising congregational space.

**Early 17th century Thomson memorial, Duddingston Kirk, Edinburgh**

Whilst fundamentally simple, such pre-Victorian post-Reformation churches were not necessarily or unwaveringly austere. And some boasted an interior feature of some decorative as well as social significance—not so much the impressive mural monuments to members of local prestigious families, but their lairdly lofts. Here, resplendent in their private galleries, often served by a private stair and retiring wing and perhaps with the family burial vault or aisle below, the local nobility or gentry could worship on a higher plane, as befitted their status! Good examples at Bowden, 1661 (no. 60) and Abercorn, 1708 (no. 62) were built for the Earls of Roxburghe and Hopetoun. Other interesting church furnishings can be seen at Lyne, Newlands (NT 161467), Borthwick (NT 368596), Aberlady (NT 461798), Dunbar (NT 681785) and Haddington (no. 68). Watch-houses, to defeat the nocturnal predations of the resurrectionist body-snatchers of the earlier 19th century, survive at Lauder (no. 61), Eyemouth (no. 13), Dalkeith New Burial Ground, Eckford (NT 707270) and Oldhamstocks (NT 738706).

If post-Reformation churches were often fairly austere, some indication of a fuller, more robust approach to life peeped out from amongst the multifarious symbols of mortality and death, carved with such care and ornamentation on recumbent slabs, table-tombs and headstones of the 17th-18th centuries—even though their more formal aim was to encourage a godly life in the onlooker by reminding him, or her, of impending death!

There would seem to have been something by way of local schools of funeral sculpture, that have led to East Lothian being termed 'Palm-frond-land', Peeblesshire the 'Realm of Full Figures', the Borders 'Portrait-with-book-shire'! The emblems may be of immortality; more soberly, of

**Pencaitland Old Kirk, East Lothian: 18th-century stone mason's headstone**
(Far left)

**Temple Old Kirk, Midlothian: 18th-century headstone to John Craig, farmer**

mortality; or more temporally of earthly trades, crafts and professions —eg Angels of the Resurrection, Winged Soul and Angel, Crown, Torches, Trees, Plants and Flowers; Father Time, Coffin, Bones, Dead Bell, Hourglass, Skull, Sexton's Tools; Farmer, Miller, Gardener, Shoemaker, Baker, Hammerman, Maltman, Brewer. . . .

Most of the older churchyards have a number of such stones; in addition to those featured below interesting examples can be seen at Peebles, St Andrews (NT 244406), Stobo (no. 72), Old Kirkurd (NT 137440), Newlands Old and New (NT 161465, 161467), Channelkirk (NT 481545), Humbie (NT 460637), Temple (NT 315587), Inveresk (NT 344720), Corstorphine (NT 200727), Cramond (NT 189768), Liberton (NT 275695), Ecclesmachan (NT 058736), Pencaitland (NT 443690), Tranent

**East Saltoun Kirk, East Lothian: 18th-century headstone to George Mill**
(Far left)

**Newlands Old Kirk, near Romanno Bridge: 18th-century Borrowman headstone**

(NT 402733), Oxnam (NT 701189). Particularly interesting, and uncommon in the south-east, are the Adam-and-Eve stones at Lyne (no. 59), Dryburgh, 1754 (NT 591316) and Uphall, 1713 (NT 060722) —with one also at Biggar, 1747.

Whilst these decorated headstones are almost exclusively 18th century (and 19th-century stones are markedly more mediocre in their carving), headstones appear early in the 17th century. The carving on the earliest is fairly rough (Southdean NT 631091; Abbotrule NT 612127), but by the last quarter of the century shaped stones were increasingly popular. They were mainly for lesser, 'respectable' folk; as distinct from the grander monuments or burial aisles.

A number of post-Reformation churches were built on the site of earlier churches, and in some cases earlier architectural features or funeral monuments have survived in part and been incorporated into the new building. Strong Norman stonework may be found, for instance, at Abercorn (no. 62) and Legerwood (NT 593434), whilst hog-backed tombstones and fragments of even earlier Anglian crosses also survived at Abercorn, Ancrum (NT 621248), Nisbet (NT 673257), Bedrule (no. 48) and Morham (NT 556725; now in NMS).

**Box pews, Bowden Kirk: watercolour by Henry W Kerr**

### 55* Ettrick Kirk, near Selkirk

*Early 19th century AD.*

*NT 259145. High up Ettrick Water on a side road about 1 km W of B 709 Eskdalemuir road.*

A 'New Kirk of Ettrick' was built early in the 16th century, though the present church dates from 1824—a typical T-shaped, post-Reformation building. Internally it remains a 'preaching kirk'. The pulpit with its characteristic sounding board surmounted by a dove, and the precentor's desk in front of it, stand in the centre of the south side; the pews face inwards from the east and west sides and from a deep north aisle. Over the west end and the aisle there are galleries reached by a stair in the tower; and over the east end there is a laird's loft, reached by the outside stair rising either side of the east door. Before the present Table was introduced, on Communion Sundays boards were simply placed over the pews immediately in front of the pulpit.

There are a number of interesting stones in the church and churchyard. A small 17th-century stone set in the south wall commemorates Sir Robert Scott of Thirlestane's son Robert who died in 1619; a white freestone tablet set inside the tower, in the wall above the door, suggests in Latin that one Walter (perhaps Robert Scott's second son, of Gamescluch, died 1609) did something 'for God, the Greatest and Best, and for the Church of Christ'. Such use of a pagan Roman formula, turned to a Christian context, was a common literary device of the period, though unusual in Scottish inscriptions. The lettering is late 17th-early 18th century and similar to that of a 1709 stone in the churchyard. It may have been erected by Sir Francis Scott of Thirlestane, grandson of Walter and great-grandson of Robert; he died in 1712.

In the churchyard are a number of very small headstones, naturally-shaped and probably glacially-rounded river boulders. They are said to have been brought from the Over Kirkhope burial ground high up the Ettrick Water, and to have been known locally as 'bulls'. One is inscribed WBIM/1691. Otherwise there are numerous 17th-18th-century headstones, several connected with the life and family of James Hogg, 'The Ettrick Shepherd', born nearby. The writer himself (1770-1835) is buried here; also his mother Margaret Laidlaw, her father William Laidlaw ('Will o' Phaup'), her husband Robert Hogg and three more of their sons.

Much of the land at the confluence of the Tilme Water and the Ettrick Water is marshy and beset with scrub and thickets. It gives a fair impression of what many a valley bottom would have been like before proper draining!

### 56* Bedrule Kirk, near Jedburgh

*Early 19th-early 20th century AD.*

*NT 599179. About 2 km S of A 698 Hawick-Kelso road, on side-road some 3 km E of Denholm; in 'centre' of village.*

On a medieval site, the present church dates to 1804, was largely rebuilt by 1877 and enlarged in 1914. It is an attractive little country church, T-plan, and close to the birthplace of Bishop William Turnbull (c 1400-54: founder of Glasgow University). It also features some remarkable moving early 20th-century stained glass windows. The east window was commissioned by Sir Robert and Lady Usher as a memorial to those who died in the Great War, 1914-1918, and incorporates stylised scenes from that war. The centre panel features a warship offshore, with marines handling equipment and marching in uniform. To the left, infantry march against a back-drop of a field gun and tank; to the right, cavalry pass by a soldier offering water to a wounded, bandaged colleague lying on the ground. All three panels provide a telling insight into the dress, equipment and techniques of the time, as well as a timely reminder of the sorrow and futility of war.

In addition to a number of interesting 17th to 19th-century gravestones outside the church, within are two fragments of hog-backed stones with shingle 'roof' patterns (see section 6), and a very small but complete sculpture of a robed figure, head resting on a pillar and hands folded upon chest as in prayer.

A little downstream from the church, 50 m above an old ford and on the west bank, is a conical mound known locally as Castle Knowe (NT 595182); it is partly natural but the top is man-made. The northern slope is relatively gentle; access was barred by a cross-trench, now a grassy terrace; and on the summit there are traces of a roughly oval rampart. It has all the appearances of a 12th-13th-century motte (see section 4).

**Gifford's Stone, 1660, West Linton**

### 57* West Linton Kirk and the Gifford Stone

*Mid 17th-late 18th century AD.*

*NT 149516. Junction of A 702 Edinburgh-Biggar road and B 7059 to Romanno Bridge; 400 m along B road.*

There has been a church at West Linton from the 12th century; the present building, however, was built in 1781—a simple rectangle with a hipped roof and a square tower and belfrey projecting from the middle of the north side. The particularly fine carved woodwork inside dates to its remodelling in 1871.

In the south-east corner of the older part of the graveyard two bee-boles, sheltered ledges for semi-circular straw bee skeps, are incorporated into the south wall of a late 18th-century burial aisle to the Lawsons of Cairnmuir and the Douglases of Garvaldfoot. Elsewhere, amongst the usual 17th and 18th-century gravestones bearing their various symbols of mortality, there ia a fine stone bearing half-size effigies of two men, arm-in-arm, in contemporary dress. Barely visible now, between them, is the Tree of Trial, with a serpent coiled around it; below their feet a coffin, two skulls, and two thigh-bones, and between their heads a crown. The stone is dedicated to John and Richard Alesander, sons of James Alesander, tenant (farmer) in Ingreston. A further stone, dated 1705, reveals a half-scale male figure wearing a buttoned coat, scarf, collar and cap:

'Here Archibald Wilson's corps lies in the Grave
Who in his Life himselfe he did behave'.

Representations of costumed figures form a particularly interesting group of post-Reformation churchyard monuments, late 17th to mid 18th century— cf Stobo (no. 72). And on the end panel of a table-tomb at Liberton in Edinburgh (NT 275695) a wider perspective provides evidence of agricultural history in 1754—plough type, plough-team, harrowing and sowing on the Braid Hills.

West Linton—a prosperous little former market town astride the drove route south, just below the crossing of the Pentland Hills—seems to have harboured one of several provincial schools of stone carving. James Gifford, a 'portioner' or farmer, was also a self-styled 'architector' and sculptor. 'Gifford's Stone' (1660) set in a cottage wall opposite the Raemartin Hotel, is an impressive monument—'Six Progenetors of Iames Gifferd wi(th)/his awne portract and eldest sone'. In 1666 he also created a cross in memory of his wife and five children. The wife's figure survives, now set above the public well.

### 58* Abbey St Bathan's Kirk, near Duns

*14th-late 18th century AD.*

*NT 758622. At Burnhouses, some 6.5 km W of Preston on B 6355 Chirnside-Cranshaws-Gifford road, take minor road N for about 10 km.*

The ubiquitous dark green paintwork on the interesting range of vernacular house types confirms that Abbey St Bathan's is very much an estate village, built just above a ford on the Whiteadder Water. It is also the site of the ancient Cistercian nunnery of St Botha founded c 1184-1200 by Ada, countess of Dunbar (or alternatively, pre-1214 by the Earl's second wife Christina). The last prioress, Elizabeth Lamb, disposed of the lands of Nunmeadow, Nunbutts and Nunflat to John Renton of Billie in 1558. Inside the church lies a very fine recumbent effigy of a nun, apparently a prioress dressed in a full tunic, her hands joined in prayer and two veils over her head. There are also the remains of a crozier within her right arm—a rare example that confirms not only that priors used the crozier in addition to abbots, but some Cistercian prioresses too. The effigy is probably late 15th-early 16th century, and was rediscovered during repairs to the church in 1856.

As to the church itself, most is late 18th century; only the east wall with its late 14th-century round-headed windows, and lower parts of the north wall remain from an earlier period, whilst the later flavour of Reformation and Presbyterianism is reflected in the wall-painted texts flanking the Table and window at the east end.

Just inside the entrance, a remarkably well-preserved early 18th-century gravestone reflects well not just upon a contemporary minister, George Home, died 1705, but on the concern of his wife, Jean Hamilton, for the endowment after her death in 1719 of a school at Abbey St Bathan's.

## 59* Lyne Kirk, near Peebles

*Mid 17th century AD.*

*NT 191405. A 72 Peebles-Blythe Bridge road some 8 km W of Peebles; on N side of road, just E of Roman fort.*

A dependent chapel of Stobo may have been sited here in the 12th century. It does not seem to have become a parish church until the beginning of the 14th century, however, whilst the present church (restored in 1888) was most probably built between 1640 and 1645 by John Hay of Yester, subsequently 1st Earl of Tweeddale. Small, narrow and of random rubble with mainly pink and grey sandstone dressings, it has a slated roof and may originally have been harled.

The only entrance is now sheltered by a late 19th-century porch, but in plan the church is essentially as it was—a narrow, rectangular building with traceried Gothic windows (east of the porch) which well illustrate a continuity of medieval forms so characteristic of early 17th-century Scottish ecclesiastical architecture. The large pointed window with simple intersecting tracery in the centre of the east gable is also original.

The church's fittings are particularly interesting. Early timber furnishings are rare; at Lyne there are a 17th-century semi-circular oak pulpit and two panelled and canopied oak pews. Small oak panels fixed to the back of each are inscribed with initials L, I, M, Y, and the outline of numerals indicates a date of 1644. The initials are of John Hay and his second wife Margaret, daughter of the 6th Earl of Haddington, whom he married in or after 1641. Pews and pulpit are original therefore, to the building of the present church.

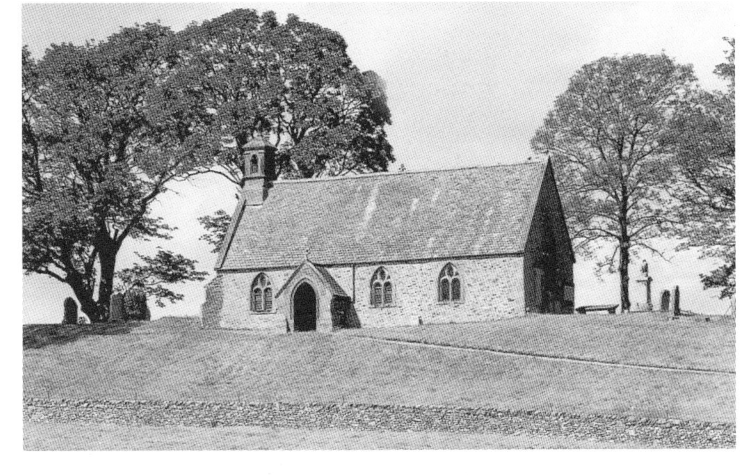

Lyne Kirk

Adam-and-Eve stone, Lyne Kirk

The font is evidently a survival from pre-Reformation times, but none of the tombstones now visible in the churchyard predates 1707. The Adam-and-Eve stone, however, at the east end of the churchyard is decidedly uncommon. Dated

1712, its west face illustrates the Fall. Adam and Eve and the Serpent are shown below the Tree and Knowledge of Good and Evil; above is a skull and the words MEMENTO MORI; elsewhere an hour-glass, for the passing of time. The stone is in memory of Janne(t) Veitch, daughter of John Veitch, tenant in Hamiltoun. She died young at the age of 16 years and 6 weeks.

### 60* Bowden Kirk, near St Boswells

*15th-17th century AD.*

*NT 554301. About 2.5 km along B 6398 W of Newtown St Boswells on A 68; in centre of village take side road S which joins A 699.*

Bowden (Bothenden in 1124) lies just south of the Eildon Hills. It has a much mutilated late 16th-century mercat cross in its attractive main street, a stone-built and slated well of 1861 and a former school, now the Post Office, dated 1831.

**Bowden Kirk**

**Laird's Loft, Bowden Kirk, before re-siting in 1909** (Bottom)

No trace survives of the original church, the property of Kelso Abbey before 1180, and the present building lies steeply above the modest river. It was said to be old, long, narrow and in need of repair in 1793, but though fully restored in 1909, it retains identifiable parts of earlier phases of building. The north wall of the nave may date in part from the 15th century; the east end dates from 1644 and the cross-aisle from 1661; the west gable and a doorway at the west end of the north wall are also 17th century.

Most remarkable, however, is the Laird's Loft, 1661, contemporary with and formerly standing against the archway leading to the cross-aisle in such a way as to divide it horizontally in two. This would suggest that the aisle was intended to have two storeys, with a retiring room behind the Loft and above the burial vault of the Kers of Cavers Carre. The Loft now stands further east; wooden-panelled and canopied, it is raised on wooden shafts. The centre panel contains the Ker shield and crest; the others are painted. On the pediment surmounting the canopy the initials STK stand for Sir Thomas Ker and DGH for Dame Grizel Halket, whilst a painted board running full length below the Loft bears the cheering verse:

> 'Behold the axe Lyes at the Tree's Root
> To hew doune these that Brings not forth
> good fruit
> And when theyre Cut The Lord into his Ire
> Wil them Destroy and Cast into the Fire.'

Outside, a sundial dated 1666 lies at the south-west corner of the church; the bell in the belfrey was made in Edinburgh in 1690 by John Meikel. It is a peaceful, rural churchyard with attractive gates and the usual range of 18th-19th-century gravestones.

### 61* Lauder Kirk

*Later 17th century AD.*

*NT 530475. On W side of A 68 just off main square in centre of Lauder.*

Lauder's parish church displays a most unusual form. Neither T-shaped nor rectangular, it is centrally-planned—a Greek cross with four equal arms spreading from a central crossing, above which four pointed arches carry the central tower.

Square to the length of the roof-ridge, this tower thereafter is octagonal. In the centre of the church beneath the tower stands the pulpit.

The north gable is dated 1673, when it was built by Sir William Bruce for the Duke of Lauderdale who simply requested that it be 'decent and large enough, with a handsom little steeple'. It has a strong vernacular character, and though repaired in 1822 and again in 1864, remains one of the best-preserved centrally-planned churches in Scotland. When built, at least two of the arms contained lofts; and there was an altar in the eastern arm. The ruined watch-house in the churchyard is considerably younger, however, built after a body-snatching raid in 1830.

A few kilometres north of Lauder, just west of the A 68 and astride the line of the Roman road, lies the church at Channelkirk (NT 481545)—a light and airy building in a perpendicular Gothic style. Rectangular in shape, and with an attractive acanthus-ornamented belfrey, its 'chief eyesore is the architectural tumour . . . which the inside stair leading to the gallery has swollen outwards for its own relief'. It was built in 1841, along with manse and garden, to replace an earlier church. The burial ground contains a number of interesting earlier stones, including two from the second/third quarter of the 18th century displaying somewhat roughly sculpted but remarkably detailed figure carvings.

**The cruciform, later 17th-century Kirk at Lauder, with octagonal tower**

## 62* Abercorn Kirk, West Lothian

*12th century and late 16th-mid 18th century AD.*

*NT 081791. At Woodend just W of Newton on A 904 between South Queensferry and Linlithgow; side road N for 3 km and turn N between houses.*

Abercorn is an ancient place. Today's quiet, secluded hamlet belies its former importance but the name itself betrays an early 'British' or 'Cumbric' presence—'the horned river-mouth',

**The Hopetoun loft, Abercorn Kirk**

probably referring to the promontory on which the church is sited, close to where the Midhope Burn meets the Firth of Forth.

Most of the surviving church is 16th century and later, with the north aisle and the belfrey rebuilt in 1893. The building was reconstructed in 1579 and subsequently three burial aisles were added to the south side—the Duddingston aisle (1603), the Binns aisle (1618) and the Philipstoun enclosure (1727). The stylish and splendid Hopetoun Loft at the east end was fitted out in 1708 using the same wood-carver and architect as engaged for Hopetoun House (no. 38). William Eizat carved the elegant foliage and coronets; Sir William Bruce also designed the two-storey Hopetoun aisle on the north side. This had its own semi-circular forecourt and private drive from the House, its own private entrance and a retiral room above, communicating with the Loft. Below is the family burial vault, whilst in the churchyard there are a number of good 17th-18th-century gravestones, some with trade symbols associated with estate crafts and trades such as the gardener.

But Abercorn is more than simply an interesting post-Reformation church. Insignificant in the south wall, sandwiched between the later burial aisles and not to be confused with the neo-Norman west doorway and arcade within, is an original blocked-up 12th-century Norman doorway. It is a simple, small doorway to what was a two-cell church. The arch is decorated with shallowly-carved chevrons whilst the tympanum, just below, carries a diamond or lozenge patterning. This tympanum is one of only two decorated examples known to survive in Scotland—that at Linton in Roxburghshire (NT 773262) has a figural relief unique in Scotland (as well as a fine Norman tomb).

Nothing survives of the even earlier Anglian monastery. But Christianity at Abercorn long pre-dates the Anglo-Normans. Bede writes that its bishop and monks fled to Whitby in AD 685 after the Pictish victory at Nechtansmere—thus confirming a see based on the site by the late 7th century. What do survive, however, are sections of standing crosses of Anglian design, presently sited just off the vestry. The predominance of abstract patterns (as opposed to carvings of human figures, birds and beasts), puts them well into the 8th century. And continuity of a Christian presence is further evidenced by two virtually complete hog-backed tombstones (and fragments of a third) of 11th-12th-century date. Their escalloped and square scaling imitates the shape of roof shingles or tiles (see section 6). The importance of Abercorn in early Christian Scotland should not be underestimated, nor its vulnerable position for so long in a frontier zone between British, Pictish, Anglian and Scottish areas of interest.

**Abercorn Kirk retains a 12th-century Norman doorway**

# 6 PRE-REFORMATION CHURCHES, ABBEYS AND EARLY CHRISTIAN STONES

**The medieval open crown steeple of St Michael's, Linlithgow, was taken down c 1821**

South-east Scotland is at least as rich in ecclesiastical buildings as in secular castles. They range from the late medieval burgh and collegiate churches, back through the great abbeys and more modest parish churches of Anglo-Norman foundation, to the Anglian monastic sites of the Northumbrian period—800 or so years all told.

In the 15th and early 16th centuries there was a real flowering of ecclesiastical architecture, particularly in Lothian. The larger towns were flourishing and their merchants and craftsmen sought to immortalise their prosperity in a grandiose show of municipal piety. Earlier burgh churches had either been destroyed (Linlithgow) or decayed; these new buildings were made to last and St Giles in Edinburgh (later 14th century), St Michael's in Linlithgow (NT 002772) and St Mary's in Haddington (no. 68) were all constructed on a particularly lavish scale. Though very different in general conception, Haddington and Linlithgow are both cruciform, aisled churches with transepts. Linlithgow is more English or French in character with a west tower, south porch and perpendicular in much of its style; Haddington has a central tower, fully developed crossing, and aisles in the nave as well as the choir. It seems to have had a crown spire like that of St Giles and (formerly) Linlithgow.

Such churches are not typical, however, of the period. More usual, equally impressive, but architecturally less inventive are the collegiate churches, endowed by the landed proprietors. But a stage removed from their baronial ancestors, they preferred to found non-monastic institutions rather than abbeys or parish churches (though some incorporated earlier churches). Within, chantry priests, choirboys and servers delivered masses for the founder's family. Most of the surviving collegiate churches are in Lothian, though the remarkable Ladykirk (no. 63) in Berwickshire, founded by James IV, might be seen as a parallel; and St Andrew's, Peebles, was established in 1543 by John Hay of Yester for a provost, 12 prebendaries and 2 choristers. Burnt by the English in 1545, the tower was strongly restored in 1882. At Dalkeith (NT 332674) and Seton (no. 64), the choirs are polygon-ended; at Corstorphine (NT 200727), Crichton (NT 380616) and Dunglass (no. 65) they are square-ended. Midcalder (NT 073673) was intended as a collegiate church, whilst Restalrig in Edinburgh (NT 283744) had the dubious distinction of being the first church in Scotland 'a monument of idolatrie, [to] be raysit and utterlie castin down and destroyed' in 1560. Its interesting, hexagonal, St Triduana's Well-House survives (no. 66).

**Temple Old Kirk, Midlothian**

Many of these churches had a semi-Baronial flavour—heavy vaulting, crow-stepped gables, battlements, partly reflecting the unsettled times and wars with England (features even more apparent at Torphichen Preceptory, no. 70), but also the fact that they were built by the same masons as the Baronial castles. To the extent that it had no parish and that it remained in private hands after the Reformation, Roslin (no. 67) was atypical. Also atypical in its effusively ornate carving, it had sought to rival the royal collegiate foundation of Trinity College Church, demolished in 1848 in favour of Edinburgh's Waverley Station. Roslin, however, like so many other collegiate churches was never completed; money ran out and the Reformation intervened.

Some of the monastic foundations in south-east Scotland were relatively late, triggered by teams of missionary mendicant friars during the 13th-16th centuries. The Trinitarian Priory of Cross Kirk, Peebles (no. 69) was founded in 1474 (though possibly from 1296, and with additional houses in Dirleton and Dunbar, (1540-48); the Franciscan friary in Jedburgh was founded in 1513 and Roxburgh c 1232-33; and the Carmelite friary at South Queensferry (NT 128784) perhaps in 1441. Most abbeys and priories, however, were firmly established by the end of the 13th century, the most notable generally being those founded by David I. Cistercians were represented at Melrose, 1136 (no. 76) and Newbattle, 1140 (destroyed); Augustinians at Holyrood, 1128 (NT 269739), Jedburgh, 1138 (no. 78) and Soutra, c 1164 (no. 71); Reformed Augustinians (Premonstratensians) at Dryburgh, 1140 (no. 77); Benedictines at Coldingham, c 1147 (no. 75), Reformed Benedictines (Tironensians) at Kelso, 1128 (no. 79); Knights Hospitallers at Torphichen, 1168 (no. 70).

Each of the monasteries presents a distinctive architectural face: the remarkable two-storey division and continuous arcading at Coldingham; the mighty north gable and double transepts of Kelso; the reconstructed 15th-century decorated magnificence of Melrose; the fine range of cloisters at romantic Dryburgh; the superbly complete nave, crossing and transepts at Jedburgh; the most harmonious west front of Holyrood; the solid, defensive central tower of Torphichen. At root, however, all these various buildings adhered to a basic plan whereby a quadrangular courtyard, surrounded by cloisters which housed the monks' domestic and administrative quarters, was attached to the south wall of the church —exceptionally, the north wall of Cross Kirk. And in addition to their spiritual lives, the monks 'cultivated their own gardens'. Not only did they establish hospitals, 'spittals', to care for travellers and the sick, they were also the first agricultural improvers, planting trees and orchards, instituting good agricultural practice, developing sheep husbandry and the woollen trade to Europe from their 'granges'. The estates linked to their endowments were vast indeed, and perhaps not entirely in-keeping with their founders' driving motives! For the wealth generated would have been enormous. Indeed, only monks could have afforded the specialist tradesmen and labourers to engineer the lengthy shaped-stone and timber flood barriers discovered close to Newstead village during the 1995 drought. Hundreds of timbers, perhaps 6 m long by 15 cm square, appeared above the water—evidence of a huge project probably designed to halt bank erosion and to maximise the agricultural potential of the fertile riverside water meadows. They are remarkably similar to the structures constructed to divert the River Wye at Rievaulx Abbey in North Yorkshire—and Melrose was founded in 1136 by monks from Rievaulx.

In introducing the monastic orders alongside Anglo-Norman barons, the Canmore dynasty was deliberately altering the political, religious and physical face of Scotland, and nowhere was this more strongly felt than in the south and east. Parish priests were also introduced, helping create a parochial division of the countryside very much still extant. Agriculturally it was no accident that each parish held a combination of fertile, cultivable land and extensive upland grazings for stock. It was no accident, politically, that so often parish church and Norman castle stood close together and that barony and parish covered much the same area—twin symbols of power and direction.

**The late 15th-century aisle, Edrom Kirk, is said to have been founded by Robert Blackadder, Archbishop of Glasgow**
(Far right)

**Stained glass window to Queen Margaret, wife of Malcolm III, mother of David I: 12th-century St Margaret's Chapel, Edinburgh Castle**

With such emphasis on abbeys and monasteries, it would be all-too-easy to forget the four Cistercian nunneries—Berwick (1153-1390/91), Coldstream (pre 1166), Eccles (NT 763412: founded 1156, with fragmentary survivals in the churchyard and 1774 parish church) and Abbey St. Bathans (no. 58). It would equally be easy to forget the 'hospitals' established both by religious orders and by secular clergy from 1164 until the early 16th century to care for the ill, infirm and poor, and to provide shelter for travellers and pilgrims. There are nearly 20 such sites in the Borders alone, including Cockburnspath, Duns, Hutton, Jedburgh, Ednam, Ancrum, Roxburgh, Rulemouth, Legerwood, Lauder and Eshiels (near Peebles), not forgetting the better-known site at Soutra (no. 71). Their social and medical importance cannot be over-estimated.

Surviving parish churches are relatively few, however, for unlike England few were enlarged or rebuilt in the later Middle Ages, and since the population was generally sparse and scattered, many small, simple churches were merely dependent chapels rather than sizeable independent churches. And where appropriated to monasteries, their revenues had equally been appropriated! Neglect and decay took its toll. The most remarkable Norman church must be Dalmeny (no. 74), though good sections survive at Stobo (no. 72) and individual features at St Andrew's, Gullane (NT 480827), St Martin's, Haddington (NT 521739), Duddingston (NT 283726), Borthwick (NT 368596), Keith by Humbie (NT 448645), Kirkliston (NT 124743), Uphall (NT 059722), Abercorn (no. 62), Linton (NT 773262), Edrom (no. 73), Legerwood (NT 593434), Chirnside (NT 870560) and Smailholm (NT 649364). St Baldred's near Tyninghame (NT 619796) must once have been as splendid as Dalmeny, though in most other churches carving and decoration had been fairly spare. Southdean (NT 631091), apart from its ground plan, is of more interest nowadays perhaps for its massive but simple, early 17th-century graveslabs.

However much or little survives, such churches were rectangular buildings, of two or three cells—nave, chancel, and sometimes a square- or apsidal-ended sanctuary. Some roofs might be vaulted inside as at Dalmeny (which like Stobo had a western tower); outside they would have been thatched or covered with wooden shingles.

Of the Christian church before David I (1124-53) there are few enough survivals. Northumbrian Christianity brought by Anglian settlers had established a bishop's see and monastery at Abercorn (no. 62) by AD 685 and there was a monastery at Tyninghame by the mid 800s—maybe even before 756, during St Baldred's lifetime. But nothing survives of these; less even than the ditched embankments associated with mid 7th-century Columban monasteries at Old Melrose (NT 588340) and possibly also at St. Abbs Head (NT 910694)—both of them promontory sites, and both established within 35 years of the Anglian victory over the British and Scots at the battle of Degsaston (603 AD). Both were founded following the foundation of Lindisfarne by St Aidan from Iona, at the invitation of the Northumbrian King Oswald. The Cumric name [Old] Melrose suggests there may well also have been an earlier British monastery.

**Mid 12th-century church of St Baldred, Tyninghame**

**Well-weathered hogback tombstone, St Helen's or Old Cambus Kirk, near Cocksburnpath**

It was the Northumbrian blend of Christianity, however, that has left the several hog-backed tombstones at the churches of Ancrum (NT 621248), Nisbet (NT 673257), Bedrule (no. 56), Lempitlaw (NT 788327), Edrom (no. 73), Old Cambus (NT 803796), as well as at Abercorn (no. 62) and at the splendidly preserved abbey on Inchcolm in the Forth (NT 189826). Dated to the 10th-12th century they are of a type thought to have been developed by Scandinavians in northern England. The sloping sides represent a roof: roof-tiles or shingles, sometimes also a roof-ridge, are carved on the 'roof', and the end panels occasionally appear as 'gables'.

Nothing remains in south-east Scotland to match the mid 8th-century Ruthwell Cross in Dumfriesshire, but particularly interesting 8th to 9th-century fragments of Anglian crosses survive at Abercorn (no. 62), with others at Jedburgh (no. 78) and at Aberlady Church (cast: original in NMS). The Innerleithen cross-shaft (no. 81) is probably late 9th century. The culture that produced such early incised Christian stones as the Cat Stane west of Edinburgh and those erected near the Yarrow Water (no. 82), Manor Water (Kirkhope: now in Peebles Museum) and Liddesdale, however, was associated with native British tribes rather than

Northumbrian Angles. The style of the Latin inscriptions, and the British personal names recorded, suggest a late 5th- or 6th-century date with affinities to similar stones in Wales and Cornwall. This then was a British Christianity, infiltrating north and east after the late 5th century —a Christianity which seems to have been independent of frameworks established by Ninian and Columba, which seems to have been established on some kind of 'parish' format, and which seems to reflect the survival into the post-Roman period of an apparently autonomous native 'state'. The inscribed fish at Borthwick Mains (no. 83) probably belongs to the same tradition. Contemporary cemeteries of stone-lined long cists, aligned east-west and without gravegoods, suggest a fairly large population of small, Christianised Celtic (British) agricultural communities, particularly in fertile Lothian, and also reflected, in part at least, by surviving 'Eccles' placenames north and south of the lower Tweed.

The Morham cross-shaft fragment and the Liddesdale Stone are in NMS, along with the exceptional Over Kirkhope 'orans'—a small, crudely cut standing figure in stone, commemorating a hermit who had chosen a life of austerity and devotion in the remote solitude of the Ettrick hills.

**The orans from Over Kirkhope**
(Far left)

**Two sides of the 8th-century cross shaft fragment, Aberlady Church**
(in NMS)

## 63* Ladykirk, near Coldstream

*Early 16th century AD.*

*NT 888476. Some 12 km NE of Coldstream, just N of B 6470 cross-border road, Swinton-Norham, close to N bank of River Tweed.*

A nearby ford on the Tweed was in use until 1839 when superseded by a wooden bridge on stone piers. Many invading armies once crossed the river at this point and tradition says that the church was built by James IV c 1500-13 and dedicated to the Virgin Mary in thanks for his deliverance from drowning whilst crossing in a sudden spate. Ladykirk is generally identified as the 'Kirk of Steill' (*stell*: a deep pool where salmon nets were set), as specified in royal accounts of 1500-13. After the Reformation the church combined the ancient parishes of Upsettlington and Horndean, both recorded in the 12th century.

It is a remarkably complete example of the final development of the Gothic style in Scotland. Greatly altered internally in the first half of the 19th century, when the west end was separated off and used as a school, in 1861 the division was removed and the church repaired and restored.

Cruciform but aisleless, the ends of the choir and transepts are rounded or apsidal. A further major feature is the pointed, stone-vaulted nave and chancel roof, strengthened by a series of splayed ribs resting on small, moulded corbels. This roof is responsible for the massive appearance of the exterior. On the one hand, the huge external buttresses, matched to the ends of the ribs, were necessary supports for the heavy roof of overlapping stones. Equally, the line from which the main roof vault springs internally determined the upper limit of the window arches—hence the large expanse of plain external walling between the tops of the aisles and the wall-head.

In the apses and north wall, the windows comprise two or three pointed lights in the traceried heads; on the south side, to make the openings as wide as possible, the arched heads are elliptical.

The upper part of the tower with its classical cuploa, said to be the work of the elder Adam, was added c 1743 and further embellished in 1882 with a Victorian clock face. The lower three floors, however, similar to towers in Northern England, seem to have been designed for defence. Some 2.5 m square internally, with walls 1 m and more thick, there is no access at ground level from the church; by contrast the only access to the upper floors is by a turnpike stair from within the church. The upper floors provided the priest's quarters, and a small window at first-floor level, now blocked up, looked into the church. Each of the three floors had a strong, substantial door and a stone vaulted roof, later pierced to accommodate bell ropes.

The lowest room has a good range of mason's marks—on the underside of the doorway arch, on the walls and on the vaulted roof. It was later used as a prison (the jougs, an iron collar and chain, hang outside), and in this respect bears certain resemblances to the larger, later tower surviving at the west end of Greenlaw Kirk (NT 711461). Built as a jail in 1696, Greenlaw's tower and now-vanished courthouse were added to the west side of the church when this was lengthened in 1712:

> 'Here stands the Gospel and the Law
> Wi' Hell's hole atween the twa!'

## 64* Seton Collegiate Church, East Lothian

*Late 15th-mid 16th century AD.*

*NT 418751. Just N of A 198 Musselburgh-Longniddry road, about 3.5 km N of Tranent; signposted.*

*Historic Scotland.*

An unaisled 13th-century parish church is represented by the ruinous side walls of a nave that may never have been rebuilt when the collegiate church was begun. By contrast, the foundations of a rectangular building protruding westwards from the south transept are those of a chapel added by Catherine Sinclair of 'Hermandston', wife of the 1st Lord Seton c 1434.

The present choir and sacristy were built in part by the 3rd Lord (died c 1478); the 4th completed the vaulting and founded the College in 1492; the 5th, who fell at Flodden in 1513, roofed the choir with stone slabs and provided glazed windows, stalls and canopies above the altar. His widow Janet Seton added the north transept in 1541, and in 1545

rebuilt the south transept so as 'to make it ane perfyt and proportionat croce kirk'. She also 'biggit up the steeple as ye see it now to ane grit hight swa that it wants little of compleiting'. It seems never to have been completed, however.

Internally, the crossing appears spatially separate from the rest of the church (cf Dunglass, no. 65), and the surviving part of the former Carmelite friary church at South Queensferry, NT 128784). The square rib- vaulted tower is also unusual in that the spire to which it is coupled is octagonal. The way in which the faces are alternately widened and narrowed allows it to be called a broach tower—though of a French rather than English type.

As with many late medieval Scottish churches, the east walls of the transepts are windowless; the choir, meantime, terminates in a three-sided, buttressed apse and like the rest of the interior (save for the crossing) is tunnel-vaulted. Around the choir there has been a stone seat; in the south wall is a 15th-century piscina or basin for washing out communion or mass vessels and next to it, unusually high up, a single-recessed sedilia or priest's seat.

Next to a second piscina in the south transept, an elaborate Renaissance monument commemorates James, 1st Earl of Perth, husband of Lady Isobel Seton, died 1611. Other 17th- and 18th-century monuments commemorate Ogilvies, Setons and Wintons.

**The crossing and chancel, Seton Colliegate Church**

**Seton bell**

(Top left)

Though well preserved the church suffered after the Reformation, and by the mid 19th century bays and windows were blocked up and one transept used as a carpenter's shop.

## 65 Dunglass Collegiate Church, near Cockburnspath

*Mid 15th century AD.*

*NT 766718. 1.5 km N of Cockburnspath a minor road branches W off A 1; some 800 m to the church, on the Dunglass estate; signposted.*

*Historic Scotland.*

Collegiate status was confirmed by James II to Sir Alexander Hume in 1450. The church may have been founded, however, in 1443, based on an earlier, probably private chapel of 1403. Dedicated

**Dunglass Colliegate Church, near Cocksburnpath**

**Sedilia and holes for either scaffolding or upper floor joists, Dunglass**

to the Virgin Mary, it had three chaplains (one of whom was also provost) and four choir boys or servers. By the 18th century it was used as a stable and barn.

Originally conceived without transepts and tower, the church was replanned as a cruciform structure before the vaulted roofs were laid. The stocky, square tower stands within, rather than above the crossing, presumably to give as wide transepts as possible. The choir, to which a priest's door enters from the south transept, retains an attractive triple sedilia (priest's seat) with corbels depicting winged and long-haired angels playing a harp and a lute. There are consecration crosses in the choir and sacristy, tomb recesses in the sacristy and transepts, and several 17th-century tombstones in the north transept. The tower, accessible it would seem only by a ladder to a doorway high above the west arch, had three storeys and a garret in the spire—the corbels once supporting the floor beams. Three tiers of holes in the vaults of the nave and choir, however, rather than supporting beams for scaffolding during construction are more likely to be later additions to support floors inserted when the church was secularised.

Dunglass was a key point on the north-south coastal route, strategically placed just north of the difficult Pease Burn gorge. Four bridges in all crossed the Dunglass Dean—two post-road bridges of 1797 and 1798 (the first collapsed), a spectacular railway viaduct of c 1840 and the A 1 road bridge of 1931.

## 66* St Triduana's Chapel/Well, Restalrig, Edinburgh

*Late 15th century AD.*

*NT 284744. Between Edinburgh city centre and Portobello, at junction of A1/London Road (Jock's Lodge), go N on Restalrig Road South. Restalrig Parish Church is close to Marionville Avenue/Restalrig Avenue crossroads; signposted.*

*Historic Scotland.*

The parish church (1836) incorporates parts of the walls of the choir of James III's 1487 Collegiate church, known as the Deanery of Restalrig. This 15th-century church had been built on the site of an earlier church, recorded in the 12th century; however, because Logan of Restalrig condemned the new Protestant church's views on sexual morality, it became the first church in Scotland to suffer at the Reformation. On 21 December 1560, the General Assembly decreed that 'his Kirk of Restalrig, as a Monument of Idolatrie, be raysit and utterlie castin downe and destroyed'. Little remained after the stone was carted away to build houses in Edinburgh and to rebuild the Netherbow Port. The undercroft of St Triduana's Chapel, however, has survived on the south-west of the later church (restored by Thomas Ross in 1906).

**St Triduana's Chapel or Well-House, Restalrig, Edinburgh** (Left)

The hexagonal ashlar building, with late gothic mullioned windows in each of the three south sides, is reinforced by a projecting buttress at each angle. Like the upper chapel, the surviving undercroft is vaulted. Normally in a polygonal building, the vault-ribs are sprung in semi-circular or pointed arcs from the central pillar to the wall-shafts. In this hexagonal building, however, whilst the hexagonal vault does indeed spring from a central 6-shafted pillar, the ribs that spring from each wall-shaft extend to that in the opposite angle, while the ridge ribs (or mid-ribs) run horizontally to an intermediate ceiling boss and then flow down to the central pillar. Four of the bosses have foliage carvings; two others have blank shields. Elsewhere, the mouldings and carvings are all charcteristic of the 1440s-1470s.

The stone benches around the wall reinforce the undercroft's use a chapel or chater house, rather than simply a well or a burial vault. That St Triduana's Chapel has periodically filled with water may be more to do with water-tables and its relatively low-lying position, though it may nonetheless, in some way, have been associated with a sacred spring. In style it is not dissimilar to a miniature version, the so-called St Margaret's Well under Arthur's Seat, close to the Palace of Holyroodhouse and removed there from near Restalrig in 1859.

The main church has a 13th-century font which lay for long in the courtyard of Craigentinny House; and in what remains of old Restalrig village, two houses date from 1678—the Wricht's House at 62 Restalrig Road South, and Dunira in a row of old houses opposite the church. In the early 19th century, Restalrig was still a tiny village—by all accounts a pretty rundown area of market gardens supplying the Edinburgh markets with fruit and vegetables and 'pick-your-own' strawberries. In return it received the capital's waste water courtesy of the 'River' Tumble (now culverted), which drained each side of the Old Town ridge.

### 67* Roslin Chapel, Midlothian

*Mid 15th century AD.*

*NT 274630. Off A 701 Penicuik-Edinburgh road take B 7003 or B 7006 E to Roslin; at crossroads, cul-de-sac SE; signposted.*

The Collegiate Church of St Matthew stands high on the west bank of the North Esk, a short distance from the picturesque ruin of the 15th-century Sinclair castle. Replacing an earlier chapel, the church was established by William Sinclair, 3rd Earl of Orkney, c 1447: 'he caused artificers to be brought from other regions and forraigne kingdomes, and caused dayly to be abundance of all kind of workmen present, as masons, carpenters, smiths, barrowmen, and quarriers . . .'.

**Flying buttresses and south door, Roslin Chapel**

**The Apprentice Pillar, Roslin Chapel**

The chapel was 'completed' by his son Oliver, though complete it is not. Cruciform in intention, and to be comparable in scale with Edinburgh's vanished royal foundation, Trinity College, only the choir was built and parts of the east transept walls. A stair leads down to the sacristy some 5.2 m lower.

The choir has two aisles, with a third transverse aisle or ambulatory east of the sanctuary. Its four eastern chapels, reminiscent of 12th-century Cistercian forms, probably reflect the influence of the destroyed late 12th-century church at the Cistercian abbey of Newbattle nearby, and Glasgow Cathedral c 1230.

Roslin is extraordinary, however, not so much for the size that it failed to attain, but for its stone carving. Every conceivable roof rib, capital, boss, arch and corbel is encrusted—whether with human or animal figures, mouldings or foliage. Such a collection would be remarkable anywhere, in any age, but much the more so given the plainness and severity of late medieval Scottish architecture—apostles, martyrs, the Dance of Death, angels playing musical instruments, the Seven Virtuous Acts, the Seven Deadly Sins. . . . Best known perhaps, but only one of a galaxy of marvels, the Prentice Pillar incorporates four strands of 'foliage' each starting from one of the base corners and spiralling through 180° to the top. And around the base, winged serpents, necks intertwined, bite their own tails. The quite recent legend (a universal folk tale!) tells of the apprentice's initiative whilst the master-mason was abroad seeking inspiration; on his return, jealous master-mason kills apprentice with mallet.

The Sinclairs of Roslin and Orkney had strong associations with the military religious order of the Knights Templar from its foundation in the 12th century until its suppression by the Pope in 1312. William Sinclair (more-or-less a contemporary of Henry Sinclair who began the building of Rosslyn Castle c 1330) had been a Templar Grand Prior; and in 1441, William Sinclair (initiator of Roslin Chapel in 1447) was appointed Grand Master of the craft masons—predecessors in Scotland of the Freemasons and other 'hard and soft guilds'.

Roslin Chapel has long been the focus of speculation. Traditionally it was said to be the resting place of the Holy Grail; recently it has been suggested that during the Crusades, Templars rescued the Lost Gospel from beneath the foundations of Herod's temple in Jerusalem and in later centuries brought it for reinterment and safekeeping to Roslin. And it has been further suggested that the Roslin carvings incorporate both Templar and Masonic symbolism.

Speculation apart, Roslin was undoubtedly the most ambitious of all collegiate churches in Scotland. Amongst so much Gothic extravaganza, however, it is as great a surprise to see still such a strongly Scottish feature as pointed tunnel-vaulting. Reminiscent of both military and domestic architecture, this underlines how Scottish and independent Roslin really is!

The Old Roslin Inn dates from 1660. It lies adjacent to the Chapel, and traditionally the innkeeper was

also the chapel's custodian. Its 18th-century re-glazed windows bear the scratched graffiti of such illustrious tourists as Robert Burns, Walter Scott, Johnson and Boswell, and the Wordsworths!

A track beside the old inn leads through woodland and across a narrow bridge to Henry Sinclair, 1st Earl of Orkney's Rosslyn Castle, begun c 1330, but mainly 15th-17th century. It was substantially destroyed by the Earl of Hertford's English army in 1544. Derelict until 1982, parts of the east range (largely late 16th-17th century) have been conserved: 2 residential floors (some rooms with 17th-century panelling) visible from the courtyard; and a further 3 service floors below, vaulted and cut into the precipitous rock-face overhanging the Glen. In the west range, the 15th-century round machicolated keep remains largely derelict, as is an associated building divided into 7 arched bays after the manner of French chateaux.

**The Seven Virtues: laying out the dead, and St Peter with the Keys of Heaven, Roslin Chapel**

**Amongst the Vices** (Top left) **and The Sleeping King** (Left)**, south aisle lintel**

## 68* St Mary's Church, Haddington, East Lothian

*Mid 15th century AD.*

*NT 518736. Just S of centre of Haddington on A 6137 to Humbie; signposted.*

*Historic Scotland (Lauderdale Aisle).*

The church of St Mary the Virgin claims to be the largest parish church in Scotland. It was built during the 'boom-time' of the late 14th-late 15th century, when greater prosperity encouraged the building or rebuilding of a number of burgh kirks. It is second in Lothian only to Edinburgh's St Giles, and is comparable in size to the smaller Scottish cathedrals. The church is cruciform, with an aisled

**Slezer's view of St Mary's Church, Haddington and the Nungate Bridge, with unenclosed, ridge and furrow field system in foreground**

nave and choir; the transepts are unaisled. Above the crossing the massive tower is thought once to have had (or been promised) an open crown in the manner of St Giles.

Stone vaulting was commonplace within, except for the timber-roofed nave. In the restoration of 1971-73, the choir and transept vaults (ruinous since their destruction in the siege of Haddington in 1548), were re-formed in fibre glass; the nave's plaster vaulting, however, is an unjustified reconstruction from 1811 when the aisle walls were raised and English-looking parapets and pinnacles added.

**Alabaster effigies within the Lauderdale monument** (Top right) **and the Lauderdale burial vault** (Right)**, St Mary's Church, Haddington**

The former sacristy projects from the north aisle of the choir. Partly pre-Reformation, it was largely rebuilt in the 17th century since when it has been used as a burial aisle and houses a remarkable Renaissance marble monument to John Maitland, Lord Thirlestane, Chancellor of Scotland under James VI (died 1595), to his wife Jane Fleming and to their son John, 1st Earl of Lauderdale (see no. 39). Elsewhere, the Scallop Shell (west end) records early pilgrimages between St Mary's and the church of St James of Campostela in north-west Spain, whilst the Colours in the nave are those of the Haddington Militia (Napoleonic Wars: 1810) and the 8th Battalion, The Royal Scots (World War I: 1914). Beneath lies the Lauderdale family vault. The churchyard contains a number of interesting 18th-century table-tombs.

The late 12th-century St Martin's Church (NT 521739: Historic Scotland) stands near the edge of the town on the by-road to Whittingehame. A two-cell rectangular building with only the nave remaining, it is an interesting ruin with 13th-century buttresses built to support the pointed barrel-vaulted roof.

## 69 Cross Kirk, Peebles

*Late 13th-late 15th century AD.*

*NT 250407. In Peebles, about 1 km N of river and A 72, and about 500 m W of A 703; signposted.*

*Historic Scotland.*

The original late 13th-century church consisted of an aisleless nave, chancel and sacristy. It forms the bulk of the surviving structure. The north wall of the nave rises to something like its original height; the east end of the south wall is also fairly complete, as well as the main doorway in the west gable. In its pre 17th-century form, the chancel seems not to have been separated from the nave.

Fordun records that a 'magnificent and venerable' cross had been found in 1261, lying on a stone inscribed with 'the place of Saint Nicholas the bishop'. The surviving fragments of a sculptured sandstone slab portraying an ecclesiastic, presumably St Nicholas, are, however, mid 16th century in date (cast: original in Tweeddale Museum). The church was apparently completed and the shrine dedicated in 1268, and a cult of St Nicholas developed, for pilgrimages are known to have been made at least from the later 14th to the early 17th century.

Consequently, the late 15th-century Trinitarian Priory church and tower were designed from the first to incorporate shrine and relics; and in order not to enclose or conceal this, the now-fragmentary priory buildings were added, unusually, to the north side of the church.

A more recent addition to the north wall is the burial site of the Douglas Earls of March, dating from 1705; adjoining the south wall at the point where formerly the feretory or repository for the saintly relics was located, stands the aisle of the Earls of Maxton and later the Erskines of Venlaw, mainly 18th or 19th century.

Abandoned at the Reformation, the cloister and associated buildings were used to isolate plague victims in 1666; and schools were held there in the early 18th century. By 1796, however, little remained.

**Cross Kirk, Peebles**

## 70* Torphichen Preceptory, West Lothian

*Late 12th—15th century AD.*

*NS 968725. In village of Torphichen on B 792 between Bathgate and Linlithgow; signposted.*

*Historic Scotland.*

The Hospital or Preceptory of Torphichen was the only Scottish seat of the Knights Hospitallers or Knights of the Order of St John of Jerusalem, a military religious order founded in 1099 which, in its religious life, followed the rules of St Augustine. Granted a charter by David I before his death in 1153, and mentioned in 1168, it stands in a sheltered little valley on the western side of the Torphichen Hills. By the late 12th-early 13th century, the aisleless nave, transepts, choir and central tower had all been built—though not necessarily all at once. In the 15th century the transepts and crossing were reconstructed and heightened; and the nave continued in use as the parish church until replaced in 1756 by the present T-plan church alongside.

**Torphichen Preceptory** (Right) **and reconstruction with cloister** (Above)

Nave and choir, which had remained low and wooden-roofed, have almost completely disappeared, as have the domestic buildings to the north; the transept and tower were used as the courthouse of the Regality of Torphichen after the Reformation—the reason no doubt for their survival!

Transepts and crossings are almost equal in size. A late 14th-century turnpike stair leads from the north transept to the mainly 13th-century vaulted tower with bell-chamber above, and when the transepts were heightened, doors were put through from the bell-chamber. Also in the north transept, the central roof-vault boss is inscribed 'IHS' encircled by 'Maria', whilst one of the ridge ribs refers to Sir Andrew Meldrum, Preceptor in the 1430s. By contrast, on the wall-plaster of the south transept a fragmentary working drawing survives for the wedge-shaped stones of one of the arches (similar constructional drawings survive at Roslin Chapel: no. 67).

The wide semi-circular Transitional wall at the west side of the crossing once led to the nave. Here two sculptured panels survive from a 16th-century monument commissioned by Sir Walter Lindsay for his maternal uncle, Sir George Dundas, whom he succeeded as preceptor in 1532. An illegible tombstone to Robert Boyd of Kipps, advocate (1645) lies in the south transept floor.

Within the Preceptory churchyard stands a cross-inscribed stone believed to mark the centre of the privileged sanctuary ground. It also bears prehistoric cup-marks. Other stones about 1.5 km from the centre indicated the limit of the legal sanctuary granted to criminals, debtors and others who entered and remained within its precincts. Such Refuge Stones lurk near Westfield (NT 943721), North Couston (NS 956707) and east of Gormyre Farm (NS 980731).

Not to be confused with the Knights of St John are the Knights Templar (founded c 1118), whose main Scottish house was at Temple in Midlothian (NT 315587) from the mid 12th century until their suppression in 1312—when all their properties passed to the Hospitallers. The surviving building at Temple cannot be earlier than late 13th-mid 14th century, though it re-uses some 12th-century masonry. There is a very fine gravestone alongside, dated 1742 and depicting farmer John Craig of Outerston in a long coat, bonnet and knotted scarf, accompanied by his two sons.

### 71 Soutra Aisle, Midlothian

*Later 12th century.*

*NT 452584. 1 km along B 6368 SW of its junction with A 68 at foot of Soutra Hill; on top of ridge.*

Though now cultivated, the top of Soutra at the western end of the Lammermuirs is a bleak place on anything but the most attractive, clear and sunny day. Its name comes from old Cumric/British *sulw tref*, homestead/settlement of the wide view. Here, in or before 1164, Malcolm IV of Scotland founded a house 'domus Soltre' as a hospice for travellers, pilgrims and poor folk travelling through Lauderdale, to and from Edinburgh and England. Dedicated to the Holy Trinity, it included an Augustinian Church and held considerable lands, particularly in East Lothian and Berwickshire—all of which (and their associated wealth) were annexed in 1462 to the new foundation of Trinity College in Edinburgh.

After the Reformation the church ceased to have any parochial charge, the buildings became ruinous and c 1850, as part of agricultural improvement, most of the stonework was carted away to build field dykes and farm steadings. Only 'ane Isle of the Abbace' remained, that had been appropriated by 1686 as a burial aisle for the Pringles of Soutra.

The surviving low, rectangular structure, about 8 m long, is widely visible and covered by an outer stone roof over a barrel-vault. The west gable has a moulded, lintelled doorway with an incised stone set in above, dated 1686, with initials referring to David Pringle and his wife Agnes Pringle. A late 18th-century grave-slab adorns the east gable wall.

Archaeological excavation in recent years has uncovered remnants of the Soutra hospital. North of the 17th-century burial aisle, a substantial range of 14th-century buildings overlie the mid 12th-early 13th-century church. Cellars with capped drains and a chute soakaway have yielded remains of cloves, opium poppy, hemlock and black henbane, all of which suggest that mixtures of herbs and grease were probably used to treat (war) wounds. Some plant-based drugs perhaps kept patients unconscious during and following operations. Others were associated with induced childbirth and abortion, both of which were illegal in connection with monks and priests. In the soakaways, limestone bands were possibly used as a disinfectant, whilst anthrax spores and evidence for scurvy further illustrate problems for the hospital's patients and staff.

Analysis of DNA extracted from blood and bones in the hospital waste pit may eventually identify diseases such as measles and tuberculosis; perhaps also 'English sweating sickness', a mystery illness that killed thousands in medieval times—a forerunner, perhaps, of contemporary flu-like infections? It may also help identify other diseases that modern medicine claims to have mastered, or that seemingly disappeared hundreds of years ago. The adjacent burial ground contains perhaps 20,000 burials from the 12th century onwards—including mass graves, presumably for the victims of plagues of smallpox, anthrax, typhus and typhoid.

South of Soutra Aisle the line of Dere Street, alias the Roman Road, and for a short way alias the Girthgate, makes its way down to the burn (NT 464567-472553). Rising again through King's Inch, through the gap between the plantations it runs on to Channelkirk and Oxton. 'Girthgate', the 'sanctuary-enclosure road', indicates its special relationship to the foundation at Soutra.

### 72* Stobo Kirk, near Peebles

*12th-16th century AD.*

*NT 182376. Halfway along B 712 Lyne-Drumelzier road, some 12 km SW of Peebles; W of road.*

In medieval times St Mungo's of Stobo was the most important church in the upper Tweed Valley, centrally sited to serve the later parishes of Stobo, Lyne, Broughton, Drumelzier and Tweedsmuir, and close to the all-important east-west route through the Biggar Gap.

The original 12th-century church (founded 1127) comprised a rectangular nave, a square-headed chancel and a west tower which, not quite square to the church, may have been built separately and certainly seems to have been rebuilt above first-floor level in the 16th century. Surviving Norman

**Stobo Kirk**

**Medieval tombstone, Stobo Kirk**

features include the plain, semi-circular south doorway, now approached through a 15th or 16th-century stone-bench lined porch whose jambs have been grooved by children, so it is said, sharpening slate-pencils in the days when the parish school was housed within! Another Norman doorway, now a window, stands in the north wall of the nave; in the north wall of the chancel, two round-headed slits, originally 12th century, retain faint traces of painted decoration.

In the 15th-16th century, the porch and two windows were added to the south wall and a much wider window to the east chancel wall. Of similar pre-Reformation date are the lower parts of the north chapel, originally a mortuary or chantry chapel, and almost completely rebuilt in 1928.

The church has some fine monuments, notably three recumbent tombstones set in the north chapel walls. One commemorates Robert Vessy, died 1473, sometime vicar of Stobo; another an unknown warrior. Probably dating to the first half 16th century, this reveals a grotesque, crudely inscribed figure of an armoured man lying on his back, hands clasped on his chest and feet splayed. The third stone, fragmentary, bears an incised mill-rynd and probably recalls a miller. Considerably earlier is part of a 12th-century coped stone, with a shingle-type decoration.

Outside, a set of jougs (a favourite early 18th-century instrument of ecclesiastical discipline)—hang beside the porch; in the churchyard stand a number of good 17th and 18th-century gravestones. John Noble's stone (1723) for instance, has a fine full-length figure in contemporary costume and with a flintlock gun; that to Elisabeth Agnas and Elizabeth Thomson (1723) pictures the united family group on an end-panel to a table-tomb; yet another (c 1730) shows a youth, perhaps of the Cunningham family, wearing a long-skirted coat with broad cuffs at the wrists.

**Edrom Old Kirk, Norman arch** (Far left) **and detail of stone carving, arch and capitals** (Left)

### 73 Edrom Kirk, near Duns

*12th century AD.*

*NT 827558. Edrom stands less than 1 km N of A 6105, about half-way between Duns and Chirnside; continue straight through village to the church; signposted.*

*Historic Scotland (Norman arch).*

The present T-shaped church, built in 1732, is one of relatively few churches retaining wall-mounted boards painted with scriptural texts—an aide-memoire for the assembled congregation: The Lord's Prayer, The Ten Commandments . . . . A burial vault in the Blackadder Aisle is dated 1668 with mid 16th-century effigies above, but the aisle itself, built by Robert Blackadder, Archbishop of Glasgow in 1499, is much altered so that only the two external, diagonal buttresses are of any great interest—they have canopied niches that held figures of saints.

Immediately to the west, however, stands a remarkably fine, large Norman doorway with elaborate capitals of late Norman date incorporating twisted scrolls emerging from human heads. The semi-circular arch consists of three equally elaborate carved orders. Two of these incorporate chevron patterns; the outermost a continuous 'embattled fret', edged with a small leaf-like embellishment. In a reasonable state of repair, the archway has been adapted as the entrance to a burial aisle.

A few kilometres further north, the ruins of Bunkle 'Old' Church (NT 808596) suggest one of the earliest Norman buildings in Berwickshire. The extreme simplicity of the apse and access arch from the chancel contrasts well with Edrom's arch and suggests a late 11th-century date. The arch is a single, square-edged order the same thickness as the wall, whilst the semi-circular semi-domed apse is covered with overlapping stones. Bunkle, like Preston church, belonged to the Bishopric of Dunkeld; the lands and church of Edrom, however, were granted by Gospatrick, Earl of Dunbar, to St Cuthbert's monks at Coldingham—a grant confirmed by David I in 1139.

Somewhat to the west, north of Earlston, Legerwood Church (NT 594434) was also originally linked to Coldingham, though transferred to Paisley from 1163. The style and the geometric and chequer pattern decoration of its chancel arch suggests a later 12th-century date. On plan the church consisted of a rectangular nave and chancel. The nave is now incorporated in the later church; the chancel arch remains one of the best examples of Norman architecture in the area, with a small protrusion on the north-west capital featuring the grinning face of a demon or imp—a favourite Norman reminder of the presence of evil! At the back of a small recess in the chancel wall, traces of red painted decoration suggest a Christogram comprising a complete circle around a chalice, edged with some kind of leafy pattern. Fragments of other such painted motifs survive nearby.

By contrast, at St Helen's or 'Aldcambus', away east of Cockburnspath (NT 803706), there is little left of the simple Norman church—though here, as at Edrom, hogback gravestones have been found.

South of the Tweed, yet another fine, small Norman church, c 1127-60, survives at Linton (NT 773262). A particularly fine tympanum above the south door features what have been described variously as two wild animals (?bears) and a bearded knight (?St George), or the slaying of a giant serpent or worm ('the Linton worm') by an ancestor of the Somerville family!

**South doorway, Dalmeny Kirk**

## 74* Dalmeny Kirk, South Queensferry, Edinburgh

*12th century AD.*

*NT 144775. Just E of South Queensferry on B 924 to Edinburgh, turn S to Dalmeny; in centre of old village turn E; church alongside.*

Situated on rising ground and dedicated to St Cuthbert, the church may have been commissioned by one of the wealthy lords of Dalmeny, either Gospatrick (died 1142) or his successor of the same name (died 1166). Quite simply it is the most complete Norman church in Scotland and the numerous masons' marks on the greyish-white sandstone inside link it with Dunfermline Abbey and Leuchars Church in Fife.

Like Leuchars (and the impressive ruins at Tyninghame, no. 22) it is well-finished and richly decorated; like those in Fife it is a three-cell structure of nave, chancel and sanctuary apse with a roofline (forgiving the ugly, squat tower of 1937) stepped from west to east. The only extension, the Rosebery Aisle, was built in 1671.

The south entrance is a superb combination of doorway and intersecting arcade above, surmounted by corbels. Its closest Scottish parallel at Dunfermline betrays influence from Durham, and a tympanum presumably once filled the half-circle below the two-order arch. Far from being decorated with simple chevrons, however, the arch is festooned with carvings. The inner arch appears to include zodiacal signs, fabulous Bestiary figures, and an Agnus Dei; the outer arch projects eight grotesque heads. And either side is a sculptured figure—that to the east a male, with a garment reaching to mid-leg, a sword, spear and triangular sword.

Inside, chancel and apse are equally splendid, and roofed with rib vaults—similar, once again, to examples at Dunfermline. The supporting corbels are carved as heads, grotesque or human according to taste; and on the south side of the chancel, a muzzled bear. The nave has only one window in the north wall to three in the south wall—a local pecularity found also at St Martin's, Haddington (no. 68).

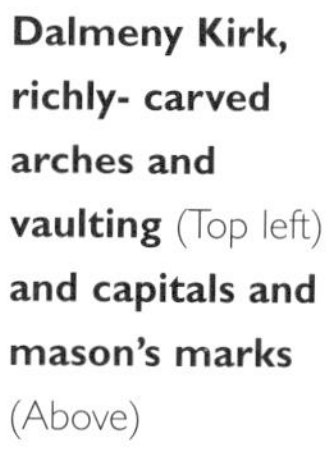

**Dalmeny Kirk, richly- carved arches and vaulting** (Top left) **and capitals and mason's marks** (Above)

Behind the tapestry on the north chancel wall is a very imperfect painted inscription, the remains perhaps of painted scriptures or lives of the saints. Inset in the apse and chancel floors are several medieval graveslabs; outdoors there are some good 17th-18th-century gravestones, but also a massive stone coffin with head-cavity and decorated on three sides—winged beast at the foot, Christ and the Apostles in thirteen arches along the side. Was this the coffin of the church's builder?

### 75* Coldingham Priory

*Early 13th-19th century AD.*

*NT 903659. 400 m E of centre of Coldingham off A 1107 coastal road N from Eyemouth.*

On a rise above the burn stands one of the most interesting of the smaller Benedictine houses in Scotland. Bede mentions a religious house at Coldingham in the mid 7th century; it was destroyed by the 'Danes' in AD 870 and a new charter granted in 1098 to monks of St Cuthbert at Durham by King Edgar of Scotland. This church was dedicated c 1100, but there is no suggestion of a priory before 1147. All the priors were English until the late 15th century when the link with Durham was finally broken, but paradoxically, whilst the monks were subject to the English king, the priors were subject to the King of Scotland. The priory was open to 'attack' therefore, in peace or in war! In 1216 it was sacked by King John; by 1509 it was attached to Dunfermline Abbey; it was burnt by the English in 1544; and after 1560 and the Reformation, it shared the fate of other religious houses. Cromwell demolished most of what remained in 1648.

Originally cruciform, with cloisters and domestic buildings adjacent to the south wall, all that remains is the long aisleless choir and sanctuary, now the parish church. Most of the church was rebuilt in 1662 with the porch added in 1854; the north and east walls, though, are largely original. The interior is particularly attractive with strong horizontal lines accentuated by the two-storey division and continuous arcading. The lower storey

**Medieval cross-slabs, Coldingham Priory**

**Arcading, Coldingham Priory**

incorporates an arcade of pointed arches; the upper division, built as a clearstory with lancet-shaped windows, contains a central passage in the thickness of the wall. Outside, the north and east walls are similarly divided with arcading; and broadly-speaking the style is late Norman/Transitional, probably dating to the early 13th century.

Not far away lie a number of interesting graveslabs—two of them commemorating priors, Radulphus (died c 1198) and Ernaldus (died early 13th century). A fine collection of medieval cross-slabs includes some with incised Latin crosses, some with Greek crosses; some displaying incised swords, one also a hunting horn.

## 76* Melrose Abbey

*Mid 12th-early 16th century AD.*

*NT 548341. Close to centre of Melrose in angle of A 6091 and B 6361; signposted.*

*Historic Scotland.*

The first Cistercian settlement in Scotland was founded here in 1136 by David I for Abbot Richard and his monks from Rievaulx in Yorkshire. They sought fertile, open farmland in preference to the bleak and restricted promontory site of Old Melrose (NT 588340: a 7th-century Anglian monastery, perhaps replacing an earlier British monastery), and by 1146 the church was sufficiently complete to be dedicated to the Virgin Mary.

By the end of the 14th century, however, much of the original structure, small and plain in line with Cistercian views on architectural embellishment, had gone—destroyed by the English in the Wars of Independence. Some 12th-century masonry survives at the west end, as well as foundations for

**Melrose Abbey: south side of the nave**

the narrow-aisled nave and the transepts where, unusually for the Cistercians, the east walls of the latter are stepped in echelon. More or less contemporary is the 'canal', sited beyond the later Commendator's House. Led from the Tweed, it may first have provided drinking water (springs later), and certainly flushed sewers and powered the corn mill. The cloister, completed late in the 12th century and almost identical in size with that once extant in the daughter-house at Newbattle in Midlothian, was sited conveniently close to this water supply, and serviced by the surviving 'main drain'.
Otherwise the present church post-dates the destructions of 1322 and 1385. Building continued into the 16th century but by then the Abbey was too impoverished and it was never completed at the west end. By contrast with its predecessor, however, the 15th-16th-century Abbey is far from austere—grandly and lavishly ornamented with capitals, bosses and corbels carved with fruit, flowers and foliage, and with numerous statues. There is a most appealing range of humorous human figures around the exterior walls—the cook with his ladle, the mason with his mallet, the fat monk. And flying high on a gargoyle—a bagpipe-playing pig.

This outward manifestation of substantial wealth would have appalled the Order's 11th- and 12th-century abbots, with their insistence on austerity, poverty and simplicity. It was a wealth founded on the ownership of 5000 acres at Eildon, Darnick, Gattonside, Newstead and elsewhere, together with some 17,000 leased acres of hill ground in the Lammermuirs (eg at Penshiel), Lauderdale, Teviotdale and the Ettrick Forest. The vast sheep flocks, tended by lay brothers, generated huge quantities of wool for export.

The reconstructed church is comparable only to Roslin Chapel (no. 67) and represents the high point of 15th-century Scottish decorated architecture; the Perpendicular tracery of the eastern chapels and of the great east window which dominates the nave also shows considerable English influence, with parallels at York and Beverley. It is a starker, cooler styling than Scotland's more usual curvilinear tracery found, with northern French influence perhaps, in the south transept window.

Though resembling its predecessors in overall plan, the new church incorporated a number of chapels opening off the south aisle of the nave, many of them containing funeral monuments. And outside, the graveyard contains many interesting 17th and 18th-century stones, covering a wide cross-section of social groups—farmer, weaver, blacksmith, builder, mason, joiner, gardener, nurseryman, merchant, manufacturer, druggist, coal agent, watchmaker, naval lieutenant, minister, writer, surgeon, architect . . . .

Melrose itself has a 16th-century mercat cross; and next to the Abbey, part of Priorwood Gardens (NTS) is given over to species of apple trees spanning nearly 2000 years.

**Melrose Abbey, Playing the Lute** (Left) **and Pig playing Bagpipes** (Below)

**Dryburgh Abbey: reconstruction by Alan Sorrell**

### 77* Dryburgh Abbey, near St Boswells

*Mainly 12th-13th century AD.*

*NT 591316. Take B 6356 Earlston-Kelso road for about 6 km SSE of Leaderfoot on A 68; turn off through Dryburgh village; signposted.*

*Historic Scotland.*

Built of pale, reddish-brown sandstone, the Abbey lies in a horse-shoe bend of the Tweed, several kilometres downstream from Melrose and a little south of Old Melrose (NT 588340), well-observed from Scott's View (NT 593342). It was founded by the Premonstratensian Order, brought from Alnwick in 1140. They were a reformed group of Augustinians and this was their first of only six houses in Scotland. As an order they were 'open'—they could go out and serve in the parishes which formed part of their endowment.

Though Dryburgh was less troubled than Jedburgh or Kelso, like Melrose it was wasted by the English in 1322, and rebuilt with the financial assistance of Robert the Bruce. Much of what survives today, however, is earlier—of 12th- and 13th-century date. The church comprised an arched nave, short transepts with little chapels on their east sides, and a square-headed presbytery also with side chapels. Much of the northern transept and its attendant chapels still stands and in St Mary's Aisle are housed the post-Reformation tombs of the Erskines, Haliburtons and Scotts. Sir Walter Scott is buried here, and nearby, outside the chapel, Field Marshal Earl Haig of Bermersyde (1914-18 War).

**West doorway and north transept chapels, Dryburgh Abbey** (Right)

**Haliburton tombstone, Dryburgh Abbey** (Left)

Like Jedburgh, Dryburgh was of modest height. But whilst at Jedburgh the main arcade extended upwards to enclose the triforium—the windowless gallery below the clearstory—here it retains a separate identity, albeit only by being 'squeezed'. It is represented above the transept chapel simply by small openings above each arch.

The 15th-century west end of the Abbey church lies flush to a high, enclosing cloister wall (where more usually would have been a range of claustral buildings). Elsewhere around the cloisters stood the refectory, warming house, library and vestry, parlour, Novices' day-room, dormitories. The Chapter House, where the monks met daily, contains a fine stone basin decorated with bird-like creatures and some late 12th-century painted plasterwork. It has a barrel-vaulted roof and an arched sedilia (priests' seat) along the east wall.

Dryburgh is often thought to be the most romantic of the Border Abbeys—gracefully shadowed by ancient cedars (said to date to Crusader times) and an 800 year old yew. 'Romance' of another strain perhaps is enshrined in an 18th-century gravestone just outside the ruined nave. William Forson, whose ancestors were tenants in Drygrange and Redpath Mills for 250 years, was exiled to Ireland for Nonconformity; he returned in 1689 to Holydeanmill where he died in 1748.

A kilometre or so north of the Abbey, close to B 6356 and above a public footpath, stands the distinctive and formidable, red sandstone, 7 m high statue of William Wallace (c 1270-1305: NT 592328), defender of Scottish independence against Edward I of England and executed in London. Complete with saltire shield, double-handed sword and suitably-inscribed urn, the statue was erected by the Earl of Buchan, friend of Sir Walter Scott, in 1874 (repaired 1991).

## 78* Jedburgh Abbey

*Late 12th-mid 13th century AD.*

*NT 650204. In centre of Jedburgh in angle between A 68 and B 6358 but set behind main streets, just above river; signposted.*

*Historic Scotland.*

Little more than the foundations survive of the monastic buildings which stood on the slope between the Abbey and the Jed Water, but the nave and the north transept are complete up to the topmost wall-head, and the tower stands as it was rebuilt in 1504-8.

The site had been occupied by a church since the 9th century; then, c 1138, Augustinian Canons were brought from St Quentin, near Beauvais in France and by 1174 the choir, crossing and both transepts were sufficiently complete to be used for services.

**Jedburgh Abbey: reconstruction by Alan Sorrell**

The nave was constructed by 1200, and by 1220 the east end was reconstructed after the removal of the original semi-circular apse. The whole church was evidently complete by the mid 13th century when attentions were turned anew to the cloisters. These were remodelled; by the late 15th century the north transept was extended, and the fine rose window added above the west door.

It is a powerful place, very much dependent upon its clustered pillars and strong bridging arches, all of which suggest authority, control and discipline. The great stone piers are carried, unusually, to the level of the triforium at first-storey level—a technique that creates an impression of height in an otherwise relatively low interior (cf Dryburgh, no. 77). There, the delicate arcading is surmounted by a light and airy clearstory. Remarkably intact in spite of constant warring between 1297 ad 1545, Jedburgh conveys the feeling of a great abbey interior more fully than any other of the Border Abbeys.

**8th century AD Anglian sarcophagus or shrine, Jedburgh Abbey** (Right)

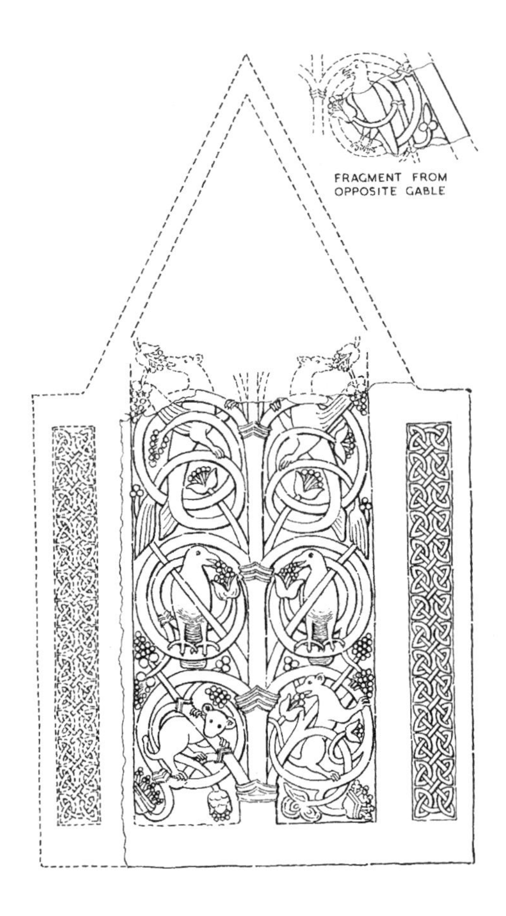


After the reformation a Presbyterian church was created within the crossing of the Abbey and transepts; and a 'new' church was provided in the west part of the nave in 1671. In 1743 the crown arch and vault of the crossing collapsed and the dangers of falling masonry doubtless partly explain why the parish church was removed entirely from the Abbey in 1875.

Within the visitor centre there are a number of important sculptured stones, notably a Roman altar slab, sections of an 8th-century Anglian shrine or sarcophagus elaborately decorated with birds, animals and vine-scroll (see section 6), several pieces of 8th-9th-century early Christian cross-heads and shafts, and a 12th-century cross-inscribed tomb-cover—possibly that of John, Bishop of Glasgow who died in 1148 and was buried at Jedburgh.

Elsewhere in the town are the fine 16th-century bastle-house (Queen Mary's House) and hump-backed bridge across the Jed Water at the foot of the Canongate, and a remarkable 'model' jail of the 19th century.

**Carved stone 'Christ' figure, Jedburgh Abbey** (Right)

**Horn comb, with intricate mouldings either side, Jedburgh Abbey** (Far left)

**The monumental west porch, Kelso Abbey**

## 79* Kelso Abbey, Roxburgh

*Late 12th century AD.*

*NT 728337. On N bank of Tweed, half-way between Coldstream and Jedburgh; centre of town, signposted.*

*Historic Scotland.*

Reformed Benedictines from Tiron in France settled at Lindean, near Selkirk c 1119. The site proved unsuitable and by 1128 they had moved to Kelso under the patronage of David I. Facing the now long-vanished burgh and royal castle of Roxburgh (NT 713338), and dedicated both to the Virgin Mary and to St John, the Abbey was to become one of the largest and the second richest of Scotland's religious houses, with granges, mills, breweries, salt pans, fisheries and other enterprises, and the revenues of 34 parish churches stretching from Ayrshire to Aberdeenshire. It also lay on the invasion route, close to the Border, and its downfall was sealed at the Reformation—by 1587 'the haill monkis of the monasterie of the abbey of Kelso ar deciessit'.

The principle survival is the Abbey's exceedingly grand and almost threatening west end, essentially a late 12th-century Norman structure in transition to a pointed style of architecture. Internally there are virtually no plain surfaces; the walls are particularly strong in decorative arcades, notably in the two surviving bays forming part of the south side of the nave. The first-storey arcades enclosed a wall passage (triforium), with another at the higher clearstory level; there are communicating stairs within the great angle buttresses.

Design in the nave is predominantly horizontal with relatively little light; in the many-windowed western transepts however, and in the great 'Galilee' porch, the lines are primarily vertical. Kelso was unusual in having transepts at the western end as well as at the east, a feature deriving perhaps from churches in Germany's Rhineland and found also at Ely and Bury St Edmunds. On plan the abbey must have resembled a double-ended cross, with a dark nave looking either way into brilliantly-lit transepts—a tunnel-effect from within.

Best preserved is the north transept with its magnificent gable. To the exterior both corners are gripped by buttresses, between which projects a stylish doorway with three recessed arches. Above the arches, an interlaced arcade is finished by a triangular pediment, decorated as at Lincoln.

Kelso also boasts an uncommon octagonal parish church (1773), the fine Ednam House (1761), 17th-century houses in Abbey Court (including the Turret House and museum) and 18th-century houses in the Woodmarket. The spacious Market Square has a Gallic feel to it; and Rennie's magnificent bridge (1800-3) replaced an earlier one of 1754, swept away in 1797.

Crosshall Cross

## 80 Crosshall Cross, near Eccles

*Middle Ages.*

*NT 760422. Crosshall Farm lies on a minor road about 1 km N of Eccles on B 6461 Kelso-Leitholm road, about 1.5 km W of A 697. Cross is about 400 m SW of farm, beside road.*

The sandstone shaft is 3m tall and set in a huge square stone base. Rectangular in section, it tapers slightly upwards and is carved on all four sides. The east face bears a roughly-incised figure of a man, his arms folded and feet turned inwards; and beneath him, a hound. The west side, by contrast, has a Latin cross with pointed ends to its arms, surmounted by shield. A similar shield, set above a sword, features on the south face; and a Latin cross placed on a calvary on the north face. On both sides of the circular 'wheel' head a plain, equal-armed cross has been cut, edged around with a marginal border.

The place where the cross stands was formerly called Deadriggs, traditionally the site of a 'bloody battle'.

## 81 Innerleithen Cross-Shaft

*9th century AD.*

*NT 332369. Set against E exterior wall of parish church, about 400 m N of centre of Innerleithen, on B 709.*

When the old parish church at Innerleithen was demolished in 1871, the lower end of an early cross-shaft was found in its foundations. All four faces are decorated with a regular pattern of cup-shaped hollows surrounded by double circles. The outer circles are linked together with vertical grooves to give a series of 'dumb-bell' patterns, pecked into the stone.

**Anglian cross-shaft, Innerleithen**
(Far right)

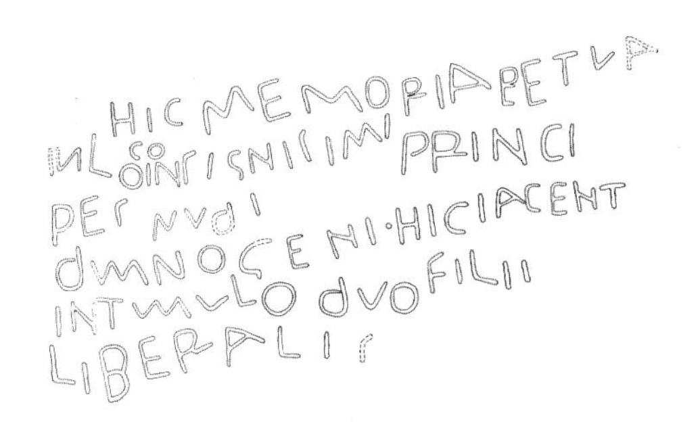

**Early 6th-century Christian inscription, Yarrow Water**
(Far left)

## 82 Yarrow Stone, near Selkirk

*Early 6th century AD.*

*NT 348274. Just over 1 km WSW of Yarrow on A 708 Selkirk-Moffat road; close to track leading to Whitefield.*

The moor known as Annan Street was first brought into cultivation in 1803-4, and the stone was turned up by the plough; it was lying flat just under the surface with human bones below. At that time there were also some twenty 'large cairns' on the moor.

Just over 1.5 m high as now set, it bears an important six-line Latin inscription, fairly roughly carved and in parts badly weathered. The letters are mainly Roman capitals, irregular and sprawling; the words are badly set out and carelessly written! Certain letters, however, provide parallels with stones elsewhere, notably in Wales and Cornwall, and help date it to the early 6th century. A brief translation would run:

> 'This (is) the everlasting memorial.
> In (this) place (lie) the most famous princes
> Nudus and Dumnogenus,
> In this tomb lie the two sons of Liberalis'.

The stone was erected, therefore, to mark the grave of two Christian British chieftains; but burial was not in a churchyard as such, rather in a small cemetery, probably the family or tribal graveyard, alongside a trackway.

The record of bones beneath the stone and of cairns on the moor cannot be dissociated with other discoveries, made in 1857, some 730 m north-east at the Warriors' Rest (NT 354277). There, about 9 m south of a standing stone, eight stone-lined cists or graves were found lying east-west Such groups of aligned graves without gravegoods are characteristic of Christian, not pagan burials, and have also been found at the Catstane close to Edinburgh Airport (presently inaccessible).

The inscription on the 6th-century Catstane suggests that 'In this tomb lies Vetta, daughter of Victricius', presumably a woman of considerable political and social importance amongst the Votadini, a British tribe whose roots and language were closely related to those who emerged subsequently as the Welsh. Much preoccupied with warring, good living and genealogy, their Christianity may have been little more than a veneer—but Christian they were nonetheless, and from the discoveries of their graves, they were fairly liberally scattered across the attractive Lothian plain.

## 83 Borthwick Mains Carved Stone, near Hawick

*6th-7th century AD.*

*NT 437141. Some 6.5 km W of Hawick on B 711 to Ettrick Water: farm stands adjacent to S side of the road: within back garden of farmhouse.*

On the north face of this 1.5 m high, roughly square-sectioned stone, is the incised outline of a fish, just under 1m long, aligned vertically—head; body and tail; fins, gills and an eye; and a line dividing body from tail. There is, however, no indication of a mouth. The outline has been made by percussion, by striking with some kind of a tool, a common technique.

**Carved Stone, Borthwick Water**

The fish was a familiar motif both in early Christian art and in the repertoire of Pictish symbols, and in this context it is likely to confirm the presence of Christian communities and to belong to the Yarrow Stone/Cat Stane tradition of early Christian stones.

The stone was formerly part of a gate-post lower down the farm road (hence the hole near the top); it then became part of the garden wall. Local oral tradition suggests, however, that it came from near Commonside beside the River Teviot (NT 4207); that it stood in the water, and that when the fish's tail could be seen it was safe to cross! It came to Borthwick, so the tradition goes, captured after a fight between the inhabitants of the two valleys.

# 7 ROMAN AND POST-ROMAN FORTS AND SETTLEMENTS

**Roman visor mask from Newstead** (in NMS)

Before the welding of the Scottish nation, begun under Kenneth MacAlpin, c AD 843, and more-or-less established by the time of Duncan I (1034-40), the landmass now referred to as Scotland (after the incoming Northern Irish 'Scotti') was inhabited by five distinct cultural groups. There is scant material evidence for Norse or Scots in south-east Scotland, a little more for Picts and considerably more for Britons and Angles. Of these, the Britons (Celts but speaking a British or Cumbric language rather different from the Gaelic of the Irish Scots) were 'native' long before the arrival of the Romans; a small number of those later known as Picts may have moved into the area from the north shortly after the Roman occupation; the Northumbrian Angles came to dominate after the 7th century.

For all that, the only material evidence for secular settlement by the Northumbrians is the site of a timber hall at Doon Hill (NT 686755: Historic Scotland)—a hill commanding the east coast from St Abb's north to Dunbar and round to North Berwick Law, Traprain Law and the northern plain. And whilst settlement names in eg *-ingtun*, *-ham*, *-wic*, *-worth*, *-bot(h)l*, catalogue the subsequent waves of colonisation, there are only three primary late 7th-8th-century Anglian names in Scotland, Coldingham, Whittingehame and Tyninghame—all of them on this narrow eastern coastal strip. The lack of other visible remains suggests not only that it was here that the first Northumbrians entered Scotland, but that there were relatively few early settlers—rather were they primarily overlords securing their position and supplies with a small number of carefully-sited strongholds and associated farms.

It would be no accident that their 7th-century hall at Doon Hill overlay the ruins of a 6th-century timber British hall (the outlines of both are indicated on site)—or that a roughly parallel sequence has been identified at Yeavering in Northumberland close to which, also on fertile coastal lowland, survive four more of the earliest Anglian names. For Yeavering, a little west of Wooller, commands the lower Merse and the more southerly section of coast either side of the (later) Border; and the whole length of this coast from the Forth to the English Tyne, inland for maybe 30-35 km, had been the territory of one of the most powerful of the native British tribes, the Votadini. When, in AD 638, the Northumbrians destroyed what seems then to have been the Votadini capital at Din Eidyn (Edinburgh), they effectively terminated a supremacy that predated the Romans with whom the tribe had clearly 'come to an arrangement', bartering freedom for economic advantage.

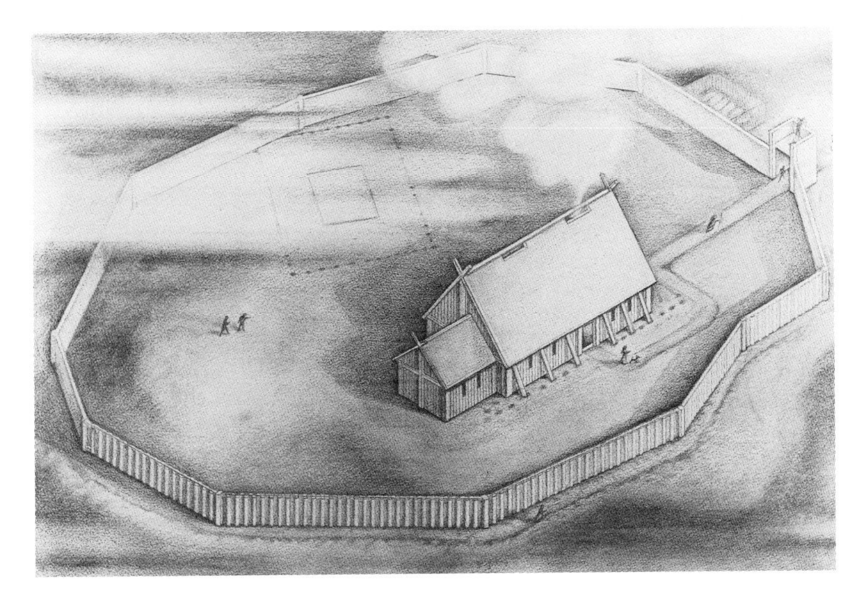

**Reconstruction drawing of Doon Hill Hall, near Dunbar**

The Roman presence in Scotland was never anything other than military. Conquest was much sought but never achieved, so that there were no Roman villas, towns or major Romanisation of native cultures, and the distribution of Roman forts, camps, roads, signal stations and training grounds in south-east Scotland related throughout to two primary routes of communication.

One route, called Dere Street in medieval times, led north from York and north-east England over the Cheviots, by Woden Law to Tow Ford and the Pennymuir Camps, on over Whitton Edge and Ulston Moor, crossing the

**Medieval Dere Street and the Roman road, near the site of Cappuck Roman fort, near Jedburgh**

Teviot at Monteviot and the Tweed near Newstead, thence up Lauderdale and into Lothian. The other led from Carlisle and north-west England, up Annandale to Crawford and the upper Clyde, thence by the Biggar Gap and along the south-west edge of the Pentland Hills, where, between West Linton and Carlops, it is revealed as a raised causeway and/or parallel lines of quarry pits. Minor link or access roads maybe led north of the Pentlands, hence the fortlet at Castle Greg (no. 89), and, in along the Ettrick Water, Oakwood Fort (no. 88). A more important link reached the Borthwick Water, in line for Trimontium (the Eildon Hills), from Annandale by way of Craik Muir; another ran east-west from Newstead along the upper Tweed and the Lyne Water, meeting the Annandale route at the upper Clyde, hence the Lyne Forts (no. 87). From Newstead, a further road would have struck out eastwards towards Berwick; whilst a 9 m-11 m wide road linked the Tweed Valley and Lauderdale, crossing the Lugate Water and over to Scroof (NT 403431), high up the Caddon Water in the south-eastern foothills of the Moorfoots.

But if the ultimate focus were the supply-ports of Cramond (NT 190770) and Inveresk on the Firth of Forth, thence to what became the Antonine Wall and beyond, an intermediate but no less vital focus was essential. This focus was Newstead or Trimontium (NT 574342), a strategic centre with some seven phases of occupation covering the period c AD 79 to AD 220. Newstead is now emerging as the largest and most important Roman site in Scotland, and one of the largest in the British Isles. Over 810 ha in extent (including associated field systems), the garrison could have held up to 2000 cavalry and infantry, with a further 1000 merchants, artisans and camp followers located in annexes outside the fort. Here there were stone- and wattle-lined wells, stock enclosures and slaughterhouses, workshops producing weapons and armour, jewellery and pottery, possibly the equivalent of a 'soup kitchen' and no doubt bars and less savoury places of entertainment. Wooden tools have been found, and an axe; also coins, brooches and roof tiles, and animal skulls and bones that were perhaps used in rituals. In all, there were perhaps some 200 buildings, some up to 20 m long, where the rich and the poor lived and worked in close proximity. On a site that was basically a frontier fort and boom town, evidence for valuable glass tableware, furniture with silver fittings and expensive jewellery suggests, nonetheless, a remarkable diversity of Roman culture. Here too are the remains of the most northerly amphitheatre in the Roman empire—where 2000-3000 soldiers, the fort governor and visiting dignitaries could view military parades and games.

**Excavation of the Roman fort at Elginhaugh, near Dalkeith**

Clearly Trimontium was a Roman outpost which subsequently grew and was settled. But whilst there is nothing to suggest continuing rebellion by the native population, there is equally little to suggest a mixing of Roman and native.They seem to have acted out their different cultures side-by-side, confirming the Roman occupation as just that—a military occupation, not a conquest and not a cultural integration. That is not to say that there were not 'arrangements' beween the two. The recent discovery of a hoard of 300 Roman coins near Peebles revealed denarii dating from the first century BC to AD 222, some 20 years after the Romans formally withdrew from Scotland. The hoard suggests a payment or bribe to a Briton to pass information on tribal movements farther north, thus helping to preserve lowland Scotland's status as a buffer zone between the frontier of the empire and the hostile north. Worth the equivalent of a Roman soldier's annual salary, the British spy presumably considered it more prudent to bury (and subsequently lose) his reward!

**Roman coin 'Imp Caes Vespasian' (77-78 AD), found at Inveresk House, near Musselburgh**

To return, however, to Newstead. Its strategic location at a key river-crossing was strengthened by the remarkably prominent and isolated nearby hills from which signals could be sent over long distances in virtually any direction. The Latin name *Trimontium* (Newstead) refers specifically to these hills—the Eildon Hills.

It was unfortunate for the Selgovae that they held so much of the land around the upper Tweed and the cross-routes to the west and south-west; also that Eildon Hill North (no. 93), close to Melrose and Newstead, was one of their major strongholds. As a native British tribe directly in their path, they had to be neutralised by the Romans; and their capital (if indeed it were still occupied) was requisitioned in the way that Woden Law (no. 91), high in the Cheviots and commanding the strategic crossing of the watershed, was also presumably requisitioned. Brownhart Law signal station (NT 790096) and Chew Green camps (NT 7808) lay high up just to the south; the multi-ramparted Woden Law perhaps proved a fine remote site to train troops in the besieging of native forts. They were accommodated in the temporary camps at Pennymuir (no. 90).

There were several waves of Roman occupation of southern Scotland. Before the last and brief, early 3rd century AD Severan campaigns, the Antonine period covered c AD 140 to the 160s/early 180s, whilst the last of Agricola's conquests of AD 79-83 were abandoned by about 100. Though subsequently refurbished, remodelled and occasionally supplemented during the later campaigns, the basic network of forts and roads laid down in the later 1st century AD was not substantially altered.

There are virtually no Roman sites east of Dere Street; the Romans were not interested in the coastal land-route and so there was no direct threat to the Votadini, who appear to have occupied the Lothian plain and Berwickshire east of Lauderdale, as far south perhaps as High Rochester in 'English' Redesdale. But the obedience of the Votadini would have been required just as that of the Selgovae, based in the uplands between Lauderdale and Clydesdale. Their capital at this time was on Traprain Law (no. 92) and they may have been entrusted with certain responsibilities by the Romans, perhaps by way of reward. By the late 4th century, however, well after the departure of the Romans, the size of Traprain Law had been reduced to some 12 ha, from a maximum of 16 ha, and a hoard of silver bullion was buried in a pit in the early 5th century AD.

By the mid 5th century, the Votadini seem to have moved out of Traprain, presumably to Din Eidyn (Edinburgh), and probably better to try and control the tribes north of the Forth who had increasingly sought to exploit southern Scotland in the post-Roman period.

That groups of Picts were penetrating south of the Forth is suggested mainly by placenames in *peffer* and *aber* along the Lothian coast, and also by names including *pit* which, because found frequently in Gaelic compounds, are unlikely to be earlier than 9th century.

Evidence of influences from the north just after or even during the Roman period is found in the souterrains at Castlelaw (no. 84) and Crichton (no. 85); there was also one at Newstead. That at Crichton re-uses considerable amounts of Roman stone, probably quarried from an as yet unidentified Roman fort. Generally found north of the Forth, notably in Angus, and probably used as underground stores or byres, they are likely to date to the 1st-3rd centuries AD.

Influence from the west, through the Biggar Gap, is suggested by the dun identified at Stanhope (NT 117291). It is contemporary with the 1st to early 2nd-century brochs at Bow (NT 461417) and Torwoodlee (NT 465384) which were probably destroyed by the Romans. These may represent an intrusive group from north of the Forth settling along the Gala Water or, as was more likely the case at Edinshall (no. 86), may have been commissioned by a prominent and wealthy local family as 'insurance' in troubled times—built by professional broch-builders from the north. In which case the well-preserved Edinshall, beside the Whiteadder Water north of Duns, would perhaps have been let stand by the Romans because it was in the heartland of the Votadini, well east of their centre of operations?

**Stanhope: a 1st to early 2nd century dun, near Broughton**

**Impression of timber entrance tower to Castlelaw hillfort**

## 84 Castlelaw Souterrain, Midlothian

*1st-2nd century AD.*

*NT 229638. Side road W from Crosshouse Farm on A 702 Edinburgh-Biggar road 5 km S of city boundary; up hill to Castlelaw Farm thence 100 m N; signposted.*

*Historic Scotland.*

The oval fort was originally surrounded by a palisaded enclosure, later succeeded by a simple rampart mainly of plain clay but reinforced with timber by the entrance.

Late in its occupation, just before the arrival of Roman forces in AD 79 or 80, further defences were added, and it was in the ditch between the two later ramparts, at the north-east end of the fort, that a well-preserved souterrain was subsequently built. The rock-cut ditch was widened and a passage constructed, lined with drystone walling that followed round the curve of the ditch for about 20 m. Its width varies from 0.9 m to 2 m, it is over 1.6 m high, and about half-way along, a low side passage leads into a large 3.5 m diameter cell. This is particularly well-built, with corbelled walls standing yet to over 1.8 m. The souterrain has yielded a brooch, Roman pottery and glass dating to the 2nd century AD.

**Souterrain between the ramparts of Castlelaw hillfort** (Below)

**Entrance to the side-chamber, Castlelaw souterrain** (Bottom right)

**Souterrain at Crichton Mains** (Left)

## 85 Crichton Souterrain, Midlothian

*2nd-3rd century AD.*

*NT 400619. Two side roads link A 68 and B 6367 a little to S of Pathhead; about half-way along southernmost, on a rise within a cultivated field, a fenced enclosure gives access to site.*

Old clothes or waterproofs and a torch are essential for this site—and care in crossing the fields. A short entrance passage below ground leads into the main curving gallery over 15 m long and 1.8 m or more high and wide. Except where it has been arched over after rediscovery, the roof is original—massive stone lintels over 2 m long and generally placed close together. The drystone walls incline inward slightly to meet the roof.

Particularly interesting and important is the re-use of around 70 stones of Roman origin. These are finely-squared and dressed, many of them with characteristic diamond/diagonal chiselling. Two such blocks stand at the entrance door; two more form the jambs of the opening at the north-west end of the gallery. The majority, however, have been placed at the top of the wall that forms the inner curve. One lintel towards the east end is carved with the figure of a Pegasus or winged horse—the emblem of the Legio II Augusta. Furthermore, one of the door jambs at the north-west end bears a groove or channel suggesting earlier use as a gutter surrounding the open courtyard of a Headquarters building in a typical Roman fort. As yet the site of a fort in the neighbourhood of Crichton has proved elusive, but clearly the souterrain was built after a Roman withdrawal.

## 86 Edinshall Broch, near Duns

*2nd century AD.*

*NT 772603. At junction of B 6365 and B 6355 3 km W of Preston (N of Duns) take road N to Cockburn Farm; thence by farm track to Cockburn East and NW via farm gates; signposted.*

*Historic Scotland.*

In the late 18th century this site was called 'Wooden's (Woden's or Odin's) Hall or Castle'. An alternative folk etymology, 'Jötun (giant's) Hall', reputedly recalls Red Etin of tale and ballad. It is a multi-period site set above a steep slope over 60 m down to the Whiteadder Water, but otherwise difficult to defend. The earliest structure is an oval fort some 134 m by 73 m, enclosed by a double rampart and ditches. (There is a hillfort on Cockburn Law, just behind: NT 765597.)

Most remarkable, however, is the broch, a well-preserved outlier of an essentially northern Scottish type of fortified building, which lies in the north-west corner of the earlier fort. Either side of the 4.9 m long entrance passage is a guard chamber set in the 5 m and more thick walls, and the courtyard has an overall diameter of some 17 m. South of the entrance an opening gives access within the walls to a short stair and passage: to the left a small chamber, to the right a further stair to the top of the wall. Elsewhere there are two further intramural cavities, each with a short passage opening either end on to a small compartment and curving to follow the line of the main wall. The small rectangular chamber just to the north and outside the entrance passage is, however, a secondary feature.

**Reconstruction drawing of Edinshall broch**

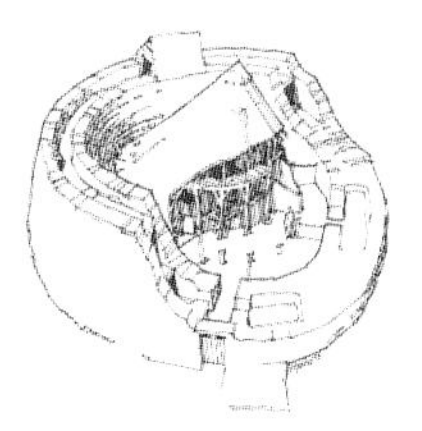

**Edinshall broch**

A roughly rectangular enclosure surrounds the broch, but this may relate rather to the last phase of occupation—an open unfortified settlement consisting of circular hut foundations and stretches of walling in the eastern half of the hillfort. In the upper angle of the surrounding field, about 90 m to the south-east, further small circular and rectangular enclosures set mainly in a line, abutting, suggest further habitation—with cultivation carried close on all sides.

The fort can probably be dated to the last years BC or early AD, prior to the arrival of the Romans; the open settlement was maybe an undefended village established in the later 2nd century AD under the 'pax Romana'. As to the broch, it seems to be the only one within the territory of the Votadini, who were supposedly at peace with the Romans. Perhaps it was built between the two Roman occupations of southern Scotland, but by whom? Were lowland brochs built by professional broch builders commissioned by leading lowland families as protection against the Romans?.

### 87 Lyne Roman Fort, near Peebles

*Mid 2nd century AD.*

*NT 187405. About 500 m W of Lyne Church on N side of A 72 Blyth Bridge-Peebles road; can be approached steeply from road bridge over Lyne Water, more gently from beside church.*

The countryside around Lyne was much favoured by the Romans. Aerial photography has revealed a fort near the attractive 18th century farmhouse of Easter Happrew, south of the river; whilst north of the river, Lyne Farm overlies a temporary camp, and a fortlet once existed a little to the north of the only visible remains.

Lyne fort was built in the Antonine period (c AD 158), probably to replace the Agricolan fort at Easter Happrew abandoned c AD 86. By the mid 2nd century, the area had been reoccupied and a road put through on the north side of the river, linking Newstead (close to Melrose) with the Clyde Valley (Castledykes) to the West.

The fort occupies a broad level plateau above a bend in the river. Weakest to defend on its eastern side, it is not surprising therefore that it faces east and was linked to the main Roman road by a branch road leading north-east. The rampart is traceable for most its length, and is particularly well-preserved along the west side (to a height of 2.5 m) and at the north-east corner. Built of turf, sometimes mixed with earth, the wall was supported either side by a narrow kerb of natural boulders. Triple ditches protect those parts of the fort lying east of the main north-south cross-street. These were the sections of wall not originally protected by annexes for camp-followers and convoys— sited on the north and south flanks, west of the cross-street.

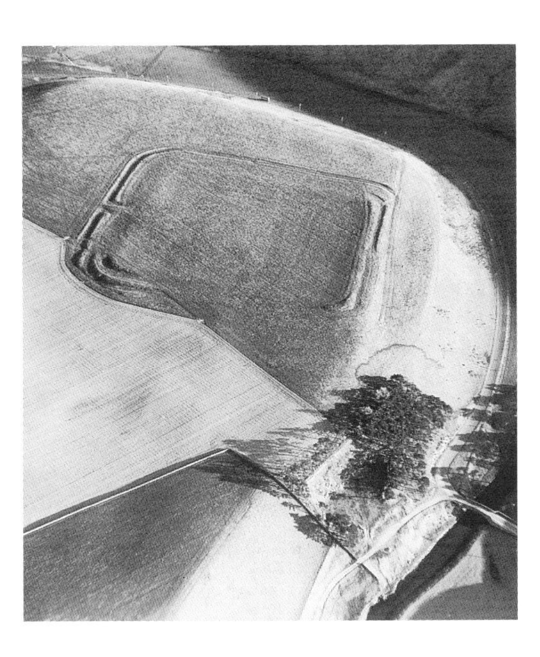

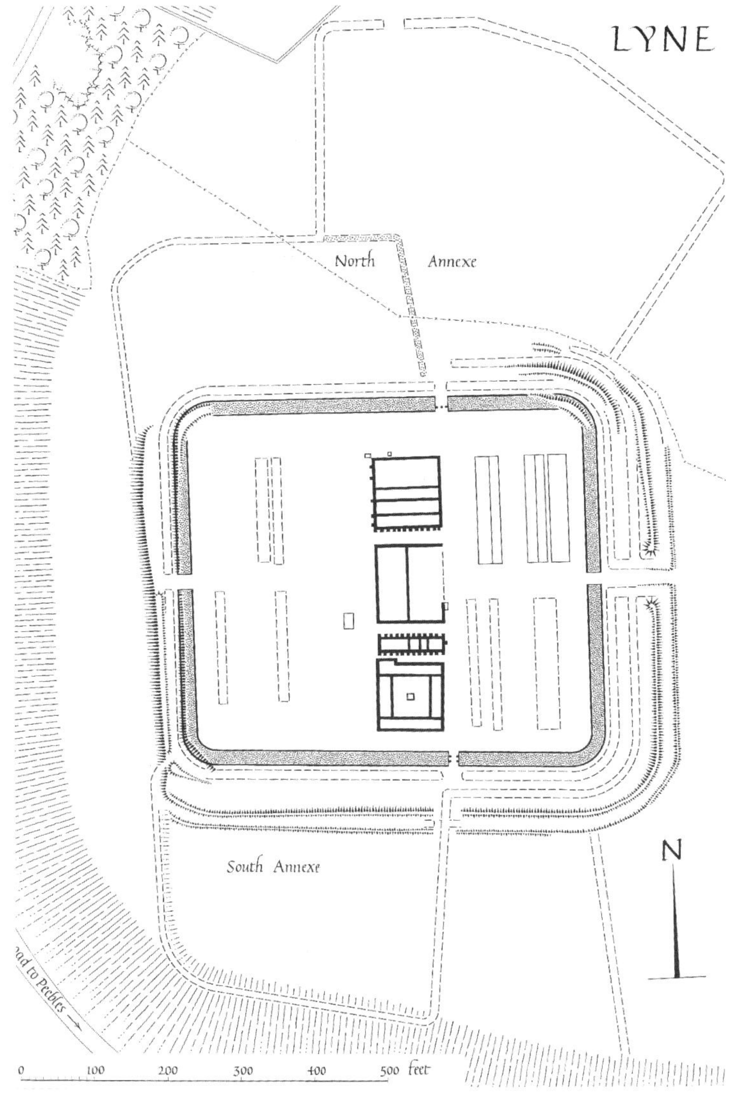


**Lyne Roman fort** (Top left) **and plan** (Above)

The positions of the gates are clearly visible; the Headquarters building would have been in the centre of the site with a granary to the south, then the commandant's house around an open courtyard. North of Headquarters was a large, square, heavily-buttressed building presumably a workshop or storehouse. Other buildings, barracks, stables and the like, ranged on a north-south axis, occupied much of the rest of the site.

The kind of garrison at Lyne is uncertain but the size of the fort (about 2.3 ha), as well as the wide streets and part of a horseshoe recovered, would suggest a cohort of cavalry.

## 88 Oakwood Roman Fort, near Selkirk

*Late 1st century AD.*

*NT 425249. B 7009 along S bank of Ettrick Water SW from Selkirk; 1 km SW from Oakwood Mill minor road climbs uphill before rejoining B road at Inner Huntley: fort on S side of this road, W of Hartwoodmyres.*

Though little more than a flat-topped, gentle grassy knoll, the site is sufficiently elevated to dominate the surrounding countryside. The outlook is particularly good to the west and north; to the east the tops of the Eildon Hills some 14-15 km distant are visible in the depression in the ridge. Given the signal-post on top of Eildon Hill North (no. 93), communication was possible direct from Oakwood to the Roman nerve-centre of Newstead.

The fort was established c AD 81 during Agricola's northward advance. During this occupation there were two phases of building, the second mainly reconditioning the defences of AD 81-86 which consisted of a thick turf-built rampart surrounded by two ditches. These are clearly visible on the west side and on parts of the north and south sides. Adjoining the south side, evidenced by a single ditch, was an annexe running over 60 m south from the south-west corner and thence east to the modern drystone dyke dividing Oakwood and Hartwoodmyres farms.

Though part of the main street running north-south is covered by a small plantation, all four gateways can be identified, set back over 9 m from the front of the rampart at the narrow end of a tunnel-shaped passage. All four gates were of timber and comprised twin portals placed side-by-side, flanked by square towers—an unusual design. The towers at the west gate were not enclosed; they were simply frameworks for fighting platforms similar to those shown on Trajan's column in Rome.

A short distance away, across the road, traces survive of a temporary camp (NT 425255), probably built to house soldiers working on the fort.

It seems likely that Oakwood was abandoned c AD 100 when most Roman troops in Scotland were withdrawn to the Tyne-Solway line. Given burning on the timber stumps of the east and west gates, identified during excavation, the occupation may have ended with a disastrous (or deliberate?) conflagration, as at Newstead. Unlike Newstead, however, Oakwood was never rebuilt.

## 89 Castle Greg Roman Fortlet, West Lothian

*Late 1st century AD.*

*NT 050592. About 50 m S of summit of Camilty Hill, a little over 1 km N on B 7008 towards West Calder from A 70, Edinburgh-Carnwath road.*

This is a fortlet rather than a full-sized fort. Standing close to 275 m above sea-level, on a slight plateau amongst what formerly were mainly peat-mosses, it may indicate the presence of a minor Roman route west of the Pentland Hills, used perhaps for troop movements into Lothian from forts or fortlets at Carstairs and Carnwath close to the River Clyde. That no such road is known, however, may suggest early construction, before the proper establishment of the Roman road network.

Almost intact, the fortlet is rectangular (some 55 m by 46 m) with rounded corners and a well-defined rampart that is best preserved at the southern end. Two ditches, with a mound between, surround the rampart except at the gateway in the centre of the east side. The roadway is some 6.7 m wide at the ditches, narrowing to about 2.7 m where it passes through the rampart, whilst near to the centre a roughly circular hollow marks the site of a well. The fortlet could have held about 80 men.

**Castle Greg Roman fortlet**

## 90 Pennymuir Temporary Roman Camps, near Kelso

*Late 1st-2nd century AD.*

*NT 7513-7514. From Morebattle, on B 6401 from Eckford to Yetholm, take minor road S through Hownam; about 12 km to junction with another minor road coming from Oxnam; W on this latter road about 1.5 km to Pennymuir crossroads.*

At Tow Ford on the Kale Water the main Roman trunk road (and the Dere Street of medieval times) comes down from the Cheviots on its way north. Passing between the best preserved group of temporary Roman camps in Scotland, it continues upwards again past prehistoric cairns and a stone circle, and between drovers' dykes to Whitton Edge (a fine broad ridge walk); thence to Shotheids, Rennieston and the now vanished fort at Cappuck. It crosses the Teviot in the vicinity of Monteviot House, and thus to Newstead, Lauderdale, Soutra and the Forth.

There are four camps bleakly situated at Pennymuir. One right down by the Kale Water (NT 757138) is badly eroded by both the river and by subsequent cultivation. A second camp (NT 756144) is bisected by the Pennymuir-Hownam road—though the western third survives sufficiently to show a trapezoidal rather than rectangular plan. The lie of the ground would not have required this; rather may it have been due to a misuse of sighting lines or to the availability of only short measuring rods!

The most visible camp, and the largest, lies to the west of the Roman road (NT 754138)—here the line of the little road from Pennymuir to Tow Ford. Most of the south side and the south part of the east side have been obliterated by rig-cultivation, but sufficient remains to show that this corner of the camp contained a separate smaller camp. Since the ditch of the latter cuts across the rampart of the larger camp it must be secondary, but like the larger version it seems to have had six gates, each of them protected by a 'traverse'—a blocking barrier set outside the entrance, allowing access only round its ends. Both camps were enclosed by a rampart formed from the upcast from a single, outer ditch.

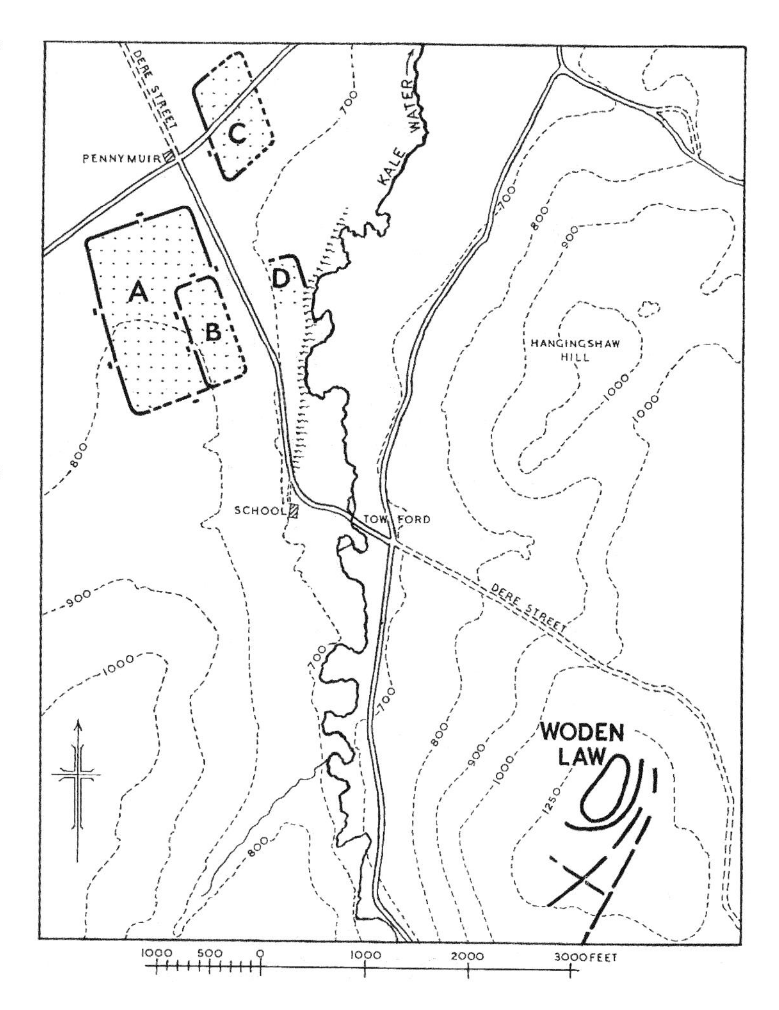


**Pennymuir temporary Roman camps, Dere Street, fort and earthworks on Woden Law**

It may be assumed that these temporary camps were training bases, providing tented accommodation for troops on exercise, most commonly perhaps on Woden Law (no. 91). The largest camp spreads over some 17 ha and could certainly have accommodated two legions—6000 men or more. It may, however, simply have been a temporary marching camp.

## 91 Woden Law Siege Works and Native Fort, near Kelso

*Late 1st-2nd century AD (?Roman works).*

*NT 768125. As for Pennymuir (no. 90) but continue S to Tow Ford; climb ESE and round back of Woden Law, thence to summit.*

The climb of Woden Law (423 m) is well worthwhile. The line of the Roman Road is quite well preserved alongside the gully rising from Tow Ford, but is even more distinct farther east, towards Hunthall Hill, as a linear mound some 8.2 m wide and 1.2 m high. It is but a short stretch to the Border, to the signal station on Brownhart Law (NT 790096) and to camps at Chew Green (NT 7808-7908). A major highway throughout the later medieval period, and equally in pre-Roman times, to the Romans it was their crucial link between York and the Firth of Forth, crucial to their conquest of Scotland. Though the road fell into disrepair after Agricola's withdrawal, it was reconstructed during the Antonine reoccupation in the 2nd century and played an important part in the 3rd-century Severan Campaign.

Equally vital was control of Woden Law, strategically situated just north of the watershed. Originally it was a native British fort, built in three stages (see section 8)—a settlement surrounded by a single, oval stone dyke, to which was then added a double rampart and intervening ditch. Both ramparts were demolished quite soon after completion, probably as a result of Roman road-building and occupation, and the site was only reoccupied by native peoples after the Romans left. Then the innermost rubble dyke on the top of the hill was built and faced with boulders.

The Romans, however, may have used Woden Law for siege practice (if the so-called siegeworks are not simply part of the native defences). They dug a remarkable earthwork of two banks between three ditches at 12 m-30 m from the fort's defences: in other words, mostly beyond the killing-range for hand-thrown missiles. Several flattened platforms on the outer bank seem to have provided sites for siege-engines, protected by the inner bank and ditch, whilst beyond the main siegework, three further independent lines of earthworks were built in the customary Roman manner of short, separate sections. These are all incomplete.

A further feature, the series of five cross-dykes spanning the easy ridge between Woden Law and Hunthall Hill, is pre-Roman however, and part of the native British defence system. Such cross-dykes are not uncommon in relation to hillforts in the Cheviots; here they guard access from the main Cheviot ridge and emphasise the importance of the site and the route.

## 92 Traprain Law Native Fort, East Lothian

*1st-mid 5th century AD.*

*NT 581746. Some 3 km SW of East Linton, minor road S from A 1 towards Whittingehame: then third/fourth side road W to hill; alternatively side roads 6.5 km E from Haddington.*

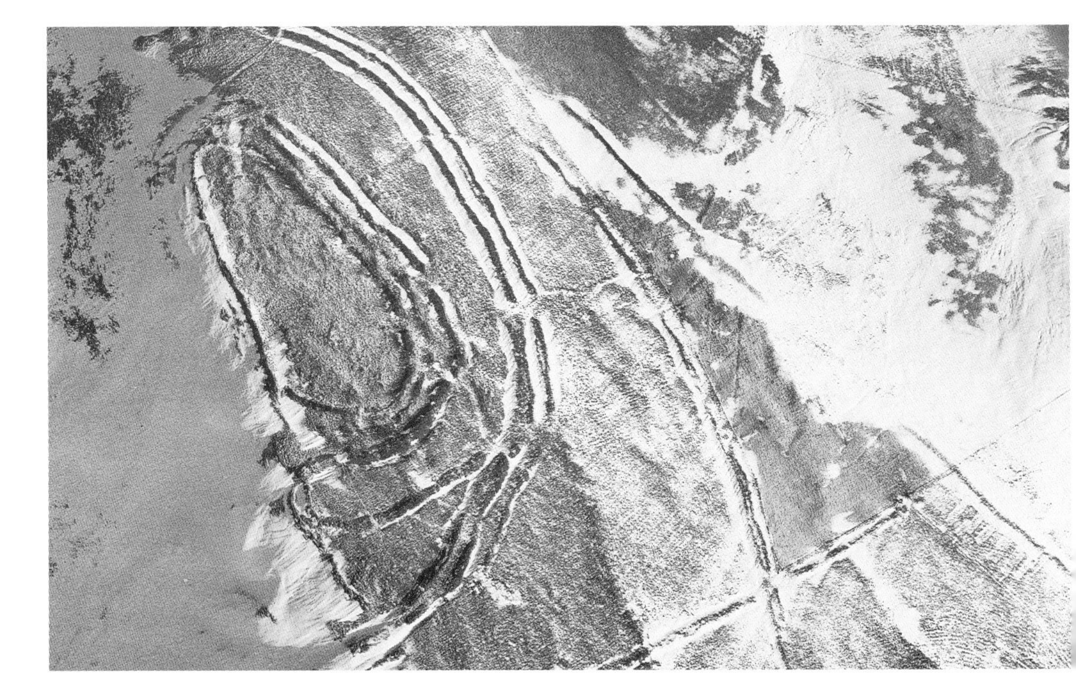

**Woden Law from the air**

**Trapain Law in 1965, when the quarry was still in operation**

Traprain Law dominates lowland East Lothian. Though quarrying has eroded the north-east part of the oval, volcanic 'hog-back' or 'harpooned whale', it remains impressive and craggy, an almost unassailable fortress with a known occupation of at least 1000 years.

One of its most prominent features is the 1.07 km long rampart of turf, faced with stone. Some 3.6 m thick, it encloses some 12 ha on the top and west side of the hill where it overlies its predecessor which then skirted lower round the north side (and now ends abruptly at the quarry). This extended enclosure, covering 16 ha, may have been built in the mid 1st century AD, shortly before the Romans arrived c AD 79; the reduced, later fort dates from late 4th century—the post-Roman capital perhaps of the Votadini.

A marginally later, early 5th-century date is given for the remarkable hoard of Roman silverware (now in NMS). It consists mainly of fragments of over 100 different objects—bowls, spoons, wine-strainer, flagons, dishes, plates—deliberately cut up, it would seem, bent and flattened, ready for melting down. Loot perhaps from a rich Roman household in England or Gaul? A Roman bribe or payment for military service? A reflection of the short-lived or two-faced nature of the 'peace'? At any rate it had been buried for security in a pit below floor level. The Christian motifs on some of the silver, whilst in no way suggesting Christianity at Traprain, nonetheless indicate the potentially Christian nature of so much of the late Roman world.

This Votadini capital, if such it was, may have been occupied until the arrival of the Angles in or after the mid 7th century AD; more likely, given the excavated finds and the state of the surviving defences, it was abandoned c mid 5th century with power transfering further west, perhaps to Edinburgh.

The earlier phases of occupation at Traprain are less easy to pinpoint. Bronze socketed axes and other items have been dated to the 6th-7th century BC, whilst pottery urns for cremation burials might suggest an occupation as early as c 1500 BC. There is little to see on the ground, though the settlement sequence may have started with a 4 ha palisaded enclosure on the summit and west slope, added to on two subsequent occasions with further 4 ha enclosures.

Some 300 m south-south-west of Traprain at NT 578741, a 2.5 m high standing stone is known traditionally as the Loth stone. Tradition suggests that King Loth was the eponymous hero of Lothian, and had his base on Traprain!

# 8 PREHISTORIC FORTS AND SETTLEMENTS

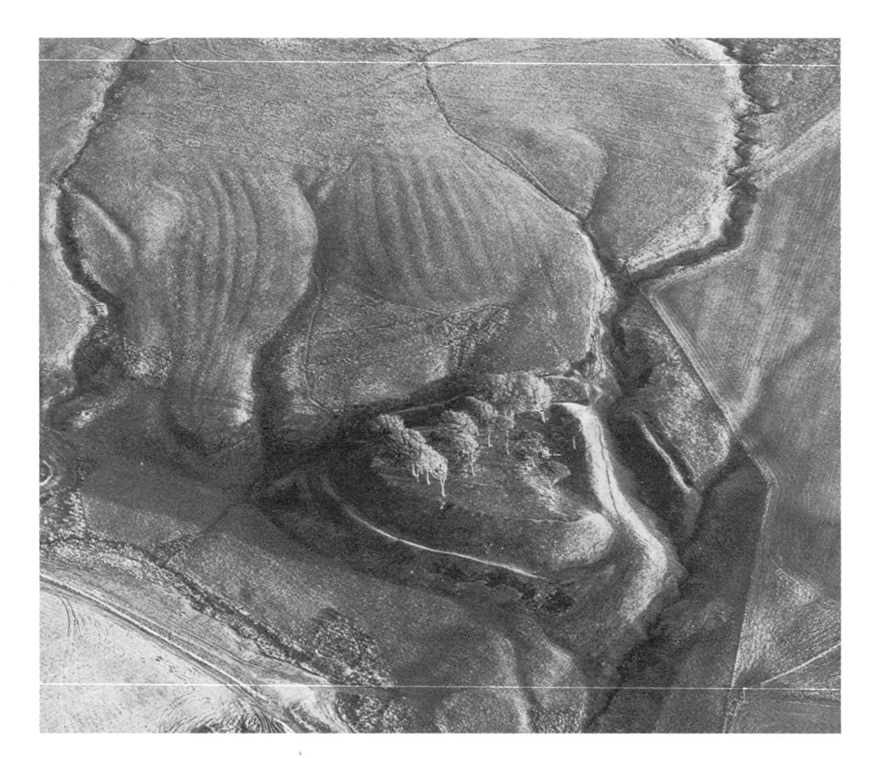

**Green Castle fort near Gifford, East Lothian**

Little enough is known of the life-style of those British tribes who lived uneasily alongside the Roman army. Some, certainly, would have provided services to the troops and would have lived perhaps in the 'vicus' or civilian settlement adjoining a fort. For many though, the enforced peace allowed them to attend more fully to their arable and livestock.

Amongst the Border hills in particular, evidence survives of their undefended settlements—low down in the narrower valleys, notably at Glenrath Hope (no. 97), at the head of Stan Hope and along the side of Dreva Hill (no. 96), higher up at Crock Cleuch (NT 833176) and Tamshiel Rig (NT 643062). Hut Knowe Rig (NT 793157), also in Roxburghshire, is particularly impressive, with a trackway leading up to the settlement entrance and enclosed fields of cord rig either side. In all these instances, traces of field-systems survive that, although known widely from southern England, are exceedingly rare in Scotland or indeed northern England. It would seem that hoe-cultivation of irregular plots continued well into Roman times and often longer, and only very occasionally did 'Celtic' fields occur, associated with ox-ploughing. Almost all these 'Celtic' fields are of the 'small square' variety, less than 2000 sq metres in extent. Exceptionally, Tamshiel Rig revealed 'long fields' within a series of walled enclosures radiating from the settlement, but the entire complex is now obliterated by forestry.

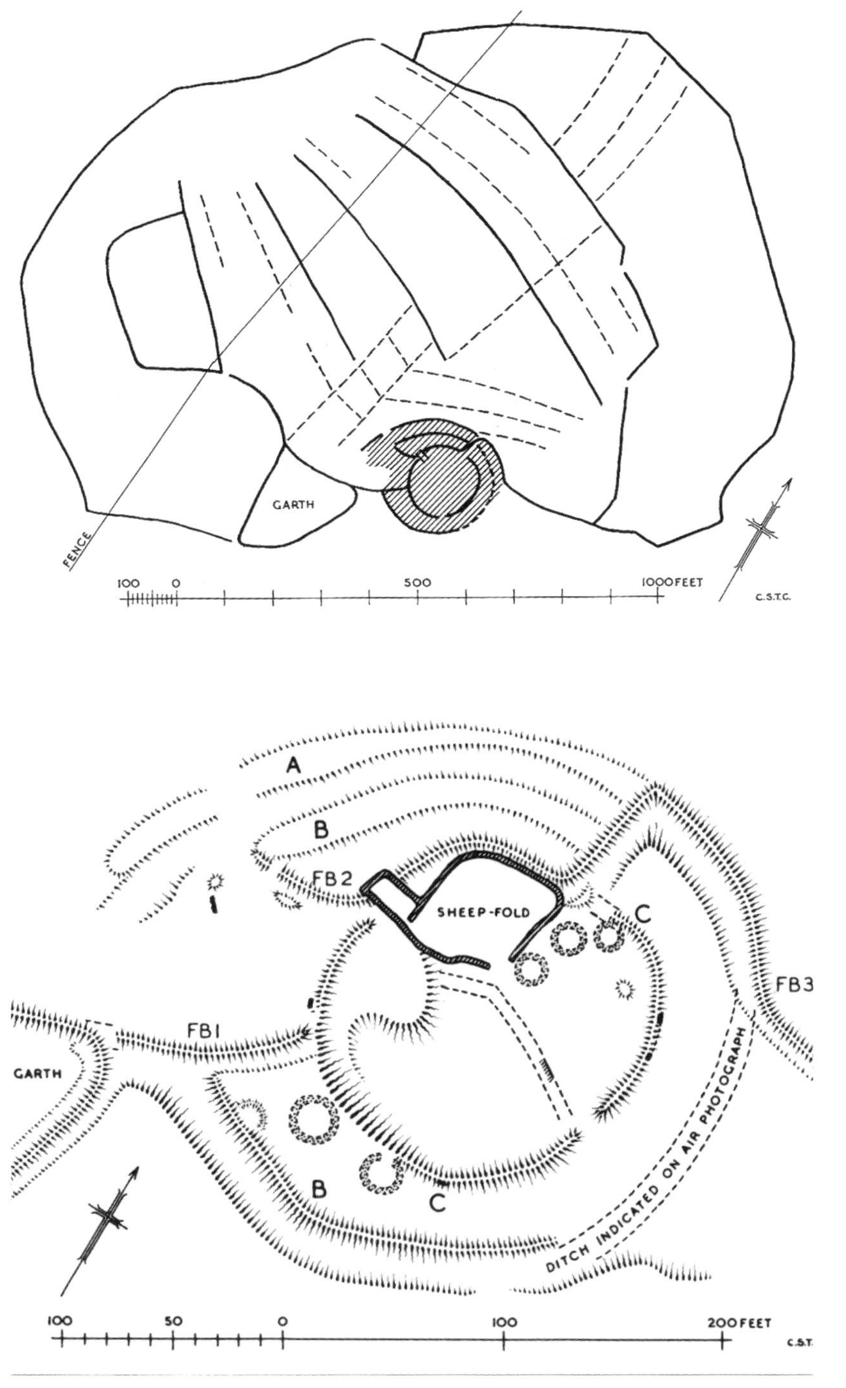


**Fort, settlement and Celtic 'long field' system, Tamshiel Rig, Roxburghshire: now afforested**

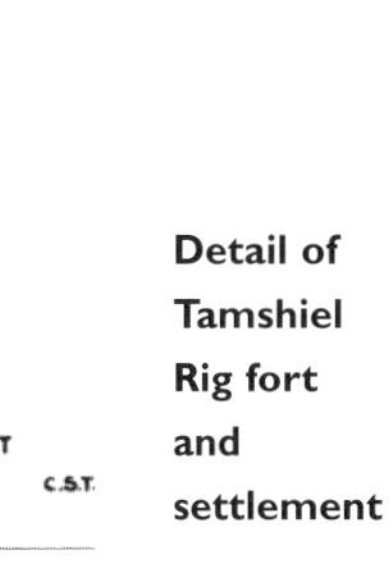

**Detail of Tamshiel Rig fort and settlement**

However sparse the remains, farming systems were becoming increasingly complex; and the many so-called 'pit alignments' logged by aerial photography across large areas of Berwickshire (from Ayton north to Bunkle Edge), Roxburghshire and the Lothian plain (here radiocarbon-dated to the late centuries BC), suggest substantial lowland enclosure and intensified agricultural settlement. Though less methodically compartmentalised, the hills also betray division—notably on White Hill, overlooking The Dod in Roxburghshire, opposite Burgh Hill (no. 109); and on Milkieston Hill by Eddleston, where they lie close to the multi-ramparted hillfort (NT 248460).

Such field systems are associated with circular stone-built houses, often enclosed within a roughly circular or oval stone-walled enclosure and opening off a sunken courtyard, the result perhaps of continued trampling by stock. In many cases, the houses have been preceded by timber-built structures; stone, however, seems to belong to (perhaps a result of) the Roman period or later, and objects recovered from sites would suggest an occupation from c 2nd century AD to maybe the 5th or 7th century at Crock Cleuch or the rectilinear Hownam Rings (no. 95).

In almost all cases the systems and settlements are associated with and in part regularly overlie the earlier hillforts, more accurately described as fortified hilltop settlements, the most prolific of all monuments in the upland areas of the south-east. The iron-working Celts had first arrived in Scotland c 600 BC, but the most prominent of their defensive settlement features developed fairly late, perhaps under pressure of an increasing population swollen by refugees fleeing northwards from the Romans. However, it is also thought that some hillforts may have been abandoned before the Romans arrived.

The ultimate design, therefore, by the 1st century AD and in evidence at least from the 1st century BC, was the multi-ramparted ring fort: generally two or three immense earthen banks with external ditches, but four or more if a site or part of a site were particularly vulnerable. Their main purpose may have been to impress and to deter, especially at such strategically indefensible sites as The Chesters (no. 101), settled first, presumably, when danger was less evident. And in some instances, the encircling ramparts were left unfinished, cut short no doubt by the arrival of the Romans—Whitehill (NT 055338), Cademuir I (no. 98).

But the extraordinary growth of the ‘rings’, defence in depth, across the south of Scotland, suggests equally a need to counteract a new kind of weapon—maybe slings but also perhaps chariots or horsemen. The Celts were traditionally superb horsemen and it is in this context perhaps that the uncommon jagged battalions of stones, *chevaux de frise*, set upright across the weaker lines of access to Dreva (no. 96) and Cademuir II (no. 98) should be seen; also cross-dykes, dug to bar the approach to Harehope Rings (NT 196445), Whiteside Hill (NT 168460) or Woden Law (no. 91).

A few forts, such as White Castle in East Lothian (NT 613686), seem to have originated with multiple ramparts and are likely to be correspondingly late settlements; for most, the extra ramparts were later additions built beyond an earlier single wall and ditch, generally of stone (Woden Law) though sometimes of earth. Occasionally there were double stone walls eg Dreva; occasionally double earthen walls eg Harehope Rings. At the Haerfaulds (NT 574500) the single irregularly oval, massive stone wall was never reinforced with further defences, though circular stone huts built into its tumble confirm occupation in the Romano-British period.

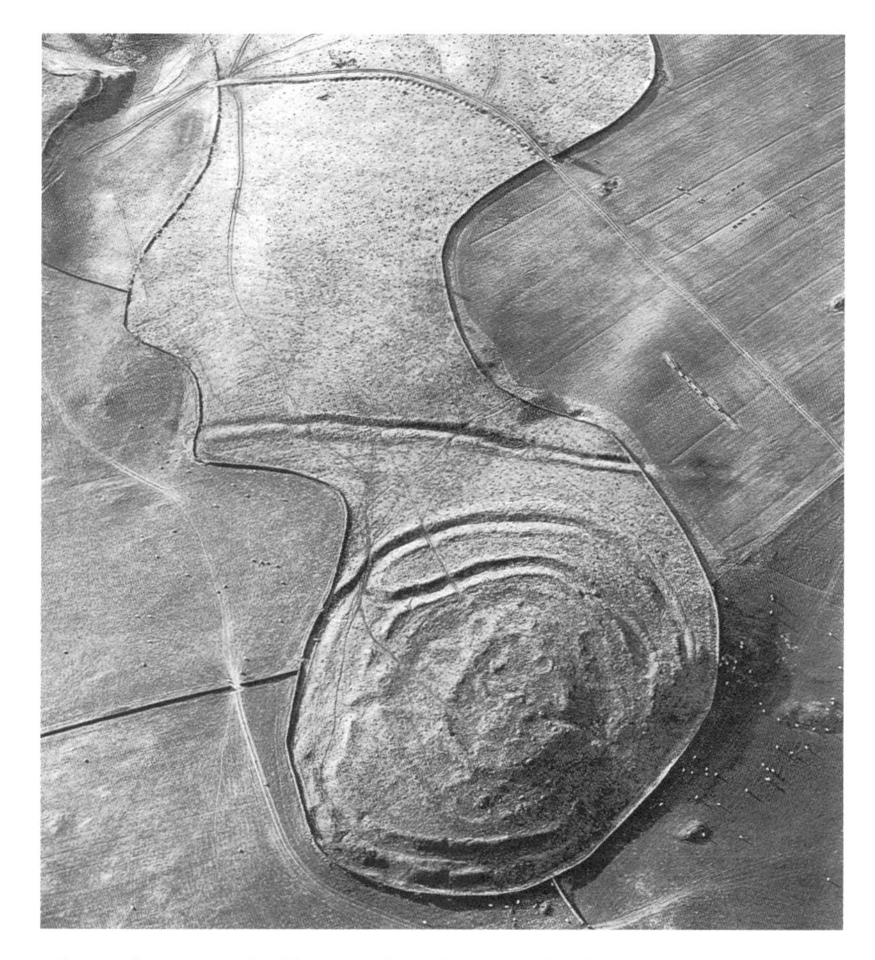

**Fortified settlement, linear earthworks and pit alignment at Milkieston Rings, Eddleston, near Peebles**

The wall at Haerfaulds may have been timber-laced, a constructional technique used at Tinnis Castle (NT 141344) and Hare Law (NT 546630). It is a technique that was introduced to Scotland from northern Germany as early as the 6th-8th century BC, but whilst valuable in stabilising a rampart or simply an entrance (Castlelaw, no. 84), the replacement of rotten timber would have required a massive reconstruction, as well as access to quantities of good woodland. Furthermore, stone alone had the advantage of not going on fire—whether started accidently from lean-to houses, or by an enemy. It was the heat from such conflagration that was sufficient to fuse granite or sandstone into the dark, vitrified, distorted lumps that betray the former presence of timber-lacing.

Vitrification apart, Hownam Rings (no. 95) shows each of the main sequences so far—a late 3rd-century AD and later, undefended settlement of stone-walled houses and homesteads partly overlying multiple ramparts strengthening a massive single stone rampart (not timber-laced). As in many other hill settlements, this stone wall was preceded by a wooden palisade: a total occupation sequence of maybe 600-700 years.

Palisades, either single or double, comprised a large number of stakes set close to each other in a narrow trench, packed around with stones. Where double, as at Hayhope Knowe (NT 860176) or Braidwood (no. 103), the

**Longcroft hillfort, near Oxton, Lauderdale**

ends looped round and joined each other at the entrance thus leaving the space between the stockades secure—perhaps for the penning of stock. Palisaded sites in south-east Scotland and north-east England can be dated from the 6th-7th centuries BC onwards.

Palisades might surround a homestead of just two or three houses—a family unit—or a larger communal settlement. Their timber-built houses can be traced by circular grooves in the ground, following round the line of sunken trenches in which the posts were set—for example at Greenbrough Hill (NT 813169) and Braidwood. Not all were sited on high ground, moreover, though these tend to have survived more effectively. Such as the Horsburgh Castle Farm site (NT 291400) in the Tweed Valley between Peebles and Innerleithen was probably the base for high-status British farmers in the centuries immediately preceding the Romans. That palisades were thought necessary at all, however, along with buried hoards of bronze work, suggests an early tension between the incoming, British-speaking, iron-working Celts and their bronze-working predecessors.

For evidence does survive on the ground of earlier more peaceful times. On the slopes of White Meldon for instance (NT 216433, 218435) or across the burn at Green Knowe (no. 104), groups of entirely unenclosed house platforms lie scooped out along the contours of the hillside, built up level to the outer face. Clusters might comprise two to twelve platforms accommodating perhaps one to four/five families with their various outbuildings—one timber building to each platform. Occupation of such settlements, though continuing presumably as long as 'open' settlements were felt safe, can be dated as early as 1000-1200 BC. They relate, therefore, to the workers in bronze who, to judge by the evidence of Traprain, were still active in the 7th and 6th centuries BC. At Green Knowe, associated small cairns, presumably clearance cairns, suggest some small-scale cultivation; the basic economy, however, was likely to have been primarily pastoral and the sites may originally have been seasonal transhumance sites that later became permanent, year-round settlements.

**Fortified native settlement and Roman signal station, Eildon Hill North**

### 93 Eildon Hill North Fort, near Melrose

*6th/7th century BC-later 1st century AD.*

*NT 555328. Via 'Eildon Walk', signposted; or golf course S of centre of Melrose on B 6359, then a steep climb to ridge. Or tracks W from Eildon village on A 6091, 1 km NW of Newton St Boswells (A 68).*

Like Traprain in its prime, this fortified British town covered some 16 ha, and the ramparts are visible from a considerable distance. Its latest feature is not native however, but Roman: a circular 10.7 m enclosure surrounded by a ditch crossed by a causeway on the north side. Inside stood a rectangular wooden signal tower, probably two storeys high, on six posts. It was a late 1st-century AD signal tower, presumably part of Agricola's defences, and visible for some 24-32 km except to the south-west (Oakwood Fort, no. 88).

At about 305 m, Eildon Hill North dominates routes along both the Tweed and the Leader Water, as well as fords on the Tweed both north and east. It commands the whole of the Merse and is clearly seen from suitable vantage points on the Cheviots. It served the massive Newstead complex, receiving and transmitting long-range messages, and was likely the key Roman communications centre in south-east Scotland. Like Woden Law (no. 91) it was doubtless too important to the Romans to be left in the hands of the natives.

The first phases of native settlement are barely evident: a single wall or rampart around the summit enclosing some 3.6 ha. In its last, most visible phase, however, the fort possessed three concentric ramparts over 1.6 km in circumference, though in places one or sometimes both of the outer lines have since slipped down the hillside. For the most part these ramparts now appear as terraces, which may have been deliberately built as foundations for the ramparts—as also on Woden Law.

Spread over the surface of the fort are some 300 hut circles: level platforms scooped out of the hill, on which timber-framed houses were built. Their number suggests a population of perhaps 2000; or 125 people to the hectare. Under these circumstances, and assuming the town to have been permanently occupied, the community could not have been self-sufficient. Society was presumably highly organised, stratified and involved in trade and localised industry in addition to agriculture.

Eildon Hill North is thought to have been the capital of the Selgovae who lived around the Upper Tweed and had smaller 'towns' on Ruberslaw (no. 94), White Meldon (NT 219427) and Dunion Hill (NT 625190).

## 94 Ruberslaw Fort, near Hawick

*Late BC/early AD-4th/5th century AD.*

*NT 580155. Farm track and hillside from Denholmhill or Whiteriggs on minor road between Denholm (A 698) and A 6088; similarly from Blawearie or Hallrule on minor road E side of Rule Water from B 6358 (A 698) to Bonchester Bridge (A 6088).*

After Eildon Hill North, Ruberslaw is the most prominent hill in Roxburghshire—isolated, imposing and with fine views to the Cheviots, the Eildons, the Lammermuirs, the hills of Selkirkshire and Liddesdale. Nearly 427 m high, its igneous summit is crowned with a fortified settlement, supplanted by a later enclosure. This later, single stone wall encircling only the actual summit has an annexe to the south; it incorporates dressed stones sometimes suggested as Roman because of their diamond-shaped chiselling and re-used when the site was reoccupied by a British community, perhaps in the 4th or 5th century AD.

These structures make considerable use of rocky outcrops as an integral part of their defences; the earlier wall or rampart, by contrast, follows a roughly even course around the hill, well below the summit, enclosing nearly 3 ha in all. It is of boulder-faced rubble build, though over 100 m is lost on the east side. There is a well-marked entrance on the south side, approached by a hollow track; two other possible entrances on the north make use of natural gullies.This then is a pre-Roman hillfort large enough to be one of the minor centres of the Selgovae whose capital was probably on Eildon Hill North (no. 93). About 4 km south-south-west, Bonchester Hill fort (NT 594117) shows a similar history.

South of Ruberslaw and west of Bonchester Bridge, either side of the A 6088, there are wide expanses of old cultivation rigs. Fairly straight, low and roughly parallel, they are unlikely to be much older than around AD 1800. Their survival is an indication of the retreat of arable cultivation from some of the higher lands; it also well illustrates the pre-improvement pattern of ridge and furrow cultivation—a necessary form of natural drainage as well as a basic working unit.

## 95 Hownam Rings Fort, near Kelso

6th/7th century BC-late 3rd century AD.

*NT 790194. 6 km S to Hownam on minor road from Morebattle (B 6401: Eckford-Yetholm); track E just N of bridge, and up to ridge; thence N.*

Over 300 m high, Hownam Rings command the ridge over which a track known as 'The Street' passes from Hownam, along the high plateau and across the Border to Upper Coquet Dale. The site is naturally protected on three sides, but is easily accessible along this ridge.

Excavation has identified at least four phases of occupation, the last dating from the late 3rd century AD and comprising an undefended settlement of circular stone-built houses and a roughly rectangular enclosure containing a single stone-walled house. This settlement lies both within and upon the abandoned ramparts of the previous phase.

Whilst it is uncertain when the triple ramparts were abandoned, they had been built perhaps in response to such new weapons as slings or chariots. They represent a major remodelling of an earlier 3.6 m thick stone wall, faced either side with stone blocks and infilled with rubble. Within the entrance to this single wall, blocked up when replaced, a quern was found, dated to the late 1st century AD. The first phase, no longer identifiable on the ground, was a simple palisaded enclosure which had been reconstructed very soon after completion on almost the same line. Originally thought to date to the 1st or 2nd century BC, radiocarbon tests now suggest these first phases to be 6th or 7th century BC—giving a total occupation span of some 700-800 years.

'The Shearers' (NT 790192-791192), a line of 28 stones, cross the plateau some 82 m south-east of the fort. Eleven of them are exposed at turf-level. Said by some to be standing stones, they are more likely the 'grounders' of an ancient field-dyke probably erected during the occupation of the fort. Such field dykes, in association with late-Roman/early-Anglian homesteads, survive at Crock Cleuch, about 5 km west-south-west (NT 833176).

## 96 Dreva Craig Fort, Settlements and Field Systems, near Broughton

*Late BC/early AD.*

*NT 126353-127353. Minor road E from Broughton to Stobo follows N side of Tweed; about 1.2 km E of A 701 it crosses lower shoulders of SE ridge of Trehenna Hill; fort is 200 m S.*

Dreva occupies a prime site, a rocky outcrop providing clear views both up and down the Tweed valley and westward to the broad and fertile bowl amongst the hills that contains the attractive village of Broughton and the key through-route to the upper Clyde—the Biggar Gap. A twin protector, Tinnis Castle and Fort (NT 141344) stands opposite, just east of Drumelzier.

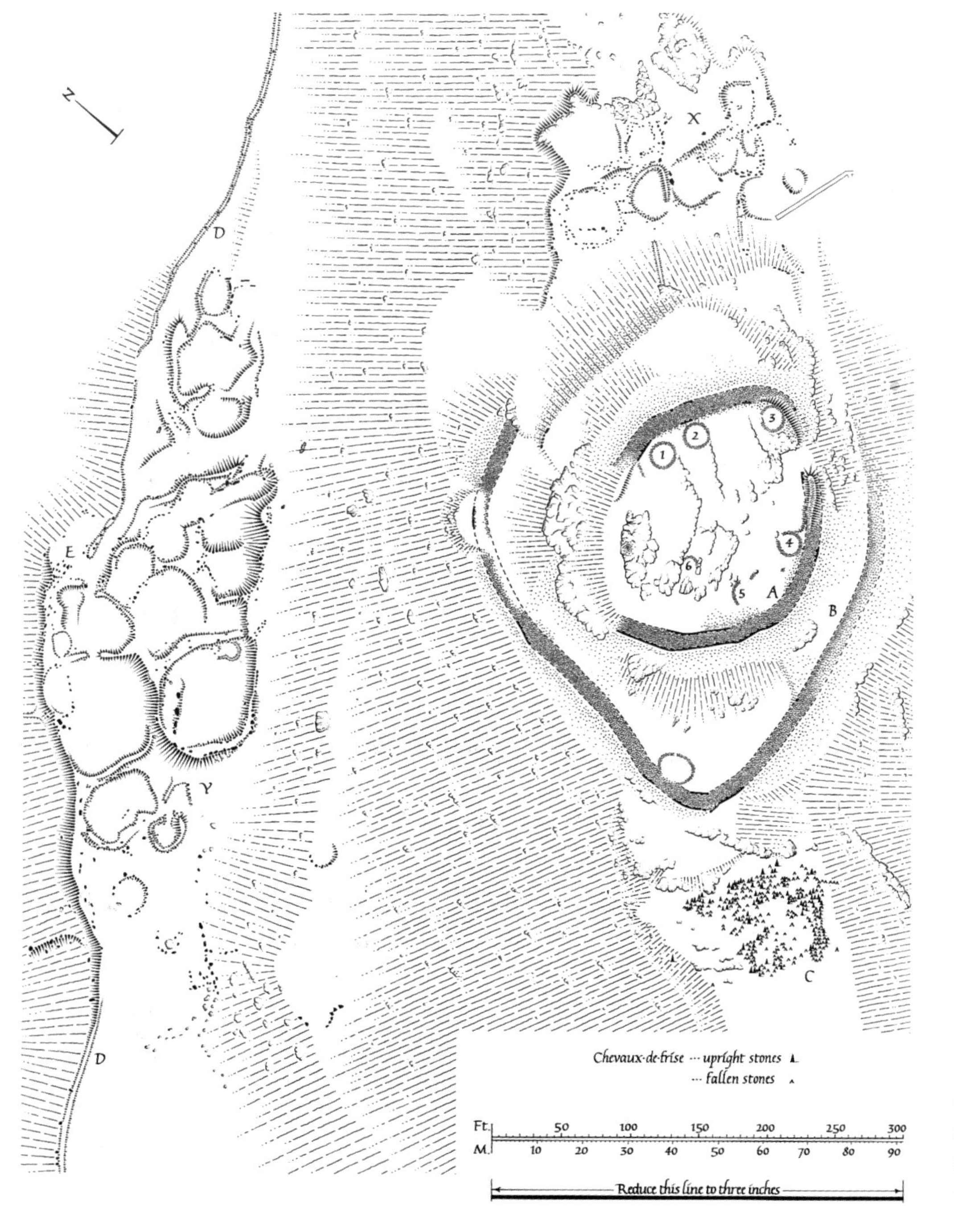


**Plan of Dreva Craig fort, settlements and field systems**

**Fort, settlement and field systems, Dreva Craig**

Built of stone, the fort consists of two walls, each up to 4.3 m thick at the base, faced on both sides with boulders and packed internally with stones. Whilst there is no evident contemporary settlement, secondary occupation within the inner wall is indicated by four stony rings and a fragment of a fifth built partly into the inner edge of debris from the wall. The entrance is by a natural gully to the east-south-east, over 3.5m wide. Of the outer rampart most survives in an area north-west by west to south-west.

The remarkable thing about Dreva is that its prominent position evidently outweighed its relative lack of natural defences. Such shortcomings were alleviated, however, by a feature that is rare in Scotland: the *chevaux de frise*. About 100 stones, protecting access up the south-west slope beyond the outer wall, still stand upright over an area of some 650 square metres; many more, either broken stumps or lying loose in the grass, must have made this instrument of defence a formidable obstacle to horsemen or chariots—or even attackers on foot. And there may well have been a similar jagged barrier on the opposite north-east side, given the number of large upright boulders scattered amongst the remains of a later settlement.

This later settlement (NT 127353) and the one below the north-west side of the fort (NT 125353) were undefended. Below the latter, and extending across the road along the slope, is a fragmentary but clearly identifiable field-system (NT 125354-130357) which even now covers over 10 ha. Although the original shapes and sizes of the fields are lost, the remnants suggest 'Celtic' fields, as at Glenrath Hope (no. 97).

Beyond, on the lower slopes of Trehenna Hill, the considerable numbers of cultivation rigs are perhaps 18th century: they are not as wide, high and sinuous as earlier rigs. The names Dreva and Trehenna, however, both contain the British placename element *tref*, a homestead.

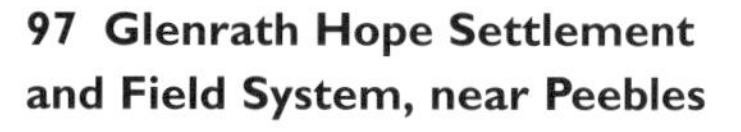

## 97 Glenrath Hope Settlement and Field System, near Peebles

*Late 1st-2nd century AD.*

*NT 213328-228323. About half-way between Lyne and Peebles on A 72 take Manor Water road S; thence farm track SE up Glenrath Burn.*

Glenrath, the 'valley of the settlement', was formerly the route of an important drove road over to the Douglas and Yarrow Waters. The hills around Glenrath are steep with screes, and snow can lie low well into March. For about 1.5 km along the northern side of the valley bottom, facing south, are plentiful traces of human settlement—some 14 ha in all. The land is criss-crossed with old dykes, field systems and traces of habitation (with later, superimposed cultivation terraces: see section 2).

The settlements lie immediately below the screes and above the cultivated ground. They are essentially the ruinous clusters of circular houses, together with small enclosures which do not appear to conform to any set pattern. The most extensive ruins are found east of the plantation; and at 'A' consist of three courts (now partly buried by falling scree), with circular houses up to 6 m diameter bonded into their enclosing walls. The only find during excavations at 'B' was a single ornamented spindle whorl.

In association with the settlements is a field system which consists partly of stony banks, presumably once dykes, running down the slope; and partly of lynchets (steep banks below pieces of cultivated ground) often topped with ruinous dykes and running along the contour. There are many clearance cairns (of stones removed from the soil during cultivation) both within the fields and on

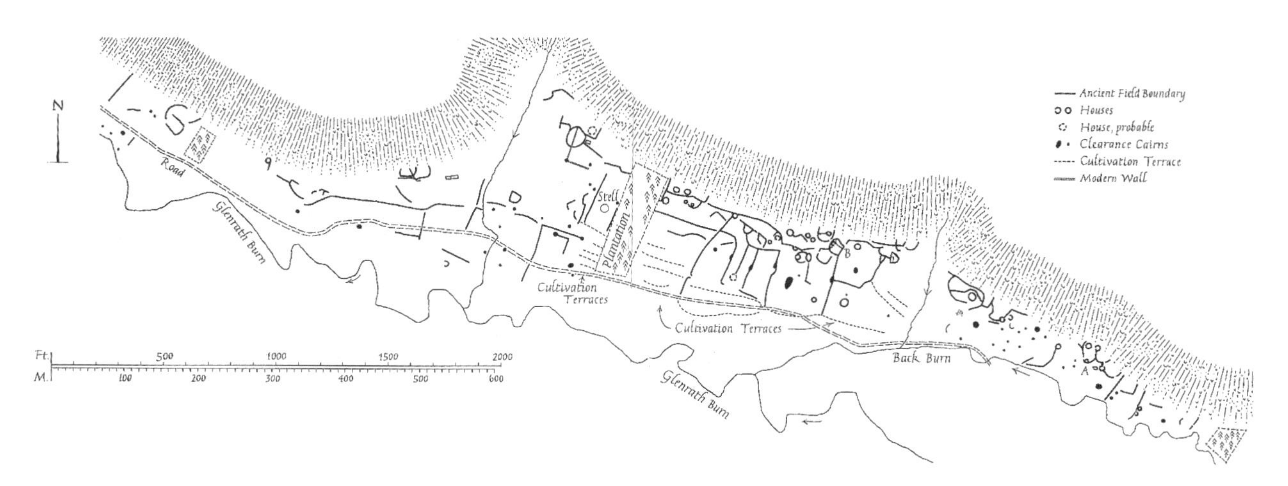


**Settlement and Celtic 'short field' system, with superimposed cultivation terraces, Glenrath Hope**

the banks; there are also a number of isolated, circular structures, apparently similar to those in the settlement and dug very clearly into the slope.

Where reasonably complete fields survive, they were clearly not larger than 0.2 ha—longer than wide in a ratio of 2.5:1. These are the so-called 'Celtic' square fields. Similar, though badly-damaged systems can be identified at Dreva (no. 96) and a fragment at Stanhope (NT 147280)—all of them in narrow locations, with limited areas of cultivable land. At Tamshiel Rig, by contrast, (NT 643062), 'Celtic' long fields were in evidence—much less common in Scotland.

## 98 Cademuir Hill Forts, near Peebles

*Late BC-1st century AD.*

*NT 230374 (I), NT 224370 (II). Track SW from Tantah, King's Muir, off B 7062 on S outskirts of Peebles (2-3 km) or by minor road King's Muir-Manor Water and path NE from below summit.*

The hills of Cademuir are a natural stronghold, bounded by the Manor Water and the Tweed, and by a former broad meander of the Tweed, now a flat and cultivated valley. Traces of hut platforms (NT 233381) and a scooped homestead (NT 234382) survive on the lower north-west slopes of the hills; whilst on the saddle (NT 237380), 485 m west-north-west of the main summit, on level ground, there are traces of platforms for two timber houses and a secondary stone-walled house within what is now simply a low stony bank.

The two fortified settlements lie on the ridge to the west. Cademuir I stands on the summit of this ridge with good natural protection on all but the slightly less precipitous south-west side. Some 2.25 ha are enclosed by a single 3 m thick wall, faced either side with stone and infilled with rubble. The original entrances are to the east and to the south-west, and except to the south-east the wall is surrounded some 6 m-12 m away by an unfinished rampart.

There are traces of at least 35 timber-framed houses within the fort, identified by circular grooves in the ground—and space for as many again. Most are about 7.6 m diameter. This suggests a site of some significance in the earlier iron age, and of more than local significance. It was, in fact, a small town but since there are no traces of stone-built houses or other secondary structures, it was probably abandoned c AD 80 after the arrival of the Romans.

**Fort and *chevaux de frise*, Cademuir Hill II**

The second, considerably smaller fort, occupies the lower western summit of the same ridge. Outside the massive stone ruins of its 6 m thick enclosing wall, subsidiary enclosures stand on terraces to the south-west, south-east and north. Its most interesting feature is undoubtedly the *chevaux de frise* protecting the north-east approach over level ground (cf Dreva, no. 96). More than 100 stones still stand over a distance of nearly 80 m, set in the outer side of a small gully so that they would have been invisible until attackers had breasted the gully and were in amongst the stones. Sudden disarray!

Both sides of this crucial Tweed Valley-Upper Clyde through-route are peppered with fortified hilltop settlements. About 3 km north-west lies White Meldon (NT 219428), the largest. A little to the west, Hamildean Hill fort (NT 187419) was never completed, perhaps on account of the arrival of the Romans; a further 4.5 km north-north-west, Whiteside Hill fort (NT 168460), above the Romanno cultivation terraces (no. 27), is particularly well-preserved and conspicuous.

## 99 Earn's Heugh Forts, Coldingham

*Late BC-late 4th century AD.*

*NT 892691. Minor road 250 m W of Coldingham N off A 1107 leads to Westerside Farm (3 km) close to Coldingham Loch; thence 500 m NE to cliff edge.*

**Earn's Heugh forts, near St Abbs**

The summit of Tun Law ends in a spectacular, precipitous cliff 150 m above the sea. To say that the twin settlements are semi-oval, semi-circular or D-shaped is to ignore the likelihood of at least half of each structure lost through erosion—an indicator of the increasing attack of the sea over 2000 years and more.

The interior of the eastern enclosure, roughly 70 m by 35 m, is encircled by the remains of a single rampart with external ditch and an entrance at the west side. A further pair of ramparts was subsequently added, overridden in turn by a similar pair added to the western enclosure. This larger enclosure follows much the same pattern—a 55 m diameter settlement perhaps, within a single wall (though apparently without a ditch), extended by the two further ramparts to a diameter of at least 80 m.

Unlike the smaller settlement which provides no evidence of house sites, here traces have been found of at least nine circular stone foundations, all lying against the inner face of the innermost wall. Such stone-built houses often accompany Roman influence in south-east Scotland, and the evidence of excavated objects dated between 150 and 400 AD, suggests that Earn's Heugh, even if abandoned during the Roman period, was certainly occupied again until at least the late 4th century AD.

Coldingham Moor, commanding the coastal route north and south, has a high concentration of fortified settlements—at least ten within a 1.5 km radius; there are other high concentrations along Bunkle Edge, commanding a fine prospect across the Merse and into Northumberland, and along the hills either side of Lauderdale, an equally important artery north.

## 100 Tollis Hill Fort, near Lauder

*Late BC/early AD.*

*NT 516580. Some 200 m W of shepherd's house at end of minor road NNE up Kelphope Burn from Carfraemill Hotel (A 697).*

Separated by no more than 4 km one from each other, fine fortified settlements hover on the hill promontories east of the Leader Water. Some are

**Tollis Hill fort**

oval—Addinston (NT 523536), an irregular silhouette on the ridge above the A 697/A 68 immediately south of Carfraemill; or Longcroft (NT 532543), up the side valley from Addinston and high above the meeting of two burns. Tollis Hill, by contrast, is an almost perfect circle, over 90 m across internally, and enclosed by a double rampart and intervening ditch. Where these defences are best preserved, towards the west and north, the inner rampart is still 3.6 m-4 m above the bottom of the ditch and nearly 1 m-1.2 m above the level of the interior. The outer rampart is rather modest and more by way of a parapet on top of the counterscarp; the distance across the ditch between the two crests, however, is almost 9 m.

A well-preserved entrance on the west, 1.8 m-2.4 m wide, is flanked either side by the ends of the ramparts brought round in a loop; and, whilst other entrances to the south and east are probably modern, that to the north might also be original.

There are a large number of hut circles within the ramparts, some of them joined together by short sections of straight walling; there are also several larger enclosures which, to judge from their size, may have been sheepfolds.

To look north and north-east to the top of the Lammermuir ridge, to look east and south-east over the slightly lower Lammermuir plateau is to appreciate the attraction of these lands. Climate permitting, they are fine lands for stock grazing, for some arable and for settlement. Some 10 km south-south-east, for instance, stands the impressive ruinous settlement of Haerfaulds (NT 574500), 'ancient folds' in Anglian times, on open moorland steeply above the Blythe Water. An oval structure, some 116 m by 73 m, it is surrounded by the remains of a massive stone wall at least 3 m thick originally, and possibly timber-faced. Many circular stone hut circles abut the inner face of the wall, some are built in its tumble; these presumably represent local building developments and occupation in Romano-British time.

Forts, cairns, stone circles litter this landscape—with a standing stone by the side of the road just east of the Tollis Hill house. And what of the west side of the Leader Water?—forts at Bowerhouse (NT 490509) and Blackchester (NT 507504); a settlement at Trabrown (NT 504487); a much earlier though now barely distinguishable henge at Overhowden (NT 486522). None of this is surprising given the strategic nature of Lauderdale to north-south communications.

### 101 The Chesters Fort, East Lothian

*Late BC/early AD.*

*NT 507782. 1.5 km S of Drem/4 km N of Haddington, on minor road linking B 1377, B 1343 and A 1, turn SE up farm track: signposted.*

*Historic Scotland.*

Though this fort occupies the greater part of a long, oval hillock, it is relatively low-lying and overlooked by a higher ridge from which missiles could easily have been launched. Vulnerability would not have mattered perhaps in its earlier periods of occupation; gradually, however, fortifications were extended providing a most elaborate system of stone and earth ramparts. Was it simply a case of a wealthy community wanting to impress? Or to present an illusion of strength to would-be attackers?

Two ramparts entirely encircle the site; to the north there are a further three lines of banking, spanning 55 m. A series of five earthworks stretches across the west end, with a further series to the east, and these may have been intended specifically to protect the entrances at the north-west and east of the fort.

The enclosed area measures some 119 m by 49 m, within inner ramparts still standing to over 2 m high. Inside, there are traces of the foundations of maybe 20 or 30 mainly circular stone buildings varying in size from 4.25 m to 12 m diameter but apparently ranged around the sides in roughly regular rows. Some overlie the ramparts, thus suggesting a period of occupation from the 2nd century AD or later.

**The Chesters hillfort**

**Hare Law vitrified hillfort** (Bottom)

### 102 Hare Law Fort, East Lothian

*6th-7th century BC.*

*NT 546632. Minor road S to Longyester from B 6355 W of Gifford; track SW towards Lammer Law for about 2.5 km, thence E along ridge between Harelaw Burn and Sting Bank Burn and on to W summit.*

Only the approach from the south-west is relatively easy; otherwise, the rocky 380 m high summit is naturally strong, difficult to attack and commands the whole of the countryside between the Lammermuirs and the Firth of Forth.

The innermost wall, something over 1 m thick and 0.5 m high encircling the summit, should be taken as relatively modern, re-using stone quarried from the north end of the fort. Otherwise, the kidney-shaped site runs roughly 61 m by 31 m, with a single stone wall around its steep north-eastern end. Around the sides, however, and especially towards the south-west, more elaborate defences were necessary. Two ramparts with external ditches cut off all access from the south-west, whilst the only entrance stands in the middle of the north-west flank—a shallow depression 3.5 m wide cutting through both the outer defences and the stone inner wall.

That the massive stone wall of this fort was timber-laced is evident from traces of vitrification in parts of the walling. Almost directly opposite the entrance, vitrified stones up to 23 cm diameter have been found on what seems to be the core of the inner east wall; somewhat to the south of the entrance, to the outside of the wall, more of the core has been exposed and suggests that the footing has been continuously fused by vitrification.

From Hare Law it is possible to see maybe seven or eight fortified sites within a range of 3 km-5 km. Kidlaw (NT 512642), Black Castle (NT 580661) and Green Castle (NT 581656) are all good examples only a short distance from a road.

## 103 Braidwood Palisaded Settlement, Midlothian

*6th-7th century BC to early AD.*

*NT 192596. A 702 Edinburgh-West Linton, 800 m SW of Silverburn; follow farm track W to Eastside for about 700 m, then strike S up slope.*

On excavation Braidwood was found not to be a conventional hillfort but rather a timber palisaded settlement with secondary earthen banks, apparently unfinished (the outer bank is now almost ploughed out). With most earthen ramparts, the ditch lay on the outside with the cast earth within; here, however, the earlier palisades were used as outer retaining walls so that the new defences were dug from within—with the ditches, therefore, also within.

The earlier settlement is best described as a single wooden palisade enclosing an oval area of about 0.5 ha. The line of the bedding trench for this palisade is still visible on the ground as a shallow groove, and it was joined at its entrance to the

**Palisaded settlement with hut circles and later earthen ramparts, Braidwood**

second palisade, some 14 m beyond, by connecting fences—providing a space between that might well have been used for impounding stock.

Also visible are traces of more than a dozen timber-framed houses; they show up as circular or oval rings corresponding to the broad, shallow trenches in which the individual timber posts were set. Some of the houses may relate to the first period of settlement; those overlying the line of the palisade, however, must relate to the later phase and indicate a lengthy occupation span perhaps into the 1st or 2nd century AD. It should be remembered that the main Roman road from Carlisle and the Solway to Inveresk or Cramond on the Forth ran close to the east of the site, having passed through Annandale and Upper Clydesdale, then round the south-east end of the Pentlands by Dolphinton and Carlops.

### 104 Green Knowe Settlement, near Peebles

*Late 2nd-early 1st millennium BC.*

*NT 212433. 4 km N of Lyne just W of minor road along Meldon Burn between A 72 and A 703; track W towards Harehope but turn S after 200 m for a further 500 m.*

Partially enclosed nowadays by forestry, Green Knowe reveals a sequence of nine unenclosed hut platforms—the largest showing evidence of three successive round-houses, some 10 m in diameter. And pottery interleaved with field-gathered stones was excavated immediately outside the door of one of the timber houses.

The fourth platform from the north end proved to be over 15 m in diameter, containing a circular house over 8 m across; its walls were 75 cm thick, made of a mixture of stone and earth or turf, faced both sides with woven withies or wattle screens. The roof was carried on eleven circular timber posts set in a circle, and the space inside divided by internal partitions fixed to stakes. There was a cobbled entrance.

Though recent cultivation has removed most of the terrace below the platforms, sufficient traces of field-banks survive, together with clearance cairns, to confirm the agricultural context for the settlement. Given its upland location, and the fact that few such platform settlements elsewhere suggest associated fields, it may be another example of an increased population converting a summer pasture to a permanent settlement—as happened with *shiels* at a much later, medieval, date.

Across the Meldon Burn, just 500 m away on the lower north-west slope of White Meldon, stand two lines each of nine similar platforms (NT 216433, 218435), many of them easily identifiable on the ground. They range from nearly 11 m to over 18 m across.

**Reconstruction drawing of a round house near Lairg, Sutherland, c 1400 BC, similar to those found at Green Knowe**

# 9 CAIRNS, STONE SETTINGS AND HENGES

**Drumelzier standing stone, near Broughton**

Timber-laced fortification of settlements seems to have been introduced into south-east Scotland c 6th-8th century BC, probably by a new wave of settlers from the continent, the iron-working Celts. And stone-walled settlements without timber-lacing had been in evidence from a similar period—signs of considerable change in the fabric of society, brought about partly by the interface of incomers and natives, partly perhaps by frictions amongst a growing local population at a time of increasing specialisation, innovation and improvement in the working of bronze.

In other words, the age of the pre-Celtic warrior aristocracy, at its height c 1000 BC, had gone; and with it the concept of a massive and permanent public manifestation, in death, of earthly power and status.

**Early bronze age burial cist, Skateraw, near Dunbar**

The first peoples to work in copper and bronze had reached Britain soon after 2300 BC. A new round-headed race from the Continent, they also introduced new kinds of burial and ritual customs, and their stone-capped cist graves often included a distinctive kind of pot or beaker decorated with bands of chevrons and bars, possibly containing a liquid gift for the gods and not infrequently revealed during ploughing or roadworks. Such cists may also contain such gravegoods as flint blades and arrowheads, pieces of charcoal, bronze or copper alloy awls, and jet buttons. A rare coal disc bead and lead necklace, discovered in 1992 when reduced water levels in the West Reservoir above West Linton revealed an early bronze age cemetery, has pushed back the earliest-known use of lead in the British Isles by some 800 years. Understandably these people's customs changed over more than 1000 years but there is a continuity of tradition, as well as change, that has been isolated at the remarkable site on Cairnpapple Hill (no. 105).

Towards the end of bronze-age supremacy, cremation burials in inverted pots placed either in the ground, in some natural mound or earlier cairn, had replaced burial of the whole body. The discovery of cinerary urns at Traprain (no. 92) confirms the occupation of that site long before the arrival of the Votadini. Urns also feature prominently in the penultimate, fourth phase at Cairnpapple where, exceptionally, the earlier round cairn had been deliberately and massively enlarged to take the urns, c 1500 BC or a little later. Yet the phase three Cairnpapple cairn, c 1800-1700 BC, also contained a cremation grave, inserted marginally later perhaps than the inhumation burial close by.

Our own contemporary society offers a choice of cremation or inhumation; change is often very gradual and practices presumably overlapped in bronze-age society, maybe encouraged by alliances between differing cultural traditions. But change in burial type was tempered to some extent by the wish for continuity of tradition within the powerful ruling caste—continuity exemplified by the enlarged burial cairn.

**Reconstructed beaker from burial cist, Skateraw, near Dunbar**

In general terms, round cairns date to the 2nd millennium BC; they are found fairly widely across south-east Scotland, sometimes in association with standing stones (Huly Hill, no. 106). They may stand singly, or in irregular groups (Nether Cairn, no. 107); they may be low down, presumably close to settlements where similar but cairnless burials have also been found, or they may dominate a hilltop or skyline. Good elevated cairns are found on White Meldon (NT 219428) for instance, on Spartleton (NT 653655) and Harestone Hill (NT 568623) and on Twin Law (NT 625548); they also litter the highest ridges of the Cheviots well above any former tree-line. Such cairns are likely to mark the burials of chieftains and to have been related to valley settlements. Their distribution in the Cheviots (there is little extension south over the main watershed) suggests association with the valleys of the lower Teviot and Tweed and such southern tributaries as the Jed, Oxnam and Kale Waters; and distribution in northern Northumberland, less dense in any case, would suggest that whatever contact there may have been was by way of the Till Valley or coastal routes, rather than across the massif. In other words, colonisation was westward from the east coast along the rivers.

River valleys would seem to have determined distribution similarly around the middle-upper Tweed and either side of the Biggar Gap; whilst a further interesting chain of cairns in the Dolphinton-West Linton area (including Nether Cairn, no. 107) indicates an important prehistoric (as later) route linking the upper Clyde Valley to the Forth.

Though they clearly indicated status of both individuals and a community, such cairns were essentially funerary. Earlier surviving bronze-age monuments were of a primarily ceremonial nature, but it is impossible to know now what caused such a break with earlier tradition around the end of the 3rd-early 2nd millennium BC. The warrior chieftains had certainly continued to use the sacred, 'elite' site of Cairnpapple, but instead of modest beaker burials, presumably ritually inserted into what was essentially a sanctuary, the enlarged burial cairn came to predominate and the standing symbols of out-moded 'superstitious' ritual were demolished—just as a priestly caste was presumably discredited?

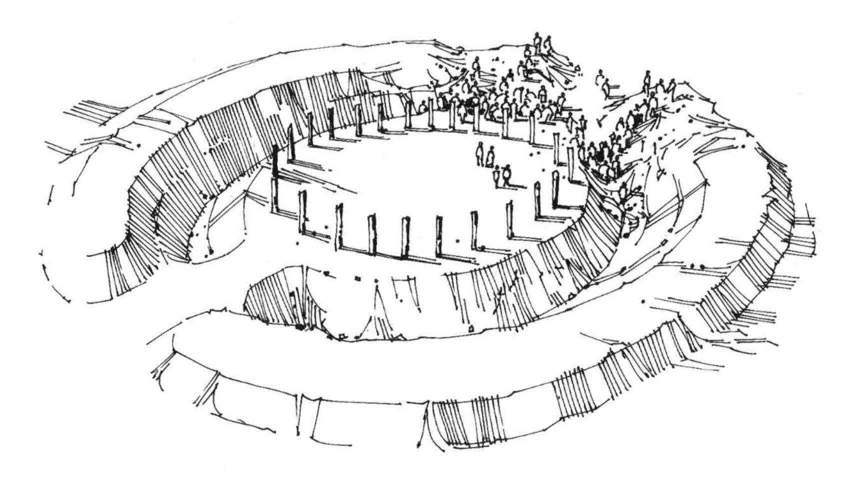

**Impression of a henge, with timber uprights and outer ditch**

Cairnpapple's phase two, therefore, was a massive henge, an egg-shaped earthwork containing a setting of standing stones, dated perhaps to c 2500 BC. The 24 large upright stones were raised close to the inner edge of a rock-cut ditch, with a bank to the outside formed by the up-cast and with entrances north and south. Here there are two entrances, but the almost vanished henge of Overhowden in Lauderdale (NT 486522) had but one entrance. As to the disposition of the stones, Cairnpapple is a Type I setting according to Thom's hypothesis that stone circles were erected according to strict geometrical principles, linked to a basic 'megalithic yard' (0.829 m). Type I settings, as also at Burgh Hill (no. 109), were based on arcs extended from two opposed Pythagorean triangles within an initial circle; Type II settings, as at Borrowstoun Rig (no. 110), simply on two overlapping circles. These last two sites are representative of an unusual group of settings, peculiar to south-east Scotland; they feature much smaller stones in rather modest 'circles' close to the ground—Kingside Hill (no. 108), Harestanes (NT 124443). (The latter name, found commonly across the south-east, merely reflects Northumbrian Angles' recognition of 'ancient stones'.)

The skill and degree of knowledge needed to construct such settings would suggest a definite and sophisticated function related not simply to the immediate vicinity of the site.

Some of the more isolated, generally single, standing stones prominent across much of the area may simply have been boundary markers; others were clearly associated with bronze-age burials (Huly Hill, no. 106); yet

**Crop marked henge at Overhowden, near Lauder**

others, like the more elaborate stone settings, may have had clearly-defined astronomical functions associated particularly perhaps with the summer and winter solstices—eg Kirklandhill Standing Stone (NT 617776), Brothers' Stones (no. 111).

Some standing stones, moreover, are decorated with cup-marks: Easter Broomhouse (no. 112), Caiystane (NT 242683). This form of decoration is found also on small stone slabs inserted into bronze-age burials (Cairnpapple, phase three), on other moveable slabs (Glencorse: NT 246626), and on natural rock outcrops (Tormain Hill, no. 114). The circular hollows may appear singly or in clusters; sometimes they are surrounded by one or more concentric circles and/or linked with grooves. Again, their purpose is obscure; could they even be decorative representations of a man-made landscape, inherited if not actually contemporary, of single standing stones, settings and sightlines?

The site at Cairnpapple, however, betrays an even earlier period. Before its visually most impressive phase, there existed a more modest irregular arc of seven cremation pits, five further surface cremations, and what seems to have been an associated triangular setting of three upright stones. A stone axe fragment originating at the Langdale 'factory' in Cumbria has been dated to c 2800 BC, which would make Cairnpapple phase one a cremation cemetery for the descendants of Scotland's first farmers—peoples whose only tools were made out of stone.

These so-called neolithic people came north from c 3500 BC. Unlike even earlier inhabitants, they were not simply hunters and food gatherers. Not only did they make pottery, but their relatively settled, apparently mainly upland, pastoral economy supported a large enough population for some to be spared for months at a time to work on rather grandiose architectural projects. To settlers originating from around the Irish Sea belong the variously distinctive sequences of stone chambered tombs covering most of Scotland; the contrasting long cairns of south-east Scotland suggest, rather, parallels with the long barrows of eastern and southern England, and a contemporary or slightly earlier migration from north-east England.

**Cup-and-ring marked stone from Hallyne, near Peebles**

The cairns were not built for single burials, but equally a population big enough to build them would not all be buried inside; rather do they seem to have been communal burials for a community's leaders, whether or not with any further ritual significance. Those that have survived—the Mutiny Stones (no. 115), and even more fragmentarily, Harlaw Muir (NT 179546), Long Knowe (NY 527862) and Broughton Knowe (NT 098388: a mere 20 m long)—stand high on moorland and suggest a strongly pastoral economy avoiding the lower-lying wet and heavy valley bottoms and heavily afforested areas. Given that a long cairn in the lowland parish of Eckford is known to have been destroyed towards the end of the 18th century, however, such upland examples may be only the survivors in a landscape where the lower lands have since become intensively altered by man.

For survival is a most quirky, chancey thing; and chance finds are often the only indicator of a prehistoric presence in an area—a flint or iron axe, arrow- or hammer-head; a spindle whorl; a dislodged cist capstone; a skull or other bones; or coins, whether single strays or a buried hoard. In particular, the chance find in 1990 of an ancient longbow is the only known evidence for tribes of hunters or primitive farmers occupying the Tweedsmuir Hills some 6000 years ago. No burial cairn this; rather some 1.3 m of bow, carved from extremely resilient yew and presumably thrown into a peat bog by the huntsman when it snapped—perhaps during a deer or wild boar hunt near to Raven Craig, high above the Moffat Water and close to the Hart Fell-White Coomb ridge. Originally 1.74 m long, with a slender tapered grip to allow the bowman to look along the line of the arrow before shooting, a reconstruction suggests a draw weight of around 16 kg (compared to the 55 kg of medieval bows). It would have been lethal at 30-50 m, but could shoot an arrow more than twice that distance in an arc. Nothing else survives of the bow, so it is unknown for instance whether the drawstring would have been of linen, animal sinew or even nettle or other fibres. It has been radiocarbon-dated to 4040-3640 BC, making it up to 800 years older than the other six prehistoric longbows discovered in the British Isles (though earlier examples are known from mainland Europe).

## 105* Cairnpapple Hill Henge and Cairns, West Lothian

*Early 3rd millennium BC-early 1st millennium AD.*

*NS 987717. From Torphichen on B 792 Bathgate-Linlithgow road, E about 1.5 km on minor road past Cathlawhill; bear right towards Craigmailing, then turn S almost immediately; signposted.*

*Historic Scotland.*

On a clear day the view from Cairnpapple's bleak and rounded hilltop ranges from the Bass Rock in the North Sea to Goatfell and the mountains of Arran in the Firth of Clyde, south to the Border hills, and north-west beyond Stirling to the Trossachs and Schiehallion. Few better spots in central Scotland could have been chosen for rituals, burials or assemblies of the highest order.

Of the five main phases at Cairnpapple (best revealed from on top of the reconstructed cairn), the most recent comprises the group of four rectangular full-length graves almost due east, close to the ditch—probably iron age, maybe early first millennium AD.

Some 1500 or so years earlier, but very much visible to succeeding generations, the site was dominated by a huge 30 m diameter stone cairn overlying the west part of the massive ditch and supported by the outer kerb of rounded boulders some 14 m away from the present cairn. Two cremations in inverted pottery cinerary urns had been placed in shallow pits within. Neither survives, but the massive effort required to build the cairn must have reflected the status of the intended occupants—for normally such urns were placed simply in existing cairns, in natural knolls or merely holes in the ground.

The cairn was an enlargement of an earlier one, 15 m across, the basis of today's reconstruction, and dating perhaps to around 1800-1700 BC. One of two graves in this earlier cairn has been retained—a short cist for a crouched burial, lined with stone slabs and drystone walling. A stone with three cup-marks was found; also a pottery Food Vessel on a small ledge. Curiously, the second cist contained cremated remains—some overlap of cultural tradition maybe separated a little in time?



**Cairnpapple Hill henge and cairns: the four main phases (omitting the late long cist burials)**

These bronze-age round cairns reflected a complete change of site function. The first overlies two socket holes for an earlier ring of standing stones—which were evidently taken down and re-used as a massive retaining kerb to support the weight of the cairn.

The previous phase at Cairnpapple was characterised by explicit ritual and ceremony rather than simple burial. Late on in this phase, perhaps c 1900 BC, two small rock-cut graves for crouched burials had certainly been constructed on the site—one of which, perhaps covered by a small mound outlined by its oval stone kerb, was subsequently incorporated and preserved within the later cairn and was marked by a single standing stone. But in essence, phase two comprised a massive oval enclosure containing an egg-shaped setting (cf Burgh Hill, no. 109), 35 m by 28 m, of 24 standing stones close to the inner edge of a wide rock-cut ditch, upcast to give an external bank. There are two causewayed entrances, to north and south, and in the centre there may have been a small, rectangular stone setting.

The first, original phase was far less impressive—seven small pits in an irregular arc within what subsequently became the western segment of the enlarged round cairn. A setting of three large stones close by was probably associated. Amongst the mixture of cremated bones and rubble, a small bone or antler pin was found; also stone axe chips, one of which came from the neolithic 'factory' at Great Langdale in Cumbria—a site dated to c 2800/2700 BC.

Cairnpapple, therefore, was a focus of prehistoric man's attention, on and off, for nearly 3000 years.

### 106 Huly Hill Round Cairn and Standing Stones, Newbridge, near Edinburgh

*2nd millennium BC.*

*NT 123726. Minor exit SW from M 8/M 9 Newbridge roundabout, 4 km W of Edinburgh Airport; or through Newbridge village, S off A 89; signposted.*

Surrounded by a modern retaining dyke, trees and shrubs, a circular mound of earth over 30 m across and 3 m high stands on a slight rise 46 m above sea-level. It is maybe 3500 years old. Stripped of our contemporary roads, villages and industrial units, the site would have had a certain prominence. A bronze rapier was recovered when it was opened in 1830.

Of particular interest at Huly or Heeley Hill is its stone circle, around 100 m diameter. Whether it was indeed a 'circle' and if so, how many stones there once were, is unknown. Certainly it would not have been concentric since the cairn is a little north-west of centre. There are three stones—one at 30.5 m north-west, over 2 m high; a second nearly 49 m south-west, 2 m high; the third over 53 m east, about 1.3 m high but apparently broken. The stones are massive, rough and unpolished just like that standing nearly 3 m high, 320 m or so east across the roundabout in an industrial estate (NT 126726). This Lochend Stone may well be unconnected with cairn and circle; alternatively it may be an outlier?

A few kilometres north-north-east of Newbridge, close to the shore walk from South Queensferry to Cramond, there is a further impressive cairn, the Earl Cairnie or Harlaw Cairn (NT 158791) standing in woodland 400 m south of Hound Point. Described in 1791 as almost 49 m across by 7.5 m high, it has been reduced by stone-robbing to about 30 m by 4.6 m, though a stony mound some 12 m from the base may indicate its original perimeter.

### 107 Nether Cairn, North Muir, near West Linton

*2nd millennium BC.*

*NT 105503. Minor road W 1 km N of Dolphinton on A 702 Edinburgh-Biggar road; after 1 km take local track N to Medwynbank, thence by track NE 1.5 km; alternatively local road and track West Linton-Medwynbank via North Slipperfield.*

On the south-east slopes of North Muir is a remarkable collection of nine or so round burial cairns, clustered at around the 280 m contour. The Nether Cairn, over 15 m in diameter and 3.7 m high, is one of the best-preserved, reasonably accessible, round cairns in the area. About 1 m beyond the present base are slight indications of a surrounding ditch about 1.8 m wide. The Upper Cairn (NT 110509), by contrast, some 730 m north-east, is even larger—over 20 m across and 4.2 m high. Now considerably overgrown, there is no trace of a surrounding ditch, whilst hollows on the east, north and west sides suggest that it has been robbed for its stone. Of the other cairns, one sited 400 m north-east of the Upper Cairn still stands about 1 m high and over 9 m across.

This chain of large, round, prehistoric burial cairns in the Dolphinton-West Linton area (there are other, more elevated examples on such Pentland summits as East Cairn Hill, NT 121595; West Cairn Hill, NT 107584; Carnethy Hill, NT 203619) seems to mark an important prehistoric route linking the upper Clyde valley with the Forth estuary. It would have left the Clyde at its junction with the Medwin Water, skirted the southern edge of the Pentlands and then followed their south-east flanks before cutting across to the River North Esk, where similar cairns existed near Roslin and Rosewell.

The small, sandstone Gowk Stane (NT 204576) stands just east of Auchencorth Farm on the east bank of the river; it is also on a direct link between

**Nether Cairn, North Muir**

the respective groups of round cairns. Moreover, the ruinous remains of an earlier neolithic long cairn—within an equally ruinous plantation dyke—survive as a low ragged mound, nearly 58 m by 14 m by under 1 m high on Harlaw Muir (NT 179546). This long cairn lies half way between West Linton and the Gowk Stane, some 90 m west of the minor roads north-east through Auchencorth Moss—evidence perhaps of the even greater antiquity of such a through-route.

## 108 Kingside Hill Stone Setting, East Lothian

*2nd millennium BC.*

*NT 627650. B 6355 Gifford-Cranshaws road, about half way between junctions with minor road SE to Longformacus and minor road NW to Garvald; old cart track N to 140 m S of Kingside Burn, then 30 m E on NW slope of Kingside Hill.*

The area around Penshiel, Mayshiel, Kingside Hill, Johnscleuch and Spartleton, around the head waters of the Whiteadder Water and its upper tributaries, the Faseny and Bothwell Waters, plays host to many cairns and hut circles, stone circles and settings. And these spread over the broad, high plateau that extends west and south-west towards Lauderdale. An area of undulating hills and upper valleys once attractive for habitation and stock husbandry, it also commands north-south communications from the Tweed Valley to East and Midlothian. Later fortified hill-settlements along Lauderdale and overlooking Yester reinforce this role.

The circle is about 12 m across, of 30 small boulders, most set on edge and the highest no more than 0.4 m above ground. A number have fallen and some are now half-covered. In the centre a larger stone, nearly 0.6 m square and as deep under the ground, rises from the middle of a slight 3 m diameter mound. It is unclear however if the latter, presumably a small cairn, is a later addition (cf Cairnpapple, no. 105).

Kingside Hill represents a group of at least 17 stone settings in south-east Scotland, unusual on account of the small size of their stones. Not far away, 30 m south of the B 6355 and about 200 m east of the Mayshiel track is a smaller setting (NT 629646), less than 3 m across. Seven stones remain in position; two lying downhill have probably been moved from the southern arc of the circle which is surrounded by a low bank some 0.15 m-0.3 m higher than the interior. The Yadlee circle (NT 654673) has stones to a diameter of 8 m, while the Harestanes at Kirkurd (NT 124443), some 15 km east of Biggar, contain five stones around a 3 m circle.

## 109 Burgh Hill Stone Setting, near Hawick

*2nd millennium BC.*

*NT 470062. Minor road S from Hawick to Skelfhill later rejoins A 7; 1 km N of Dod, gate access to gentle N shoulder of Burgh Hill; climb to summit.*

The nearby hills were quite well settled in the iron age by British tribes, and subsequently by

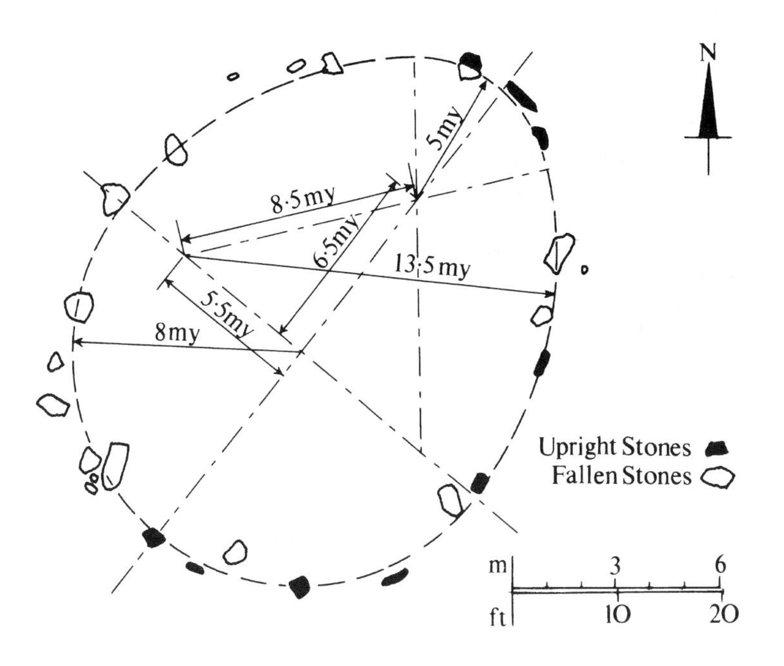


**Burgh Hill stone setting**

Northumbrians for whom the Catrail (NT 4804-4904: a considerable linear earthwork just visible from Burgh Hill towards The Pike, south-east across Dod Burn) may have been a temporary 'frontier' before the mid 12th century.

Burgh Hill, at 306 m, in addition to its roughly rectangular fortified hill-settlement, hosts a setting of 25 stones, 13 of which are still erect. It is some 2.5 km north-west of the Tinlee Stone (NT 484038), a standing stone set on rising ground above Dod Burn.

The setting is low on the ground; it is egg-shaped, some 16.5 m by 13.4 m and, like Borrowstoun Rig (no. 110) is believed to have been constructed according to clearly defined geometrical rules involving a megalithic yard calculated at 0.829 m. But whilst Borrowstoun is termed a Type II setting (based simply on two overlapping circles), Burgh Hill, like Cairnpapple's much larger ring of standing stones, is termed Type I. It is based on an initial notional circle and on further circles linked to pythagorean triangles placed back-to-back at the centre point of the diameter of the original circle! In this particular setting, the first circle has been calculated as 16 megalithic yards in diameter; the longer sides are arcs of 28 my diameter circles, the tip is part of a 10 my diameter circle based on the apex of the triangles.

Regardless of such megalithic mathematics, the factors that determined the overall size of a setting (geographical limitations apart) are still unknown; as also the reasons why they were built at all, whether ritual, ceremonial or astronomical.

## 110 Borrowstoun Rig Stone Setting, near Lauder

*2nd millennium BC.*

*NT 557523. From Newbigging, half way between Carfraemill and Lauder on A 697 Kelso road, take farm road NE past Burncastle/Earnscleugh for about 4 km; then strike up E side of valley, doubling back 1 km S (the fit might strike up E, lower down valley).*

High on the plateau (350 m) some 32 small stones survive, some barely showing above the heather, 10 of them still upright, and none more than 0.6 m high. They form an egg-shaped setting nearly 46 m by 43 m, most of the stones lying on a 41.5 m true circle (50 megalithic yards), but the western segment formed on the arc of a separate notional circle 25.6 m or 31 megalithic yards in diameter whose circumference passed through the centre of the larger circle. The perimeter of the setting was determined by straight lines joining the outer arcs of the overlapping circles. This, at least, would be the theory suggested in recent decades—that our ancestors had devised careful mathematical formulae linking an apparently standard unit of length, the 'megalithic yard', to basic geometrical shapes (cf Burgh Hill no. 109).

## 111 Brothers' Stones, near Earlston

*2nd millennium BC.*

*NT 619360. Brotherstone Farm is half-way (4 km) along minor road from Leaderfoot (A 68) to Smailholm (B 6397); farm track N 200 m, then 500 m NE to top of hill.*

Brotherstone Farm has a traditional courtyard steading with a farm-chimney indicating a one-time steam-powered barn threshing mill. Near the top of the gentle little hill beyond are two large standing stones, set as a pair nearly 13 m apart and packed around their bases to keep them firm. The south-easterly, larger stone stands nearly 2.5 m high; the north-westerly to 1.6 m. Both are of considerable girth and taper slightly towards the top.

Some 250 m down the north-east shoulder of Brotherstone Hill (NT 621362) stands a much bulkier, equally tall mass of rock 2 m high. Evidently split off from an outcrop, it too is packed around the base with broken stone. Known as 'The Cow Stone', its alignment between the smaller of the Brothers' Stones and Hareheugh Craigs a little south-west of Hume Castle may—or may not—be significant!

## 112 Easter Broomhouse Standing Stone, East Lothian

*2nd millennium BC.*

*NT 680766. Minor road S from E end of Dunbar (A 1087) crossing A 1 to Spott; farm road SE to Easter Broomhouse; 200 m SSW on broad ridge.*

A red sandstone monolith stands 2.7 m high and 1.8 m in girth on the summit of a broad ridge less than 50 m above sea level and overlooking the coast around Dunbar.

East Lothian has always been in the forefront of agricultural improvement and the two deep grooves cut in the stone near its base were made by the wire cable of a steam plough rubbing against it! However, other markings are much older. Over half way up the western side are three cup-marks each about 90 mm wide and 13 mm deep, in the shape of an inverted triangle.

In Lothian there are some 35 surviving standing stones; of these five or six cluster between Traprain Law and Dunbar. Whether or not the Witches' Stone (NT 669752) is such a stone, two lie just south of Traprain (no. 92)—one in the old stackyard of Standingstone Farm (NT 577736); the other, the Loth or Cairndinnis Stone (NT 578741), has been moved to the side of its field in the interest of efficient cultivation. The impressive Kirklandhill Stone (NT 617776) and the Pencraig Hill Stone (NT 581768), by contrast, are both visible from the A 1; Kirkhandhill, in particular, has been suggested as a marker, linked to the conical peak of North Berwick Law over which the sun would set at the summer solstice—its most northerly point.

## 113 Caiystane, Swanston, Edinburgh

*2nd millennium BC.*

*NT 242683. In Caiystane View, close to junction with Oxgangs Road on S edge of Edinburgh, 1 km W of traffic lights at Fairmilehead (A702); signposted.*

*National Trust for Scotland.*

This massive standing stone stands emasculated in the pavement of a surburban street. One of three in this part of Edinburgh, all lie close to ancient trackways from the south which took the higher ground fringing the Pentland Hills, then made their way northwards towards Wester Craiglockhart Hill, Blackford Hill, Castle Rock and Arthur's Seat, one or other side of Duddingston Loch and the Burgh Loch. Each one of these hilltops once held an iron-age fort, and may well have been settled in much earlier times too.

The thick, broad, 3 m high Caiystane bears cupmarks on its east face, some 50 cm from the ground; it is also known as General Kay's Monument or the Kal Stane. Traditionally it is said to mark the site of a long-past battle between the Picts and the Romans—the former recalled perhaps in the name of the Pentland Hills.

The Catstane stands in the grounds of Kingsinch School (NT 274706: viewable from The Inch public park between the A7 Gilmerton Road and A68 Old Dalkeith Road); the third is at the end of Ravenswood Avenue (NT 282704), just south of the park.

## 114 Tormain Hill Cup-and-Ring Markings, Ratho, near Edinburgh

*2nd millennium BC.*

*NT 129696. From B 7030 to Wilkieston 1 km SW of Ratho, take track through woodland shelter belt where it diverges S from roadside; 500 m S to top of hill.*

Tormain Hill affords fine views of the Pentlands, west Edinburgh, the Forth Road Bridge and the West Lothian landscape, with the Ochils beyond.

The low summit ridge, at about 140 m, shows a number of natural rocky outcrops; at least eight of these, within an area some 12 m by 6 m on the highest part of the ridge, bear a rich collection of man-made markings. Four or five sets of markings are clearly visible, especially with a late afternoon sun; the rest are overgrown with turf.

The markings vary from a single large cup on one rock, to a set of circles, concentric rings and grooves—as well as cup-marks—on another at the southern end of the group. This particular boulder, though split and rather worn, shows traces of 20 cups varying from 13 mm to 50 mm in diameter; at least seven cups are surrounded by single rings and in two instances the rings are connected by shallow grooves to simple cup-marks. The largest cup on this stone is circled by one complete ring, with three additional concentric arcs linking up four of the other rings.

Such markings were made, in the main, with small picks or driven punches—and a tedious, lengthy task it undoubtedly was. As a form of ornamentation they feature on fixed natural outcrops such as Tormain Hill (was it a special place of meeting or ceremony?), on smaller more 'portable' slabs, on standing stones, on or within burial cists. They may be clustered, several of one or various designs together; or singly. Outside Glencorse Parish Church, for instance (NT 246626), the upper surface of a slab of stone, less than 1 m long, is covered with at least 22 cups, some with faint rings, and five cup-and-ring markings with radial or connecting grooves.

## 115 Mutiny Stones Long Cairn, near Longformacus, Duns

*3rd millennium BC.*

*NT 622590. About 7.5 km NW of Longformacus on minor road joining B 6355 to Gifford; follow track 2.5 km SW from tight V-bend, past Killpallet to burn; cairn 100 m W. Alternatively N from farm road to Byrecleugh by Wrunk Law, 3 km NW Longformacus.*

'The Mittenfull of Stones' in 1794, subsequently 'The Meeting Stones', currently 'The Mutiny Stones', the cairn is aligned north-east/south-west on Byrecleugh Ridge, overlooking the Dye Water. Reached after a good, bracing walk, it is a striking example of a rare long cairn, over 85 m long and between 7.6 m and nearly 23 m wide. Even though considerably robbed to provide stone for nearby sheep-stells, it stills rises to 2.5 m at its eastern, wider end.

Though normally considered a burial mound, evidence of burials has never been identified and a wider ritual significance should not be ignored.

**Mutiny Stones long cairn**

# 10 A GLIMPSE OF EDINBURGH

**Slezer's view of the Nor Loch, High Street and Edinburgh Castle, from the mills at Dean, late 17th century**

*'A windy toon o cloods an' sunny glints;*
*pinnacled, turreted, stey an' steep grey toon; . . .'*

*'Steeple an' toor an' battlement stand bauld,*
*an' gaze ootowre the kindly lands o Forth. . . .'*
*George Campbell Hay*

**Slezer's view of the old town, Arthur's Seat to Edinburgh Castle, early 18th century**

No city in Scotland has been so variously presented as Edinburgh; its buildings and townscape have been interpreted, misinterpreted and re-interpreted in a maze of exhibitions and experiences, trails, tours, guides and literature. It remains appropriate, nonetheless, at least to refer to some of the better (and lesser) known features of Edinburgh's 'monumental' heritage—an Edinburgh defined on an Old Town/New Town axis but also as an extended urban area bounded by once-isolated villages such as Cramond (no. 5), Corstorphine, Colinton, Swanston (no. 20), Burdiehouse, Liberton, Gilmerton and Portobello. The names themselves suggest well over 2000 years of human settlement; the archaeological evidence over 4000 years.

**The Union Canal aqueduct at Slateford, with the railway viaduct behind**

It is only within the last 150 or so years that these small, separate communities have gradually been assimilated into a greater Edinburgh. Thus came the canal into Fountainbridge, railway viaducts to Warriston and Slateford, large-scale coal-mining to Gilmerton, brickworks to Niddrie, quarrying to Craigleith and Craigmillar, limekilns to Burdiehouse (see no. 23), gas-holders to Granton; all manner of industries and manufacturies sweep across from Leith to Sighthill.

Could it be, therefore, that such 20th-century municipal housing schemes as Craigmillar, Oxgangs, Wester Hailes and Pilton might be seen as tomorrow's 'monuments'? And to what? Will they eventually engender the same interest as those later 19th century cooperative housing 'colonies' for working people at Stockbridge, Haymarket, Abbeyhill, Slateford (see no. 3) and behind Fountainbridge at Rosebank Cottages and Rosemount Buildings—the counterpart of the Victorian/Edwardian middle-class tenements of Marchmont, Bruntsfield and Comely Bank, and of the more relaxed stone-built acres of Trinity, Grange, Blacket, Morningside and Murrayfield? Or regardless of their architectural 'interest', will they be swept away like the slums of the Old Town, leaving East Craigs, Barnton, Bonaly and Fairmilehead as uncomfortable reminders of the more—or is it the less acceptable face of later 20th-century social and political engineering?

Earlier townscapes are set correspondingly closer to the centre of the city. Edinburgh's neo-classical grid-square New Town, for instance, which first siphoned off the wealthier and higher classes from a 'come-all-ye' Old Town, was begun in the later 18th century. The Georgian House (NTS) in Charlotte Square forms a part of the first development, completed by 1800—though the earliest houses are in Thistle Court, 1767, just west of St Andrew Square and of much the same date as what remains of George Square, 1763-64, south of the Old Town. Whilst the palace fronts, wide streets and spacious squares and circuses impress, so also do numerous

**Granton's gasholders date from 1902 (with delicate steel lattice-work), 1933 and 1967**

other individual buildings of the 18th and 19th century—Register House on Princes Street, 1774-78; Royal Bank of Scotland, St Andrew Square, 1772-74, Royal Scottish Academy, 1832; National Gallery of Scotland, 1845; Old College, South Bridge, 1789. The various skyline observatories and monuments on the Calton Hill, 1776-1832, set above the former Royal High School, 1825-29, form a memorable group; St Bernard's Well, beside the Water of Leith, 1789, has an elegance all of its own; the Palmhouses, 1834-58, within the Royal Botanic Garden cannot fail to attract (also the new glasshouses, 1965).

Some 'vaguely classical' forms continued into the Victorian period, but elaborate embellishment was more in tune with the times. Once again, many of the more notable examples are institutional, and a little further out—Donaldson's School on Haymarket Terrace, 1842-54; Daniel Stewart's College, Queensferry Road, 1849-55; Fettes College, Inverleith, 1862-70; Royal Scottish Museum, 1861; Craig House Asylum, Craiglockhart Hill, 1893 (now part of Napier University). St Mary's Episcopal Cathedral, 1873-79, in Palmerston Place, stands alongside the much earlier, once rural and lairdly Easter Coates House, 1615.

Developments beyond the Water of Leith were hastened by the building of the Dean Bridge, 1832; developments north and south of the Old Town had earlier been linked by the North Bridge, 1772 and the South Bridge, 1788—best seen from Market Street and the Cowgate below. The North Bridge, like the completely artificial 'Earthen Mound' to the middle of Princes Street, crossed what remained of the Nor' Loch; the South Bridge overflew the old track out through the Grassmarket to the common grazings, peat-mosses and woodland on the Burgh Muir. This area once stretched from Duddingston to Merchiston and south to the Blackford Hill; it survives vestigially in the Meadows and Bruntsfield Links.

**Charlotte Square: Georgian street furniture and Georgian House kitchen**
(Far right)

For the 'oldest Edinburgh' was restricted by the troughs gouged out by Ice Age glaciers as they flowed eastwards either side of the hard volcanic Castle Rock. On the 'tail' of glacial deposit subsequently arose the domestic settlement associated with the fortified 'crag'. Or rather, the Burgh of Edinburgh was associated with the royal castle; the Burgh of Canongate, below the old Netherbow Port, went with the canons of the Abbey of Holyrood.

The Canongate was always an area of less dense population and of larger and more substantial houses, courtyards and closes, whether built after or before the Union of the Crowns—Moray House, 1628; Acheson House, 1618; Whitehorse Close, 17th century; Canongate Tolbooth, 1591; Huntly House, 1570. By contrast, the Burgh of Edinburgh (parts of whose mercat cross and tolbooth are preserved at Abbotsford, no. 31) was always more congested, with narrow wynds and closes separating multiple-storeyed 'lands' set upon pieces of ground stretching back from the main street and known as 'tenements'. Gladstone's Land (NTS), 1617-20, with its surviving outside stair, represents one such building, contrasting with Lady Stair's House, 1622, behind; also Moubray House and the so-called John Knox's House, 15th-16th century—the sole survivor of a timber-fronted town house. By the later 17th century the slum 'lands' were being replaced by more fashionable tenements, as we now call them, set around wide open squares—Mylne's Court, 1690 and James Court 1725-27, off the Lawnmarket. Riddle's Court and Bailie MacMorran's House, 16th century, represent an earlier courtyard phase comparable with structures in the Canongate. Of more recent 18th- and 19th-century date, Ramsay Gardens was romantically extended by Patrick Geddes, creator of the nearby Camera Obscura, 1895-96. Alongside, the former Castlehill Reservoir, 1849, is a considerable contrast—built to replace an earlier, smaller reservoir of 1676. From this original cistern, water was led in elm-wood (earlier, lead) pipes to 10 smaller cisterns or wells in the old town—of which examples survive outside John Knox's House, in the Grassmarket at the foot of the West Bow, in the Cowgate and elsewhere. The water came from four springs at Comiston—the Swan, Hare, Fox and Lapwing springs (NT 239688)—supplemented from 1760 by springs at Swanston (no. 20). The springs are still in use.

**Gladstone's Land, Lawnmarket**
(Far left)

**Painted ceiling from Pinkie House, Musselburgh**
(in Huntly House Museum)

After the Union of the Crowns, 'defence' was a much less crucial factor and the design of buildings became increasingly more attractive and elaborate—the Tailor's Hall, in the Cowgate, 1621; Parliament House, 1629-40; George Heriot's Hospital, 1628-50; the remodelled Palace of Holyroodhouse, 1674-78. Up until the Union, however, fortification had been of considerable importance—particularly defence against the English. Parts of the Flodden Wall, 1520s-1530s, survive at the foot of the Pleasance and at Bristo Port; the shell of the only surviving tower, with gun-loops, stands in the Vennel, south of the Grassmarket. The long-vanished 'ports' were gateways in and out of the city, passing through the massive walls that looped round from the south side of Edinburgh Castle (Historic Scotland). The present castle spans the 11th-18th centuries; as a massive and instructive national monument it is pre-eminent, though as evidence for the development of fortification it is quite overshadowed by Craigmillar Castle (no. 48), beyond Arthur's Seat. Smaller-scale tower-houses, the houses of the lesser lairds and merchants, remain scattered beyond Old Edinburgh in what was once a rural landscape—Cramond, Merchiston, Liberton and, fragmentarily, at Craiglockhart. Many others have been incorporated in later houses.

**Part of altar retable from Mary King's Close, High Street**
(in NMS)

As for the Church, the post-Reformation is well-represented by Greyfriars Kirk, 1620, the first to be built in Edinburgh after the Reformation; by the Tron, 1640s; and by the Canongate Kirk, 1688: subsequently by the New Town's St Andrew's Church, George Street, 1780-85 and by the former St George's, 1811-14, in Charlotte Square. Greyfriars and the Canongate Kirks also possess remarkably interesting graveyards; there are others at Old Calton, Dean, Pilrig and Grange, in addition to those associated with the old 'village' churches of eg Liberton, Cramond, Restalrig, Corstorphine, St. Mary's Leith. A tiny, original Jewish cemetery survives in Sciennes House Place, where the facade of the old House yet remains as the rear elevation of the tenements (NT 262722).

**Palace of Holyroodhouse and Holyrood Abbey**

**Royal Pew, High Kirk of St Giles**

The pre-Reformation, former Collegiate Churches at Corstorphine and Restalrig date to the 15th century, though of the latter, only the remarkable St Triduana's Chapel/Well-House survives (no. 66). St Margaret's Well, now rebuilt at the foot of Arthur's Seat, bears a close resemblance; it is but a short distance from the ruins of St Anthony's Chapel and Hermitage, also 15th century. From the same period, nothing survives of Trinity College Church other than the altar panels now in the National Gallery of Scotland; the recently-restored Magdalene Chapel in the Cowgate, however, represents the very last pre-Reformation church to be built in Edinburgh. The High Kirk of St. Giles, though originally a Norman foundation like Duddingston, was remodelled in the 15th century and restored in 1829. Its open-work crown dates to c 1500. The other major Norman works are St. Margaret's Chapel in Edinburgh Castle and Holyrood Abbey (Historic Scotland), founded by David I in 1128. The nave and its fine west front survive—mainly late 12th-13th century.

**Mons Meg, when it stood proud on the battlements of Edinburgh Castle** (Far left)

**Helping the wounded: Scottish National War Memorial, Edinburgh Castle**

Of the former agricultural and other villages of 'Edinburgh', most no longer or barely survive—either quite swept away (Tipperlin and Picardy) or largely submerged by residential development (Morningside). An identifiable nucleus of certain settlements does survive however—Restalrig has its old cottages as well as its Well-House; Cramond, its bridge, tower-house, mansion, iron mills (no. 5) and the nearby Lauriston Castle; Colinton, a session house, offertory house and mort-safe in its churchyard beyond the old village street; Liberton, its tower and House beside the Braid Hills ; Corstorphine, its collegiate church and dovecote; Newhaven, its harbour and the remains of a fishing community; Dean, its former mills, granary, Well Court, Telford bridge and ancient ford; Duddingston, its Causeway, watch-tower and partly Norman church. R L Stevenson's Swanston, moreover, retains an identifiable rural setting—both the separate Swanston House and the 18th-century thatched village which survives below the Pentlands alongside a later square of farm cottages (no. 20).

Evidence of an agricultural past is also evident from the rare mid 18th-century 'agricultural' table-tomb in Liberton Churchyard, a reminder of the remarkably dense systems of parallel cultivation rigs yet preserved amongst the whins, grassland and bunkers of the Braid Hills, Easter Craiglockhart Hill, Corstorphine Hill (east slopes) and Prestonfield, just south of Arthur's Seat. The fine 16th-century beehive dovecote at Corstorphine (Historic Scotland) is complemented by later, larger and rectangular examples at Nether Liberton (with a water meal-mill opposite, converted to a dwelling) and in the Hermitage of Braid. Post-improvement farm steadings survive in whole or in part at Swanston, Liberton and Lauriston—a further reminder

**Lectern-style doocot, Nether Liberton**

**Beehive doocot, Corstorphine** (Left) **and nesting boxes** (Far right)

of how contained Edinburgh was, even well into the 20th century. Indeed, in 1800, the city spread no further than from Holyrood to Tollcross and from the University to Queen Street. Beyond, amidst a gentle rural landscape, stood the numerous country houses of Edinburgh's merchants, lawyers and gentry: 16th-17th-century Stenhouse Mansion (Historic Scotland/NTS) and Lamb's House in Leith (see no. 12: NTS); 16th-18th-century Craig House; 16th-19th-century Lauriston Castle, Craigcrook Castle and Craigentinny House; early 17th-century Easter Coates House; mid 17th-century Dalry House; late 17th-19th-century Prestonfield House and Cramond House; mid 18th-century Gayfield House; late 18th-century Inverleith House, Mortonhall House and Hermitage of Braid, with its nearby ice-house.

As late as the 16th century, so many marshes and lochs still surrounded the town that French writers referred to it as 'Lislebourg', the 'island town'; and the principal route north-south followed the latter-day Pleasance, past the Netherbow Port, west around Calton Hill, and down as the 'wester' road to Leith-Leith Walk. As a town it had first developed in the 12th century, when burgh status was granted by David I. Mainly or partly Gaelic names such as Braid, Corstorphine, Dalry, Craiglockhart, Drumsheugh, Dunsapie, betray the 'Scottish' ruling presence from the 10th, century after the eclipse of the Northumbrians, but very little by way of structures survives for this period, or for earlier times. A late 6th-century symbol stone found below the Castle Rock (now in NMS) betrays a Pictish presence, though the Viking-period rune-stone now standing in Princes Street Gardens is a later gift from Sweden! As for the Romans, the partially-visible fort at Cramond (no. 5) and the Eagle Rock (NT 184774) on the shore across the Almond (where the eye of faith should perhaps discern Mercury or the three Mother Goddesses, rather than an eagle?), point to the strategic importance of the area to the Romans—complementary to now-vanished harbour and fort at Inveresk. The discovery in 1997 of a stone statue of a lioness devouring a human confirms the importance of Cramond, for it is a high-status tombstone.

The most prominent prehistoric monuments, by contrast, are those in Holyrood Park (NT 2773). Discernable fortified settlements certainly survive on Hillend Hill (NT 245662) above Swanston, and on Wester Craiglockhart Hill (NT 228700), but little remains on Blackford Hill. It is within the Royal Park, however, that the most plentiful, though again fragmentary evidence of ramparts is found—on Dunsapie Hill, Samson's Ribs, the east side of Arthur's Seat itself and Nether Hill, Salisbury Crags. Moreover, there are multiple cultivation terraces around Dunsapie and above Duddingston Loch, as well as a number of homestead sites close to the Queen's Drive just south of Dunsapie Loch. These are more likely to be of later 'Dark Age' or medieval date, however. The earliest settlement feature is a row of six circular hut platforms on the Dasses, above Hunter's Bog. Again, the eye of faith helps to pick them out!

**Cultivation terraces, enclosures, scooped settlements and defences, Arthur's Seat**

Back through time to c 1500 BC, cup-and-ring stones from Blackford Hill, the Braid Hills and Saughtonhall now lie in NMS. Ruinous bronze-age burial cairns, however, can be traced on Caerketton Hill (NT 237662) and Galachlaw (NT 253683), whilst other conical cairns once stood not far from the Caiystane (no. 13), a fine and stocky standing stone in Caiystane View, Fairmilehead. There are further standing stones at the Cat Stane, Kingsinch (NT 274706) and at the end of nearby Ravenswood Avenue(NT 282704). All are close to the main lines of access from the south, passing west of Duddingston Loch and either side of the former Burgh Loch.

The one factor, indeed, which unites man through time in Edinburgh is the shape and form of the land. Regardless of building styles and materials, racial and cultural overlays, it was the forests, marshes, lochs and firth that dictated man's exploitation of the area; and most particularly the craggy volcanic hills. Still today they stand as oases amongst the lava-flow of stone, brick and concrete trickling past towards the unsuspecting—maybe all-suspecting—countryside.

**18th-century tombstone in Liberton Churchyard: using an old Scots plough, probably on the Braid Hills**

*'I'll wave the sour and moaning heart away,*
*For in my head I nurse a magic day*
*When once I walked upon the Blackford Hill*
*In sun, after a week of rain and chill;*
*For at my feet there lay nine shades of green*
*That kings and southern eyes have never seen.'*

*Stuart MacGregor*

**Pictish symbol stone from below Edinburgh Castle**
(Far right)

# MUSEUMS

Museums and interpretation centres are a growth industry in south-east Scotland. Look out also for small, specialist collections at Historic Scotland and National Trust for Scotland monuments, and at country houses, country parks and nature reserves. Displays cover a wide range of relevant themes and periods.

Generally only the big national and local authority museums are open all year. Others are usually open from Easter to September/October, though not necessarily all day/every day. Some are open at weekends out-of-season; many levy modest entrance fees. For further details enquire locally at Tourist Information Centres or Local Authority Community Services/Leisure/Education Departments, or contact the Scottish Museums Council, County House, 20-22 Torphichen Street, Edinburgh EH3 8JB (tel 0131 229 7465).

## BORDERS

### Coldstream

**Coldstream Museum**, Market Square. Small local history and regimental museum on site of HQ of original Coldstream Guards.

### Eyemouth

**Eyemouth Museum**, The Auld Kirk. Lively introduction to history of Berwickshire's fishing industry.

### Galashiels

**Galashiels Museum**, Nether Mill, Huddersfield Street. Development of textile industry, health, education and housing in 19th-century Galashiels.

**Old Gala House**, Scott Crescent. Late 16th-century house with 17th-century painted ceiling and 20th-century painted wall; displays about the House, its inhabitants and the early growth of Galashiels.

### Hawick

**Drumlanrig's Tower Museum**. Displays about the Border reivers, set in restored towerhouse 'rescued' from former dilapidated hotel.

**Hawick Museum & The Scott Gallery**, Wilton Lodge Park. Local archaeology, natural history, and development of industry in Hawick, particularly hosiery and knitwear; 19th-20th-century Scottish paintings.

### Innerleithen

**Robert Smail's Printing Works** (NTS), High Street (see no. 4).

### Jedburgh

**Jedburgh Castle Jail**, Castlegate. 19th-century jail is only surviving Scottish example of a Howard Reform Prison. Displays include prison life, short history of Jedburgh and area.

**Mary Queen of Scots' House**, Queen Street. Story of Mary Queen of Scots displayed in fine example of late 16th-century bastle house.

### Kelso

**Kelso Museum,** 17th-century Turret House (NTS). Displays include Victorian school-room, 19th-century market place, reconstructed skinner's workshop and Kelso Abbey.

### Lauder

**Borders Country Life Museum**, Thirlestane Castle. Borders domestic, rural and agricultural life over the centuries.

### Melrose

**Priorwood Garden** (NTS), beside Melrose Abbey. Includes orchard illustrating history of the cultivated apple.

**Trimontium Museum**, Ormiston Institute. Small collection of finds from the nearby Roman site of Newstead (main collections are in NMS, Edinburgh).

### Peebles

**Scottish Museum of Ornamental Plasterwork**, The Cornice, 31 High Street. Re-creation of late 19th-early 20th-century plasterer's workshop detailing main ways of creating ornamental plasterwork.

**Tweeddale Museum & Gallery**, High Street. Small museum within Chambers Institution, with interesting range of local material and publisher William Chambers's own collection. The Picture Gallery is an original Victorian gallery.

### St Abbs

**St Abb's Head Visitor Centre** (NTS/SWT), Northfield Farm Steading. History/natural history of area within and around St Abb's National Nature Reserve.

### Selkirk

**Halliwell's House Museum**, Market Place. Local historical material (including Royal Burgh of Selkirk) alongside fascinating collection of ironmongery, including farm and household tools/utensils. Housed in late 17th-century cottages/former ironmonger's shop.

### Walkerburn

**Scottish Mueum of Wool Textiles**, Tweeddale Mill. History and processes of wool-working; old tartans and patterns; dyeing; spinning and weaving demonstrations.

## EDINBURGH

**Camera Obscura**, Castlehill. Unique Victorian system of revolving lenses and mirrors housed in rooftop 'observatory' provides extensive panoramas (on fine, clear days) of Edinburgh's Old/New Towns.

**City Art Centre**, 1-4 Market Street. Good late 19th and early 20th-century works by Scottish artists; Edinburgh topographical and historical paintings periodically on display.

**Cramond Maltings**, Old Cramond Village. Small visitor centre outlining history of Cramond from pre-Roman times to present-day.

**Georgian House** (NTS), 7 Charlotte Square. Fine late 18th-century New Town house, furnished as for 1760-1820.

**Gladstone's Land** (NTS), Lawnmarket. Fine 6-storey 17th-century Edinburgh merchant's tenement home, with good painted ceilings and reconstructed cloth merchant's booth.

**Huntly House Museum**, 142 Canongate. Edinburgh's local history in restored 16th-century town mansion: reconstructed room interiors; silver, glass, pottery, shop signs, domestic/municipal life.

**John Knox's House**, 45 High Street. Items relating to John Knox and the Scottish Reformation, in restored 15th-century home of James Mossman, Goldsmith to Mary Queen of Scots.

**Lauriston Castle**, Cramond Road South. Late 16th-century tower house with 19th-century additions; interior preserved with prosperous Edwardian furnishings and 'family' collections.

**Museum of Fire**, Lothian & Borders Fire Brigade HQ, Lauriston Place. Displays and equipment, including pumps and fire engines, illustrate development of firefighting (mainly 19th-20th century) and history of UK's oldest municipal fire brigade.

**National Gallery of Scotland** (NGS), The Mound. Important/extensive Scottish collections, Scottish artists and Scottish topographical /historical interest amongst its international collections (see no. 37: Paxton House).

**Newhaven Heritage Museum**, Fishmarket, Newhaven Harbour. The story of Newhaven and its people; fishing, boats, gear, customs and superstitions, community life; re-created scenes.

**The People's Story**, Canongate Tolbooth, Canongate. Everyday life of the people of Edinburgh, 18th century to the present day, with re-created scenes.

**National Museums of Scotland** (NMS), Chambers Street. Scotland's foremost archaeological, ethnographic, scientific, technological, fine arts and natural history collections (including weapons, silver, textiles, mining, lighthouses, transport/communications, water power, geology, evolution). New Museum of Scotland will open in 1998.

**Scottish National Portrait Gallery** (NGS), Queen Street. The people behind Scotland's history—kings, queens, statesmen, inventors, soldiers, chieftains, agriculturalists, writers, poets etc. National photographic archive.

**Scottish United Services Museum** (NMS), Edinburgh Castle. Uniforms, weapons, personal relics and equipment from Scottish regiments and militias.

**The Writers' Museum**, Lady Stair's Close, Lawnmarket. Restored 17th-century Old Town house containing collections relating to Robert Burns, Sir Walter Scott, RL Stevenson.

## LOTHIANS

### Cousland

**Cousland Smiddy**. Preserved early 18th-century village smiddy, with tools, equipment, smith's cottage and garden.

### Dunbar

**Dunbar Lifeboat Museum**, The Harbour. Small collection of models of early lifeboats and examples of rescue equipment, set within working lifeboat shed.

**Dunbar Under Ground**, Townhouse, High Street. Local history and archaeology, including spinning and weaving, and finds from local excavations.

**John Muir Museum**, High Street. Birthplace of John Muir, founder of the modern conservation movement and the USA's National Parks. Kitchen and bedroom furnished in early 19th-century style.

### East Linton

**Preston Mill & Phantassie Doocot** (NTS). Restored and working 18th-century watermill, with nearby dovecote (see no. 24).

### Ingliston

**Scottish Agricultural Museum** (NMS), Royal Highland Showground. Comprehensive collections relating to Scottish agricultural and rural life, Highland and Lowland—cultivation and harvesting, livestock, peat-cutting, forestry, fishing, crafts and trades, building techniques; lots of tools/equipment; seasonal rounds-of-work; reconstructed cottage interiors.

### Linlithgow

**Linlithgow Museum**, Annet House. Small local history collections and displays.

**Linlithgow Union Canal Society Museum**, Manse Road Basin. Brief history of Scottish canals, particularly the Union Canal, set in old canal stables. Occasional canal-boat trips.

### Livingston

**Almond Valley Heritage Centre**, Millfield, Kirkton. 18th-century farm steading, water-powered corn mill/mill machinery; shale oil museum with reconstructed worker's cottage and 'shale mine'.

### Newtongrange

**Scottish Mining Museum**, Lady Victoria Colliery. 19th-century colliery with exhibitions, steam winding engine, furnaces and reconstructed walk-in coalface; classic mining village (see no. 1).

### North Berwick

**North Berwick Museum**, School Road. Interesting displays of local archaeology, social/local history, natural history, fishing, golf; Bass Rock.

## Prestongrange

**Industrial Heritage Museum**, Prestonpans. 19th-century Cornish beam engine, colliery steam locomotives ('steam days', in season), displays of coal-mining and other local industries; large disused brickworks adjacent (see no. 2).

## South Queensferry

**Queensferry Museum**, Old Council Chambers, High Street. History of the former Burgh and building of the Forth Bridges.

**Swedish rune-stone in Princes Street Gardens, Edinburgh**

# BIBLIOGRAPHY

**Adams, IH** *The Making of Urban Scotland*, London, 1978.

**Breeze, DJ** *Roman Scotland: A Guide to the Visible Remains*, Newcastle-upon-Tyne, 1979.

**Burl, A** *The Stone Circles of the British Isles*, London, 1976.

**Butt, J** *The Industrial Archaeology of Scotland*. Newton Abbot, 1967.

**Cadell, P** *The Iron Mills at Cramond*, Edinburgh, 1973.

**Cruden, S** *The Scottish Castle*, Edinburgh, 3rd edition, 1981.

**Cruden, S** *Scottish Medieval Churches*, Edinburgh, 1986.

**Dixon, PJ** *Southdean, Borders: An Archaeological Survey*, Edinburgh, 1994.

**Douglas, G & Oglethorpe, M** Brick, *Tile and Fireclay Industries in Scotland*, Edinburgh, 1993.

**Dunbar, JG** *The Architecture of Scotland*, London, 2nd edition, 1978.

**Dilworth, M** *Scottish Monasteries in the Late Middle Ages*, Edinburgh, 1995.

**Fawcett, R** *Scottish Medieval Churches*, Edinburgh, 1985.

**Fawcett, R** *Scottish Abbeys and Priories*, London, 1994.

**Fawcett, R** *Scottish Architecture from the Accession of the Stewarts to the Reformation 1371-1560*, Edinburgh, 1994.

**Fenton, A** *Scottish Country Life*, Edinburgh, 1976.

**Fenton, A & Walker, B** *The Rural Architecture of Scotland*, Edinburgh, 1981.

**Gifford, J, McWilliam, C & Walker, D** *The Buildings of Scotland: Edinburgh*, London, 1984.

**Gilbert, JM** *Hunting and Hunting Reserves in Medieval Scotland*, Edinburgh, 1979.

**Haldane, ARB** *The Drove Roads of Scotland*, Edinburgh, 1952.

**Hanson, W & Maxwell, GS** *Rome's North West Frontier*, Edinburgh, 1983.

**Hay, GD & Stell, GP** *Monuments of Industry*, Edinburgh, 1986.

**Hay, G** *Architecture of Scottish Post-Reformation Churches 1560-1843*, Edinburgh, 1957.

**Henshall, AS** *The Chambered Tombs of Scotland, Vol 2*, Edinburgh, 1972.

**Hume, JR** *The Industrial Archaeology of Scotland: 1 The Lowlands and Borders*, London, 1976.
**Gilbert, JM** *Hunting and Hunting Reserves in Medieval Scotland*, Edinburgh, 1979.
**Gow, I & Rowan, A (eds)** *Scottish Country Houses: 1600-1914*, Edinburgh, 1995.

**Jaques, R & McKean, C** *West Lothian: An Illustrated Architectural Guide*, Edinburgh, 1994.

**Lindsay, J** *The Canals of Scotland*, Newton Abbot, 1968.

**McKean, C** *Edinburgh, Portrait of a City*, London, 1991.

**McKean, C** *Edinburgh: An Illustrated Architectural Guide*, Edinburgh, 1992 ed.

**MacKie, EW** *Scotland: An Archaeological Guide*, London, 1975.

**McNeill, P & Nicholson, R (eds)** *An Historical Atlas of Scotland, c 400-c 1600*, St Andrews, 1975.

**McWilliam, C** *Scottish Townscape*, London, 1975.

**McWilliam, C** *The Buildings of Scotland: Lothian (except Edinburgh)*, London, 1980.

**Maxwell, GS** *The Romans in Scotland*, Edinburgh, 1989.

**Millman, RN** *The Making of the Scottish Landscape*, London, 1975.

**Morton, RS** *Traditional Farm Architecture in Scotland*, Edinburgh, 1976.

**Munro, RW** *Scottish Lighthouses*, Stornoway, 1979.

**Naismith, R** *Buildings of the Scottish Countryside*, London, 1985.

**Nicolaisen, WFH** *Scottish Place-Names*, London, 1976.

**Omand, D (ed)** *The Borders Book*, Edinburgh, 1995.

**Parry, ML & Slater, TR (eds)** *The Making of the Scottish Countryside*, London, 1980.

**Ritchie, A** *Scotland BC*, Edinburgh, 1988.

**Ritchie, G & A** *Edinburgh and South-East Scotland*, London, 1972.

**Ritchie, G & A** *Scotland: Archaeology and Early History*, Edinburgh, 1991.

**Ritchie, A & Breeze, DJ** *Invaders of Scotland*, Edinburgh, 1991.

**Royal Commission on the Ancient and Historical Monuments of Scotland.** Inventories have been published for the following areas included in this volume: *Berwickshire*, 2nd ed 1915; *East Lothian*, 1924; *Midlothian and West Lothian*, 1929; *City of Edinburgh*, 1951; *Roxburghshire*, 2 volumes, 1956; *Selkirkshire*, 1957; *Peeblesshire*, 2 volumes, 1967.

**Shaw, JP** *Water Power in Scotland*, Edinburgh, 1984.

**Skinner, B** *The Lime Industry in the Lothians*, Edinburgh, 1965.

**Strang, CA** *Borders and Berwick: An Illustrated Architectural Guide*, Edinburgh, 1994.

**Tabraham, C** *Scottish Castles and Fortifications*, Edinburgh, 1986.

**Thomas, C** *Britain and Ireland in Early Christian Times: AD 400-800*, London, 1971.

**Thomas, J** *Midlothian: An Illustrated Architectural Guide*, Edinburgh, 1995.

**Tranter, N** *The Fortified House in Scotland*, Edinburgh, 1962-70.

**Whyte, I** *Edinburgh and the Borders: Landscape Heritage*, Newton Abbot, 1990.

**Whyte, I & K** *Exploring Scotland's Historic Landscapes*, Edinburgh, 1987.

**Wickham-Jones, CR** *Arthur's Seat and Holyrood Park, a visitor's guide*, Edinburgh, 1996.

**Willsher, B & Hunter, D** *Stones: 18th Century Scottish Gravestones*, Edinburgh, 1978.

**Willsher, B** *Understanding Scottish Graveyards*, Edinburgh, new edition, 1995.

**Rosslyn Castle, Midlothian**

# INDEX OF PLACES

Places within central and inner Edinburgh are listed under 'Edinburgh'; places outwith this area, including the one-time 'villages' of Edinburgh, are listed under their own name - eg South Queensferry, Dalmeny, Duddinston, Kirkliston, Newbridge, Balerno, Cramond, Corstorphine, Colinton, Swanston, Liberton, Burdiehouse, Craigmillar, Restalrig, Leith, Newhaven, Granton.

Printed in Scotland for The Stationery Office by (3808)
Dd 293088 C50 05/97